WITHDRAWN

PLURALISM, CORPORATISM, and CONFUCIANISM

PLURALISM, CORPORATISM, *and* CONFUCIANISM

Political Association and Conflict Regulation in the United States, Europe, and Taiwan

HARMON ZEIGLER

TEMPLE UNIVERSITY PRESS *Philadelphia*

Temple University Press, Philadelphia 19122
Copyright © 1988 by Temple University. All rights reserved
Published 1988   Printed in the United States of America

The paper used in this publication meets the minimum
requirements of American National Standard for Information
Sciences—Permanence of Paper for Printed Library Materials,
ANSI Z39.48-1984

Library of Congress Cataloguing-in-Publication Data

Zeigler, L. Harmon (Luther Harmon). 1936–
     Pluralism, corporatism, and Confucianism: political association
and conflict regulation in the United States, Europe, and Taiwan /
Harmon Zeigler.
        p. cm.
     Bibliography: p. 229
     Includes index.
     ISBN 0-87722-529-X (alk. paper):
     1. Corporate state. 2. Pluralism (Social sciences) 3. Pressure
groups. 4. Conflict management. 5. Sociology, Confucian.
I. Title.
JC478.Z45 1988
320.3—dc19   87–20161
                                                          CIP

Designed by Adrianne Onderdonk Dudden

To the politics and government majors
at the University of Puget Sound

CONTENTS

Preface   ix

1   *Thematic Continuities: Pluralism and the Corporatist Critique of Pluralism   3*

2   *The Creation and Maintenance of Political Organizations in a Pluralist Society   33*

3   *Group Behavior and Government Performance in Societal Corporatist Settings   67*

4   *Corporatism and the Shape of Policy   89*

5   *State Corporatism in Asian Society   117*

6   *Factions in Encompassing Organizations   147*

7   *Bureaucratic Encounters   163*

8   *Pluralism, Corporatism, and Confucianism: A Reprise   185*

Notes   197

Bibliography   229

Index   243

PREFACE

This book compares interest groups in three political settings: pluralism, societal corporatism, and state corporatism. As used in the United States, "pluralism" has come to mean a system of multiple, competing interest groups that, through bargaining and compromise, contribute to the shape of public policy. Power, while not equally distributed, depends more on commitment and organizing skill than on social position or economic influence. The meaning of "pluralism" in this book is not so restricted. I use it to refer to a political process in which interest groups organize, attempt to exert influence, and survive or disappear largely without arousing the participation or concern of government bureaucracies. European political scientists allude to pluralism in this way, and used in this manner, the term carries very little ideological baggage. According to this meaning of the word, the United States is the most pluralist nation in the world.

But in the United States, the battle between pluralists and elitists (those who do not believe that group competition is open, and who think that inter-elite competition is usually trivial) engages deeply felt ideologies about what ought to be, and equally strongly supported empirical theories addressing the distribution of political influence. Although I touch on these disputes in the sections considering critiques of pluralism, the thrust of the book is in other directions. The main line of inquiry is directed toward motivations for group membership, the consequences of pluralism, societal corporatism, and state corporatism for policy, and the functions of "encompassing" organizations. While the phrase "encompassing organizations" was not introduced by corporatist theorists, its evident utility for corporatism must not be overlooked. Encompassing organizations are said to address themselves to policy in ways that belie their origins as representatives of narrower, less communal, interests.

Chapter One sets forth the two competing theories—pluralism and corporatism—in both their normative and empirical configurations. "Traditional" group theory, which assumes a politically aware "potential" group membership longing to be united, is challenged by micro level theories of choice, which conclude the opposite: it is "irrational" to join an organization even if one agrees with its goals. The dispute between "shared attitude" and "rational choice" models is displaced by theories of corporatism, a means of regulating or constraining interest group activity by bringing "peak" economic associations into the policy formation and implementation process.

In Chapter Two, the two contenders in pluralist interest group theory are tested with a sample of members of interest groups in the United States.

Chapter Three opens a fresh line of inquiry, addressing the "so what?" question. Does it matter whether a nation is pluralist or corporatist? Societal corporatism, the democratic European and Japanese variant, describes a political system in which the state, principally through relevant bureaucracies, orchestrates group conflict. Selected peak associations are included in policy making and implementation. Societal corporatism refers to governments that regulate, constrain, or inhibit the free flow of organizations. The European corporatist governments have established a client-patron relationship with peak associations (principally labor and business) and undertake the policy formation process in concert with them. Groups do not come and go; they are firmly imbedded in the policy process.

Chapter Four continues to explore correlates of corporatism and pluralism, but concentrates on the most ambitious claim yet made for corporatism: its ability to guarantee stability. The intent here is to discuss the encompassing organization in a milieu in which such claims are treated seriously.

State corporatism—authoritarianism—defines an institutional arrangement that is similar to societal corporatism, but with less freedom of association and organization. Although there are major differences between authoritarian and democratic governments, the regulation of interest groups is not one of them. The "original" theorists of corporatism were fascists, and a lingering association between corporatism and fascism persists. Irrespective of the symbolism, the essential difference between societal and state corporatism is the location of policy initiative; in state corporatism, it invariably rests with the bureaucracy, while in societal corporatism it may not.

Perhaps because corporatism is so focused on peak associations that claim a representational monopoly, those who examine it rarely concern themselves with individual motives for joining or sustaining membership in these organizations. The research question is whether the corporatist mode of conflict resolution makes any difference in government policies.

The use of the industrial democracies for the "so what?" question is inescapable. We need a manageable sample of governments, and for better or worse, the empirical indicators of corporatism and pluralism are European in origin. The twenty-one industrial democracies supply a wealth of statistical information about themselves, and political scientists have seized upon it to add their own refinements. The theorists have *not*, however, spent much time worrying about why people join organizations; aside from an occasional article, they care mostly about macro-level questions: what does corporatism look like and does it yield a discernable pattern of policy outputs? It would have been ideal had the Europeans examined the questions of individual choice that have so absorbed the Americans, but in more collectivist societies the question may be less significant. Put another way, it is unlikely that theories of rational choice, which treat the potential group member as a consumer deciding whether to buy a "good," would have appeared in a less aggressively individualistic civilization.

State corporatism is the subject of Chapters Five, Six, and Seven. Here the focus is not so much on policy outputs as on the role of encompassing organizations, believed by their admirers to provide stronger commitments to unity than is true of interest groups in societal corporatist settings, and especially true of groups in pluralist countries. State corporatism appears most prominently in the Asian non-Communist countries and in Latin America. Among the most notable practitioners of state corporatism are Taiwan, South Korea, and Singapore.

Taiwan is the subject of a detailed analysis of state corporatism.

Chapters Six and Seven are devoted solely to this small island nation. The Kuomintang, Taiwan's governing party, can trace its ideological and organizational beginnings back to the turn of the century. Although it has governed Taiwan only since 1949, it was active in the overthrow of the Manchu dynasty and still claims Sun Yat-sen as its creator. Because Taiwan is a "soft authoritarian" government in its mode of interest group regulation, it is a good candidate for comparison between "state corporatism" and the societal corporatism of Europe.

Taiwan has an interesting role in the history of ideas. Initially it was the center of the "China lobby," a failed lobbying effort to persuade the United States not to recognize the People's Republic of China. More recently is has become the darling of free market economists, as its economic performance far exceeds that of mainland China. It is also the symbol of the continuing, and vitriolic, debate in the United States about the Chinese mainland. During the McCarthy period, with the United States engaging Chinese troops, the defeat of the Nationalists in 1949 became the center of charges of disloyalty. Chiang Kai-shek, yet another corrupt dictator who gained our favor by being anti-Communist, was to be "unleashed" to liberate the mainland. As time went by, the mainland became a beacon of hope for the American left, and Taiwan remained a symbol, although a fading one, of American opposition to Mao. Memories that remained were of Chiang and his wife, rumored to be the model for the Dragon Lady in the comic strip *Terry and the Pirates*.[1]

However "interesting" Taiwan may be, its selection for this project involved its meeting an explicit criterion that accompanied the beginning of my research. I needed a state corporatist system that had enjoyed both high economic growth and substantial reduction of income inequalities. Since state corporatism generally requires an authoritarian government, Japan was excluded (although, as we shall see, its mode of conflict regulation is in some respects authoritarian). South Korea achieved high growth but with high inequality. Costa Rica is an example of a high-growth, high-equality country. Its political system, a stable democracy, nevertheless exhibits some of the characteristics of the more authoritarian Latin American corporatism: socioeconomic exclusion of the majority, control of wages, and patterns of income distribution.[2] But neither its growth nor its income equality are on a par with the Asian countries. We are left with Taiwan and Singapore. Both enjoy high growth rates, although Singapore is wealthier. However, Taiwan's better performance on income distribution made it more attractive. It is the model high-growth, low-inequality political-economic system. As Gary Fields observes:

Taiwan is in the admirable position of combining rapid economic growth, sharply reduced inequality, and widespread alleviation of poverty. . . . It is one of the very few low-income countries in the world to be developing so rapidly. . . . Taiwan's development success—and indeed it is a success in terms of alleviation of poverty, reduction of inequality, and promotion of overall economic growth—offers an important lesson. There can be little doubt that Taiwan's development strategy had the effect of benefitting *all* her people, more or less.[3]

Not surprisingly, Taiwan maintains a massive and reliable archive of economic and political statistics. Fields' reference to Taiwan as "poor" comes from 1972 data. The data in Chapter Five, from 1984, give Taiwan a per capita gross national product of $3,400. The 1986 data, not yet published, put Taiwan's GNP per capita at $4,300. Taiwan is wealthier than South Korea ($2,100), Maylasia ($1,900), Thailand ($860), the Philippines ($660), but not as well off as Japan ($10,600) or Singapore ($7,260). Living styles are hard to judge; by most of the standards in use today, Taiwan would be classified as in the "upper middle" group. A good unobtrusive indicator of the changes in Taiwan's life style are the appearance in Taipei of pet shops and reducing clinics!

While income growth has continued at an impressive rate, reduction in income inequality has abated. Between 1964 (when statistics became consistent and reliable) and 1972 the Gini index declined by 9 percent to .318. (The Gini index measures the deviation of actual income distribution from a theoretically perfect one; hence low scores, meaning a closer approximation to the line of perfect equality, indicate less inequality.) During this period, the income of the poorest decile grew by 109 percent while that of the richest decile grew by 53 percent. The richest 10 percent earned

4.08 times more money than the poorest 10 percent. The Gini continued its downward slide until 1980 (.303), but edged up to .313 in 1983, where it has remained. The richest decile now earns 4.40 times as much as the poorest, 22.5 percent of all earned income. If, as Edward Muller and Mitchell Seligson believe, land reform contributed to declining inequality, the lack of recent decline is understandable. Land reform was completed by the 1960's.[4] Taiwan is compa-rable to Japan (where the richest decile earns 22.4 percent) and the United States (23.3 percent). Its income distribution is more equitable than South Korea's (27.5 percent earned by the richest decile) and much better than the other high growth/ inequality reduction country, Costa Rica (39.5 percent). No appreciable inequality decline has occurred since 1972 in any of these countries.[5] Different data in Chapter Five are in agreement with this information. Taiwan's record is treated more thoroughly in Chapter Six. The ability of government to redistribute income is taken up in the concluding chapter.

The book concludes with a reassessment of the costs and benefits of modes of conflict regulation. In today's context, these remarks are surely conservative. I suggest that efforts to emulate other governmental systems are unwise and unnecessary. With Japan being all the rage these days, readers will, I trust, disassociate themselves from this adulation. In any case, the differences between modes of conflict regulation, while profound, are not so great as to make any of them preferred.

In highlighting the similarities and differences among these three kinds of conflict resolution, the book touches upon political culture and history, especially in the portions dealing with Asia, where the influence of Confucianism is readily apparent. Confucianism is not a set of religious dictates; rather it is a "secular religion" whose perspectives color family relations, interpersonal interactions, and politics. Confucianism offers a detailed rationale for the encompassing organization, since the major thrust of its ideology is toward unity rather than conflict.

Confucianism once was the "official state ideology" of the early Chinese emperors, but has become so secularized in the past three hundred years that it is now a part of a broader Asian culture. It is a system of ethics based on two tenets: groups are more important than individuals, and society should be organized hierarchically. Confucianism is a delineation of the appropriate relationship between the various occupants of the hierarchy: husband to wife, son to father, sister to brother, subject to ruler, ruler to subject, and so on. If each occupies his or her designated status and behaves toward superiors or inferiors in compliance with the appropriate style, social conflict can be avoided. Thus serious conflict is regarded with more dread in "Confucian" societies than in the United States or Europe, because it implies a deterioration in the hierarchy.

The writings of Confucius and his disciples are available and accessible; still, Confucianism is not a formal body of thought as is, say, Marxism. It lacks the urgency, the need for explicit and detailed profession of belief, that more structured religions or ideologies require. But although "Confucian" countries vary substantially in their mode of conflict regulation, they adhere (usually) to a minimum package of cultural expectations.[6]

I lay no claim to expert knowledge, have cast my lot with a group of colleagues who know more than I, and have been well served by them. Usually they felt that my naiveté provided them with insights that their immersion had caused them to neglect. Notice that I said "usually." Sometimes I was told, "You can't do that. It's like comparing apples with oranges." It seems to me that comparing apples and oranges is likely to be more fun than comparing apples with apples. Why not compare apples and oranges? They are both fruit grown on trees. Besides, why would anybody want to compare apples with apples? The difference between a Red Delicious and a Rome Beauty, while apparent to those who grow and sell them, has proved too subtle for my unrefined palate. But the political science analog to comparing apples to apples is what most of us do. We compare European parliamentary democracies with each other, and we compare Asian authoritarian governments with each other. A conspicuous, and glorious, exception is Robert Holt and John Turner's *The Political Basis of Economic Development*, which compares France (from 1600 to 1789), Japan (from 1603 to 1868), China (from 1644 to 1911), and England (from 1558 to

1780), countries whose economies were "pre-take-off" and whose politics were "traditional."[7]

But suppose we did compare apples and oranges. I do not deny that some comparisons are foolish, as the comparisons of Guinea, France, and the United States, and of Austria, Switzerland, and Lebanon, on my desk remind me. But I have found, and presented in this book, a good reason to compare Japan and Spain. They have both moved from authoritarianism to democracy and both find ways to avoid much of the latter. South Korea and France offer another fruitful comparison. In reading Peter Hall's superb analysis of economic policy in England and France (Why this comparison? Would any one ever think to question?), it seemed to me that France and South Korea had as much in common as France and England.[8] Both were driven by the same ambition, to play in the big leagues of international commerce and industry, and both did it the same way: by making the costs of avoiding mergers exceed the benefits of small enterprise. They created conglomerates.

In gathering the data, analyzing it, and writing the book, I have been struck by the high quality of the previously published research, but also by its narrow focus. Those who pursue corporatism to the limits of their endurance rarely consider Asia; corporatism remains European and Iberian. Until recently, the corporatism literature also ignored Mancur Olson, who has written arguably the most influential criticism of pluralism, and whose examination of international economic growth directly challenges the corporatist premise. He, until recently, reciprocated by steering clear. One reason for specialization is prudence. Weaving together themes from disparate cultures is unlikely to yield a book as tightly argued as we might hope. And, while I investigate three political cultures, I rarely draw any direct comparisons.

On the other hand, the insights about conflict, its avoidance, and encompassing organizations to be gained from studying Confucianism are formidable. A culture with the premise that conflict is unnatural is as corporatist as you could ask. Since I found the Taiwanese joined organizations for many of the same reasons the Americans did—to get ahead—the comparison seems apt.

My goal is exploration; I have tried to set out some ideas and some data analysis that will get the various subdisciplines talking to

each other. And though I address a variety of questions, most attention is on two: Why do people join groups? And does the mode
of conflict resolution "matter?" The first question is ideally addressed in the United States; the second in Europe, since it has a
population of governments large enough for statistical analysis.
The chapters dealing with Taiwan ask both of these questions, and
also inquire into the phenomenal economic growth of the Pacific
Rim. Taiwan, like the United States, is a fine example of its genre.

I am in the debt of a large number of people who provided me
with most welcome help and criticism. As most of you know, ours
is a discipline in which turf protection is the first, possibly the only,
commandment. I am pleased to report that some of my colleagues
welcomed me to their turf, and helped me slightly reduce the odds
of making a fool of myself. Their help required unusual generosity.
Area specialists spend years learning how to avoid telling their
dinner host that his Hovercraft is full of eels, and rightly suspect
those who have not paid their dues. Richard Kraus, Robert Lane,
John Orbell, Donald Share, Maria Chang, Daniel Lev, Michael
Baer, and Gerald McBeath were colleagues in the truest sense of
the word, reading carefully and showing no mercy. Their time, efforts, and patience are greatly appreciated. As you might have gathered, the usual disclaimer—the merits theirs, the faults mine—is
more appropriate than usual.

Chalmers Johnson, Michael Veseth, Gus Di Zeraga, and Richard Kraus guided me toward sources that would have remained un-
known to me without their efforts. James Gregor, visiting at the
University of Puget Sound in 1985–1986, was generous with his
time and patient with my ignorance.

In Taiwan, Tsai Cheng-wen and Hu Fu guided me through the
Byzantine maze of politics and power on Taiwan. Wei Yung was
especially helpful in sharing his knowledge of Taiwan's politics and
economics. Thomas Lee, Dean of Graduate Studies at Tamkang
University, provided opportunities for colloquia and the exchange
of ideas. The following people spent many hours refining my
knowledge of the Taiwanese variant of Asian politics: Tsiang Yien-
si, Robert P. Parker, Fredrick Chen, Chen Li-an, Chao Yao-tung,
Livingston Merchant, George Lee, Chien-Jen-chen, Henry Yu-shu

Kao, Thomas B. Lee, and Esther Kuo. Fred C. H. Lee and Fei Lung-lui were able to arrange interviews with everyone I needed to see, and practiced the art of Chinese hospitality flawlessly. Jeane Tchong Koei Lee, President of the Pacific Cultural Foundation, which sponsored my research, opened doors that were once locked. David Chao and Nathan Yu-jen Lai eased the burden of developing a routine for research and living. Simon Wang, who accompanied me on most interviews, made this book possible; without his help I could not have completed the research.

In addition to the Pacific Cultural Foundation, I was aided by the Guggenheim and Ford Foundations. I am grateful to them for both their support and patience.

The University of Puget Sound provided the ideal surroundings for research: ample computer time, excellent software, and knowledgeable and reliable support. Tom Aldrich, Pat Taylor (who steadfastly maintained, like the priest at Boys' Town, "there is no such thing as a lost file"), and Joan Sodderland were especially helpful in this regard. Daren Bush and Glen Kuper of UPS were outstanding assistants who put in hour upon hour of time tracking down obscure references and collecting information. They, and I, remain in awe of Doris Braendel at Temple, who found errors where none of us did and made us fix them.

At the University of Washington, colloquia chaired by Donald McCrone provided an opportunity for me to bounce ideas and data around and, in so doing, enabled me to correct some mistakes that should have been obvious but were not.

Finally, credit should be given to those who, at various stages of this project, performed as entrepreneurs, putting me in touch with the right people, telling me when I was barking up the wrong tree, and assuring me that "just one more" revision would fix the book. They are: Doty Breibart, Ed Artinian, Willis D. Regier, Irving Rockwood (who, as an editorial consultant, never sent me a bill), and Jane Cullen of Temple, who took the baton over the finish line.

Finally, I wish to express my esteem for Heinz Eulau, who is a model of professionalism, acumen, and personal warmth.

PLURALISM, CORPORATISM, and CONFUCIANISM

ONE

THEMATIC CONTINUITIES: PLURALISM AND THE CORPORATIST CRITIQUE OF PLURALISM

Pluralism is best understood as the belief that advanced industrial democracies, especially the United States, generate a system of multiple, competing elites (including interest groups) that determine public policy through bargaining and compromise. The ideas of the social contract theorists of the seventeenth and eighteenth centuries were precursors of pluralism. Hobbes, Locke, and Madison believed that individuals were both rational and selfish: they tried to maximize their own positions and were capable of recognizing and acting in their own self-interest. It was rational for people to contract to create a government because otherwise life would be "solitary, poor, nasty, brutish, and short."[1] The heart of the doctrine is the belief in rational choice. The rational person became integral to pluralism and, ironically, equally central to corporatist critiques.

PLURALISM AND INDIVIDUALISM

Additionally, both pluralism and corporatism contain elements of normative *and* empirical theory. The most frequently derived normative variant of individualism is the doctrine of limited government. If government exists because it serves a purely utilitarian function, its intrusion into personal life must be carefully constrained. The building block of society is the individual. Assessments of government could be undertaken in individualist terms: is a proposed course of action likely to enhance or impede the individual's ability to achieve his or her goals?

The implied belief in equality of political opportunity is pluralism's most contentious tenet, but one not important to this book. More consequential is the pluralist commitment to the rational individual. According to the pluralists' conviction, people join groups because they believe it is to their political advantage to do so, just as they entered into the abstract social contract through which the state was created.

Pluralism is therefore a variant of individualism. If individualists believe that the purpose of government is to shield personal liberty, the pluralist modification furnishes the means for accomplishing this purpose. Individualism leaves to our imagination the means whereby citizens participate in decision making. Pluralism specifies that most (some would argue all) participation is engaged in by active leaders who represent the interests of passive followers.

Decisions are a result of elite bargaining and compromise. Elite competition, generally expressed by organized interest groups, helps to safeguard individual nonparticipants from governmental abuse, since no set of interests is likely to be ascendant indefinitely. A particular interest will win in some years, lose in others, win in some arenas, lose in others, win on some issues, lose on others. When people join organized groups, pluralists believe that the joiners expect that the group will at least be competitive in the political process. Pluralism does not argue that political resources and political influence are equally distributed, but rather that they are widely dispersed.

The ability to influence a decision is often not a result of other resources, such as economic influence; it is a consequence of how much stake a given group has in a decision. If a group regards the decision as a matter of life or death for its members, it will try to acquire participation and influence, and will generally succeed. The resources of pluralism are interest, skills in organization and leadership, information, and commitment. Public policy is not necessarily a majority preference: it is at worst an equilibrium struck between the competing interest groups. Policy thus is a reasonable approximation of the preference of the passive, and it is the best estimate we can hope for.

Interest Groups in Pluralist Theory

Interest groups are the linchpin of pluralist theory. They move from necessary evils (in Madison's mind) to agents of connection for the pluralists. At the very core of pluralist theory is belief that *individuals* can best convey their needs and desires to the government through concerted group activity.

In a large, complex society one stands little chance of being heard—much less of being able to affect the governmental decision-making process. However, so the argument runs, when a number of people who share a particular concern unite, their collective voice speaks with more command than the sum of their individual voices. Thus, for pluralists, interest groups are channels through which people realize the democratic ideal of legitimate and satisfying interaction with government: "Voluntary associations are the prime means by which the function of mediating between the state and the individual is performed. Through them the individual is able to relate . . . effectively and meaningfully to the political system."[2]

The Rise and Decline of Traditional Group Theory

Pluralism as group theory and pluralism as individualism are mutations of the work of the "original" group theorist, Arthur Bentley, who maintained that governmental institutions were nothing more than dependent products of "lower-lying political groups" and that individual needs, desires, aspirations, or values were generally of marginal importance. Ignored at the time that he was writing on politics (1908), Bentley's ideas burst upon the scene in the 1950's and 1960's, only to fade away into obscurity again a few years later. Nowadays, David Truman is more often given credit for the original systematic presentation of interest group theory.

To the pluralists, Truman provided the notion of "overlapping" group affiliations and "shared attitudes." People are presumed to have a variety of interests, so that it is thought unlikely that any single group will circumscribe *all* the salient interests of its many members. Moreover a sizable number of persons who agree on any one issue will more than likely not agree on a host of other issues. Therefore groups not only proliferate but also tend to restrict the scope of issues of concern in order to concentrate on the one area in which all members share a common interest.

The individualist roots of pluralism are also well expressed by the belief that shared attitudes are the base of group activity. In perhaps the most famous passage in *The Governmental Process* Truman argues: " 'Interest group' refers to any group that, on the basis of one or more shared attitudes, makes certain claims upon other groups in the society for the establishment, maintenance, or enhancement of forms of behavior that are implied by the shared attitudes."[3] Truman narrowed his definition: shared attitudes are not just the similar ways of viewing the world that many categories of people share; they are only those attitudes that inspire people to join a group. The problem was that Truman appeared to be defining himself out of existence.

Truman's followers trooped obediently to Congress and produced volumes of case studies, usually entitled something like "A Bill Becomes a Law," or "The Dance of Legislation." But more systematic studies of Congress, especially those based on interviews with representatives and senators, revealed that many of them rarely saw lobbyists, and paid attention to only a few of those they saw.[4] The implication was apparent: rather than occupying center stage, interest groups were marginal to the routines of politics.

Where had all the groups gone? It appeared that *The Governmental Process* was either encased in an earlier era or wrong. There is also the possibility that Truman's work has been misunderstood. Truman was very much the Bentleyan, and as a result sought to avoid "reification" (the attribution of independent reality to an analytical concept). Recall that organization is simply a stage in the development of interaction, based on shared attitudes. If the shared attitudes are stable and intense, an organization will "ratify" them. People who have shared attitudes but have not yet begun to interact are a "potential" group.

To Truman, both an organized interest group and a potential interest group are part of the governmental process: "The fact that one interest group is highly organized whereas another is not or is merely a potential group . . . is a matter of great significance at any particular moment."[5] There are interests without organizations, but since political scientists who sought to test Truman's research paradigm needed *something* to study, they substituted formal organizations for the less precise notion of "interests." The discovery that interest groups were not invariably major actors in any policy dispute neither confirmed nor refuted Truman's work.

Now began the lamentable tendency for fragmentation in research that led to needless internecine struggles. There could be interests without organization, but there could be no organization without interests. Shared attitudes need not result in institutionalization, especially if the shared attitudes are not central to an individual belief system. In 1960, when *The Governmental Process* appeared, survey research was the preferred research technique of the vanguard of "the behavioral revolution." Yet survey research was rarely used to assess the existence of shared attitudes in subgroups of the sample. Students of interest groups concentrated on observing the policy process, questioning the active participants, and reconstructing the history of legislation, but not assaying the merit of the idea that the existence of an organization *proved*, or *required*, shared attitudes.

THE BASIS FOR MEMBERSHIP:
INDIVIDUAL AND GROUP GOALS

Mancur Olson's[6] *The Logic of Collective Action: Public Goods and the Theory of Groups* is generally credited with exposing Truman's most extensively discussed error: his belief that shared attitudes were the foundation of formal organizations. But Olson was willing to accept as a given the existence of shared attitudes, because it made no difference to his argument whether shared attitudes existed before the formation of an organization, since he was talking exclusively about the individual's decision to join (presumably) an *established* organization. He assumes the existence of a large number of people who share a common interest in a collective good. Economists had long employed the distinction between *collective* goods and *selective* goods, the former being goods that are not amenable to discriminatory distribution within a given potential or "categoric" group. These kinds of groups in Truman's marvelously time-bound phrase, are composed of "persons of a given age level, . . . those of similar income or social status, . . . people living in a particular area, as Westerners, and . . . assortments of people according to an almost endless variety of similarities—farmers, alcoholics, insurance men, blonds, illiterates, mothers, neurotics, and so on."[7]

When a city purifies its water, it is providing a collective good, for all who use the city water supply benefit equally. It makes no difference whether a group is merely categoric or has started to jell because of shared attitudes. There can be no discrimination among water users. On the other hand, if a city distributed home purification devices to some but not all water users, those devices would be *selective*. In the latter instance, not all members of the water-using public would benefit equally from the good in question.

Whenever we differentiate collective from selective goods, it is essential to identify the group to which we refer, for the universality of benefit is determined by the particular set of people in question. Assume a categoric group of all college students in the United States. Suppose that, taking its cue from most industrial democracies, Congress enacted a law providing a three-hundred-dollar-per-month cost of living allowance to all college students. Such a stipend would be a collective good for students as a categoric group. However, if one were to define the categoric group as all persons of college age, then the monthly allowance would become a selective benefit. Additionally, when a collective good is made available in equal amounts to all persons, it is not necessarily equally valued by each recipient. The three-hundred-dollar stipend may be of less value to students from wealthy families than to those who are less well off.

The Rational Individual Choice

Olson's contribution was to apply this classification of rewards to interest group theory. He argues that the mere existence of a joint interest in a collective good (shared attitudes) is not a sufficient condition for *rational* people to unite in organized group activity— or for an individual to join an existing group—unless the "potential" group is very small. The argument rests squarely on the same rationality assumptions so critical to individualist social contract theory, and to its pluralist offshoot. The rational person who pools resources in the pluralist scheme to gain an advantage in policy choice will *not* join such a group, according to Olson's thinking, because he or she will realize that, as long as others organize, the value added to the group by his or her membership will be insignificant. Moreover, since the good in question is collective (since policy choices ratified by public bodies are collective), he or she will benefit from an organized group's acquisition of the good regardless of whether he or she participates in the process by which it is obtained.

Since group membership is *never* without a price for the individual, Olson deduces that no rational person will incur the costs of organizational participation unless (1) the anticipated payoff resulting from such participation is appreciably higher than the probable payoff resulting from nonparticipation, and (2) that payoff exceeds the costs of group membership.

The economic analogy—the interchange of political and economic motives—is Olson's major error, as will become apparent when we examine empirical assessments of individual motives for joining.

The Flaw in Economic Models

Olson judged political attitudes to be of no value in group organization. But surely this is an extreme position. It is, as is Truman's, based on the assumption of individual rational behavior. Unlike Truman, however, Olson believes that individual behavior can be explained solely by a desire for economic gain. Olson does acknowledge, in a throwaway phrase, the importance of "erotic incentives, psychological incentives, moral incentives, and so on."[8] However, it is inaccurate to allege that these theoretical assumptions are newcomers to political science.[9]

Individual pursuit of rationally understood self-interest is the foundation of pluralism as well as of individualist political theory. Pluralism is not a uniquely American contribution to group theory, but the idea of selective benefits is. The dispute between traditionalists and Olson's adherents is an argument that requires a strongly individualist culture. It takes absolute freedom of association as a given and implies that people operate on a foundation of rational self-interest. They will join either because it is to their individual economic advantage (Olson) or their political advantage (Truman) to do so.

Individuals are not given much of a collective conscience by Olson, which is a reasonable conclusion within the context of the culture of the United States, but not in a comparative setting. Other cultures are more collectivist, and it is likely that the motivations that Olson attributes to individuals are moderated substantially by a person's ability to identify with a collective goal. David Marsh's study of the Confederation of British Industry leads him to speculate about the likelihood that British interest groups do not fit the Olson theory, as many of their members join because of the expectation of collective goods, fully aware that their individual decision to join will not enhance the probability that each member will personally acquire more of such benefits.[10]

What *was* new in Olson's work was the *deductive* application of economic models. Starting from his theoretically *a priori* statement of motivation, Olson shows why only selective benefits will serve to encourage group membership. If we believe that each person has only one goal—his or her economic advancement—it is hard to see why Olson is not correct. All physicians benefit from American Medical Association lobbying on Medicare caps (maximum allowable fees) and restrictions on the eligibility of marginal occupations—usually chiropractic physicians and naturopaths—for insurance coverage. All used car dealers benefit when intense lobbying defeats legislation requiring the display of a car's condition on its windshield. Social scientists christened the rational rejection of collective goods as a sufficient cause for organizational membership the "free rider" problem; in a somewhat different context, the late Elvis Presley, when asked why he did not marry, gave a fine definition of the problem: "Why buy a cow when you can get milk through the fence?"[11]

So we are left with two major theories, each asserting a single cause for the existence of interest groups: shared attitudes or selective goods. James Q. Wilson has captured the irony in the fact that the two theories end up espousing simple explanations. He observes that Bentley himself argued against the investigation of individual motives, as their complexity would lead researchers into a labyrinth of complex theory from which little explanatory precision could be expected.[12] Olson's decision to infer rather than to examine individual attitudes is as Bentley would have preferred.

Efforts Toward Synthesis

Two recent works, Terry Moe's *The Organization of Interests* and John Hansen's essay "The Political Economy of Group Membership"[13] do what neither Truman nor Olson ever did: they investigate the actual reasons that people say are important in their decision to join (Moe) and examine change in membership as a result of the availability of individual discretionary income (Hansen). They find, not surprisingly, that people join organizations for different reasons, depending on the organization, the individual, and the nature of the times. Moe examines the motives of members of the Minnesota Farm Bureau, the Minnesota Farmers Union, the Minnesota Retail Federation, the Minnesota-Dakotas Hardware Association, and the Printing Industries of the Twin Cities. Hansen studies membership surge and decline in the American Farm Bureau Federation, the League of Women Voters, and the National Association of Home Builders. Moe's sample of organizations is most likely to yield the "Olson response," as it consists of economic organizations. Hansen's subjects of research also are Olson-type organizations, except for the League of Women Voters. Fortunately for us, they both happened upon the Farm Bureau.

Moe finds that Olson is largely correct: in three of his five organizations (Printing Industries, Hardware Association, and Farm Bureau), the main reason for joining was to obtain services. But for the Retail Federation and the Farmers Union, lobbying, a collective good, was more important. When asked what they would do if the organization stopped providing services, and only lobbied, a majority in all organizations save the Farmers Union said that they would drop out, and a majority of the members of all associations revealed that they would *not* drop out if lobbying were stopped and services were maintained. However, a majority is not everybody. In four of five organizations, minorities ranging from 23 to 43 percent *would* drop out if lobbying were ended but services were not. Moe concludes that Olson is right, but so is Truman. While the provision of selective goods is more important than shared attitudes, for a good many members, political reasons are pivotal:

> For a balanced perspective on interest groups, then, an exclusive emphasis on their nonpolitical foundations will not do—nor, obviously, will the traditional emphasis on politics. Both the nonpolitical and political bases for membership need to be taken into account and their organizational implications mapped out. Both have their own special roles to play.[14]

Hansen's conclusions parallel Moe's. The Farm Bureau, which Olson correctly singled out as a massive service-providing organization, enjoyed its greatest membership growth during periods of rapid economic expansion: the period during and after World War II and the decade of the 1970's. Selective benefits attracted new members only when farmers had enough money to pay dues. On the other hand, Hansen infers a political motive by examining the relation between farm aggregate income and membership increase. When farm income was lagging, each additional 5 percent increase in farm subsidies (for which the Farm Bureau claimed substantial credit) was accompanied by a 1 percent increase in membership. When farm income was up, a *100 percent increase* in subsidies was required for a comparable membership increase.[15] A perceived threat was a strong inducement to join. As Truman had argued, the "disruption of established patterns of behavior" or "disturbances" are of major import in the dynamics of group membership.[16]

Hansen's study of the League of Women Voters provides a chance to see an answer to Moe's question: would you remain a member without selective goods? The League offers virtually no selective benefits. The major Trumanesque disturbance for the League was the entry of women into the work force. Employed women have more discretionary income, but employment outside the home contributes to a more militant egalitarianism than the League represents.[17] The formation of the National Organization for Women in 1969 is roughly coincidental with the loss of membership by the League, although its lack of selective goods makes the League membership less stable than the Farm Bureau. In a sense, the National Organization for Women became the responding organization when the disturbance occurred.[18]

With the Home Builders, Hansen has his best case: membership surges when income is threatened, as happened with the Farm

Bureau. Building subsidies propelled Farm Bureau membership up-ward when income was low, but not when income was high. He concludes, as does Moe, that "individuals do indeed join interest groups in response to collective benefits."[19]

Joining an Organization and Creating an Organization

Traditional group theorists—and for that matter many of their critics—pay no attention to the distinction between *joining an exist-ing group* and *organizing a group*. The former is an easy decision, with minimal effort involved. You just sign up, pay your dues and, if your personal calculus of costs and goods is favorable, remain a member. But what of the time and expense involved in creating an organization from scratch, rather than attracting members? Truman and Olson are silent on this point, and it is here, rather than in their assumptions about shared attitudes or selective benefits, that they make their gravest miscalculation.

Truman presents his "disturbance" theory in pure form: distur-bances yield an organizational response; organization leads to coun-terorganization; the group formation process is one of "waves." The disturbance theory is an essential one for pluralism, for it suggests the sort of equilibrium for which the theory is renowned. If each group creation is itself a disturbance that leads to a countervailing organization, the group process contributes to an approximately even spread of political resources: no group will exist for long with-out a challenge. Organizations are believed to "have sprung from the disruption of the established patterns of behavior." Just as the individual choice is a political one, so is the creation of an organi-zation a rational response to a threat.

Before considering alternatives to Truman's explanation of the origins of organizations, we remark that his tormenter, Olson, is equally guilty of confusing the creation of organizations with indi-vidual choices to join. Both Olson and Truman discuss the origins of labor unions in somewhat similar terms. Both agree that local unions preceded national ones. For Truman, local unions began in order to combat "merchant capitalists" and to resist the competi-tion of immigrants. Once the unions were underway, "in . . . wave-like fashion," employers' associations emerged as a reflexive answer.

Labor's counter was the creation of national organizations, a process encouraged by improvements in transportation. Truman contends that this process (wave to disturbance to organization to counterorganization) illustrates "the generic process whereby any association is formed."[20]

Olson too uses the language of spontaneity: early unions "sprang up," and became national in response to "market forces." Market forces—the same transportation and industrialization disturbances mentioned by Truman—are given the same explanatory assignment by Olson. Truman explains, "Local organizations were no longer able to control wages and working conditions."[21]

The Entrepreneur

Surely neither the pluralists nor their detractors believe that political organizations—universally dominated by active elites—had somehow transformed ordinary people into political activists. If people are so apolitical that they need at least *some* selective goods to remain in an organization, how do these same dullards suddenly emerge with an organization, a headquarters, a charter, a goal, and a mission? Of course they do not. The history of organizations is replete with examples of the patient labors of entrepreneurs. Just as people join organizations for different reasons, entrepreneurs also have differing needs. Whatever the motives, group formation is the province of an elite. Even "mass movements," when they become mass organizations (ideologically, rather than in terms of membership), do so because of entrepreneurs.[22]

Entrepreneurs are not necessarily individuals, in the sense that the word is normally used in economics. Governments, foundations, as well as individuals play the role of entrepreneur. The active participation of governments in the creation of interest groups is a much neglected, but often essential, component in their formation. Because interest group theory in its pluralist incarnation has tended to concentrate on societies with freedom of association, conflict-based political systems, and market economies, it has neglected the important role of governmentally encouraged organizational monopolies.

CORPORATISM

Corporatism is often used to describe fascist societies (such as Italy and Nazi Germany).[23] However, even though the association lingers, it is inaccurate. Fascism requires mass state powers and the emotional commitment to a charismatic leader.[24] Corporatism to the contrary connotes at least a partnership between the state and its component interests, albeit with a dominant partner. Moreover, its rational/bureaucratic mode of policy evaluation is not at all similar to fascism. Enemies of corporatism dread and fear its deference to "nonpolitical" experts and its inability to hold bureaucracies accountable to elected bodies, and they believe that corporatism is merely a device to pacify labor unions. They do not worry about its appeal to the most ignoble of human emotions.[25]

Corporatism's modern usage (often as "neocorporatism") contains fewer negative overtones, and instead is said to be a characteristic of the consensus-oriented democracies such as Austria, Switzerland, and Japan, of authoritarian Latin American governments, and of Asian governments heavily influenced by Confucian theories of harmony. In these settings the close interaction of groups and government is supposed as a matter of course. But in the pluralist societies, the role of government in the origination and maintenance of organizations is not taken as seriously as it should be.

We should distinguish between those organizations serving a well-defined, narrow constituency of some import for economic policy and the larger, more symbolic ones with vague goals. Their origins and member expectations are not similar. In both pluralist and corporatist societies, the more narrowly focused economic organizations have more voice and influence and are more likely to have been organized in closer collusion with government.

Organic Statism

The two conflicting views of the relationship between the state and the individual find their way into virtually every philosophical or theoretical discussion. Social contract theories are not far from the surface of modern pluralism, and collectivism finds its modern expression in corporate, or organic, theories of the state.

Alfred Stepan's extraordinary essay highlights flawlessly the disparate and incompatible tenets of pluralist and corporate theories, with unambiguous explanations about how each produces different assumptions about interest groups. Of pluralism he writes:

> In the liberal-pluralist approach the main normative, empirical, and methodological concern is with individuals who, pursuant to their individual economic and political interests, together make up society. In pluralist theory, people may form into groups, but because they all have a variety of concerns, they associate themselves with many and diverse groups whose interests may clash. A methodological and normative assumption among both political and economic thinkers in the liberal-pluralist tradition is that it is inadmissible to use the notion of the general good. Instead, individual utility for the constituent members of society is most nearly achieved when people are able to pursue freely their own economic and political interests.[26]

Stepan places pluralism squarely within the individualist political tradition, and as a result also distinguishes pluralism as a normative philosophy from pluralism as an explanatory theory. Pluralism sets forth both a system of government, with interest groups as the central representative component, and a preferred distribution of influence, with interest groups roughly evenly balanced in power or influence.

Corporatism and Organic Statism

Stepan's explication of corporatism stresses its procedural components:

> Corporatism refers to a particular set of policies and institutional arrangements for structuring interest representation. Where such arrangements predominate, the state often charters or even creates interest groups, attempts to regulate their number, and gives them the appearance of a quasi-representational monopoly along with special prerogatives. In return for such prerogatives and monopolies the state claims the right to monitor representational groups by a variety of mechanisms in order to discourage the expression of "narrow" class-based, conflictual demands.

Philippe Schmitter's definition is similar in its emphasis on the *exchange*, the bargain, between groups and governments:

Corporatism . . . is a system of interest representation in which the constituent units are organized into a limited number of singular, compulsory, noncompetitive, hierarchically ordered and functionally differentiated categories, recognized or licensed (if not created) by the state and granted a deliberate representational monopoly within their respective categories in exchange for observing certain controls on their selection of leaders and articulation of demands and supporters.[27]

This definition does not include any dimension of authoritarianism, but the language suggests an intrusive state; the essence of corporatism is its control or monopolization of the demand-making process.

THE COMPONENTS OF CORPORATISM

Whether the bureaucracy is constrained, at least symbolically, by an elected executive or legislature does not matter very much. Corporatism describes both Switzerland and Mexico, one vigorously democratic and the other a one-party monopoly with an unsavory reputation for electoral fraud. But surface distinctions to the contrary, both of these governments meet Schmitter's requirements.[28]

We reiterate the distinction between societal corporatism (the democratic variety with regularly held elections and clear legal limits on the bureaucracy) and "state corporatism" (single-party systems with vague constraints on bureaucracy). Whether this distinction is important for policy outcome or for the structure of bureaucratic encounters with interest groups is not apparent. The topic is addressed more fully in Chapter Three.

Authoritarian and Democratic Variants

There are procedural differences between democratic (societal) and authoritarian (state) corporatism. Among the most important are the location of initiative in policy implementation, the extent to which bureaucracies regulate organizations or organizations capture bureaucracies, and the degree of coercion available to the state.[29] The distinction between societal and state corporatism is based largely on the degree of dependency. In societal corporatism, interest groups are autonomous from, and at worst equally balanced with, the bureaucracy. In state corporatism, interest groups are dependent, auxiliary organizations. Societal corporatism is the European variant, while state corporatism is the authoritarian Latin American and Asian mode.[30] They are species of the same genus.

The balance between the state and interest groups has preoccupied students of corporatism, irrespective of its type. Neither "societal corporatism" nor "state corporatism" can be regarded as terms that describe a static division of authority. Alliances between groups, the economic decline of others, and the ebb and flow of will in the bureaucracies tilt the balance one way or another. To some writers, these distinctions are trivial; they impede our understanding of the fundamentally *authoritarian* nature of *all* corporatist governments. Amos Perlmutter represents this way of thinking. He writes that "the old corporatism was conservative, royalist, and an expression of historical authoritarianism. The new corporatism . . . represents modern authoritarianism."[31] In the same fashion, J. T. Winkler defines corporatism as "an economic system in which the state directs and controls predominately private-owned business according to four principles: unity, order, nationalism, and success."[32] But these views neglect the many varieties of corporatism that its students propose. Much of the dispute is perceptual: when do differences become significant? Even though I downplay such differences, I do not propose oversimplification or invective.

Interest Intermediation

Schmitter prefers to write of intermediation because he doubts that any interest group, whether in a pluralist or in a corporatist system, is any more successful in translating member attitudes into group demands than are other political institutions such as political parties. But Alan Cawson offers an interesting counterproposal. Rather than regarding interest groups as competitors with political parties for the job of representation, he believes that societal corporatism is actually an "extension of pluralist theories of the distribution of power in modern societies." The only genuine departure from pluralism is state corporatism, invariably authoritarian. Theories of representation do not impede governmentally induced cooperation in state corporatist systems. Cawson believes that state corporatism "emerges from the imperatives of an authoritarian regime—which has been established suddenly after a crisis or *putsch*—to mobilize the consent of the population for its policies." Thus the fundamentally different nature of state and societal corporatism can be attributed to different origins, one a slow evolution and the other a more radical or abrupt departure from past processes.[33] I admire, but do not accept, his argument.

In executing their intermediation function, however, organized groups in corporatist theory are almost a polar opposite from those in pluralist theory. Of paramount importance, they are likely to have legitimate monopolies on the representation of functional interests. Unlike the American pluralist interest group system, where there is fierce competition for the same clientele and substantial membership turnover, corporatist organizations are almost like guilds.[34] Guilds legitimate *vocations*. Corporatist theory reflects this focus with its view of representation as one of "functions." Individuals are not represented; rather groups of vocations or occupations are the foundation of representative government. As Peter Williamson concludes, "The structure of representation can, therefore, be regarded as consensually-orientated, designed to allay conflict, particularly class conflict, through adopting a corporate basis of representation that upheld the common good."[35]

The strong corporatism of European countries and the weak corporatism of the United States and Canada is sometimes attributed to the enduring tradition of the guilds of the Middle Ages, which in England and France were either formally represented or consulted even as geographical representation was taking hold.[36] Neither of these two countries, however, is strongly corporatist.[37]

Other frequently cited antecedents of corporatism are, especially concerning its Iberian forms, "the Common Roman legacy, the strength of Christianity, . . . and empire building."[38] But it is unlikely that the Iberian culture is uniquely suited to corporatism, for the Confucian traditions of Asia are equally inclined toward corporatism, as are the Northern European countries. It *is* probable that certain ways of life, among them Iberian and Confucian, where there is strong emphasis on group identification, are more receptive to corporatism than are the more individualistic cultures, such as that of the United States. The forerunners are not so much explicit tenets of appropriate behavior as found in a particular religion, but rather those that appear as a common thread running through all religions. Roman Catholic countries are apt to be corporatist, but so are the Northern European countries, which are predominately Lutheran. The common thread is religious homogeneity.[39]

Given its rich and varied historical and cultural antecedents, corporatism is certainly not synonymous with authoritarianism, for the European corporatist countries are all strong democracies. Of course it is not imperative that the intermediation function be carried out only in representative democracies; authoritarian systems can be equally responsive—if they choose to be—to the needs (not demands) of interest groups.[40] None of the variants of corporatism has anything to do with socialism, although socialism posits a collective good, as does corporatism. Only the monopolization of the demand-making function is similar.

Stepan seeks to distinguish corporatism both from its normative rationale, organic statism, and from Marxism. In classical Marxist thought the state is an instrument of oppression, initially at the bidding of the ruling class and, in its transitional phase, of the proletariat. In either organic statism or corporatism, the state is not necessarily oppressive; on the contrary it is liberating, in the tradition of Rousseau and the collectivist romantics. Organic statism and corporatism are compatible with authoritarian or even totalitarian regimes, but they need not be so. Fascist governments may be corporatist, as may democratic ones. The seminal idea of corporatism, and to a lesser extent organic statism, is that geographical representation is inadequate and that functional representation should replace or augment it. Governments would create and sanction occupational associations—farmers, electricians, computer programmers, and the like. In some forms of corporatism such organizations have been given authority for policy implementation; in others they are legitimately influential in policy formation. In every case, corporatist systems confer quasi-public, often monopolistic, status on interest groups. *The goal is invariably enhanced or augmented representation.*

Pluralist Responses

In pluralist systems such incorporation is eagerly sought by most groups but achieved by only a few, and often at the expense of their legitimacy. "Capture theory" decries situations in which interest groups are said to control, or at least manipulate, the public bureaucracies created to regulate them.[41] The allegedly cozy relationship between private associations and public bureaucracies led to Theodore Lowi's condemnation of *normative* pluralism. He argues that the democratic state has become little more than a holding company for interest groups. Lowi calls such a circumstance "interest group liberalism," after considering and rejecting corporatism because of its "unwanted connotations" (Italian fascism and conservative Catholicism).[42] More radical assertions about ruling class hegemony agree with Lowi's assessment. By contending that the consequence of normative pluralism is a concentration of power narrow enough to reject the assumptions of analytical pluralism, such critics are saying that industrial democracies drift, or consciously move, toward corporatism. The most arresting manifestation of the anti-pluralist perspective is Olson's *Rise and Decline of Nations*,[43] which alleges that governments that behave as Lowi believes the United States behaves have sacrificed healthy economic growth: "On balance, special-interest organizations and collusions reduce efficiency and aggregate income in the societies in which they operate and make political life more divisive."[44]

The Conception of the Public Good

A central assumption in these kinds of criticism is the objective existence of a public good. Since the public good, in this view, is not merely the balance of demands among competing groups, it can be realized only if "narrow" group conflicts are avoided. Corporatism thus details a decision-making system in which conflict is subordinate to cooperation, a set of circumstances possible only if the state regulates the ebb and flow of group behavior. Whereas pluralist analysis begins with the premise that conflict is either healthy or unavoidable, corporatism insists that it may be pathological. The divisive effects of conflict are amplified by the free access of any person to any group, and by the consequent multiplication in the number of groups demanding the redress of grievances though public policy. Corporatism therefore seeks to limit the number of available groups, sanctioning a few "peak," or encompassing, organizations. These peak organizations are *incorporated* (hence corporatism) into the policy process, a device whereby the state hopes to maximize compliance and cooperation.

The idea of the public good among theorists of corporatism is as emphatic as it was with Rousseau's "general will." In organic theories of the state, both the centrality of the rational, self-interested individual of pluralism (and, of course, liberal individualism) and the centrality of class (in Marxism) are rejected in favor of the idea of people as members of a community. Hence "common good" is not merely a pseudonym for a narrow interest, as is true in pluralism. Conflict can be channeled and sanitized by subordinating narrow interest to the larger good. Stepan rightly points to Aristotle as a proponent of such a view, even though the pluralists claim him as well, and traces the notion of the public good through the doctrines of medieval Catholicism to modern corporatism. He contends that these doctrines share a belief that the "moral center of the organic-statist vision is thus not the individual taken by himself but rather the political community whose perfection allows the individual members to fulfill themselves."[45]

Corporatist Views of the Common Good

Organic statism and corporatism are thus distinguished from Marxism (or socialism) and fascism as well as individualism and pluralism. Fascism glorified the state and defined the common good and the needs of the state as indistinguishable; Marxism and socialism regard the state as the instrument that will eliminate the autonomy of interest groups and replace it by a collectivism achieved by the "new socialist being." Again, however, the common good and the interest of the state are fused. Corporatism is rather a system *depen-*

dent on the existence of groups that, in cooperation with a powerful central state apparatus, are integral participants in the process whereby the common good, the public interest, is defined.

That it *can* be defined is a view completely contrary to the dogma of pluralism. John C. Calhoun's assertion that the common good, "instead of being the united opinion of the whole community, is usually nothing more than the voice of the strongest interest or combination of interest; and not infrequently a small but energetic and active portion of the people," finds its echo in Truman's synthesis: "In developing a group interpretation of politics . . . we do not need to account for a totally inclusive interest because one does not exist."[46]

The Centrality of Conflict

Pluralism deems conflicts normal and healthy. Madison's oft cited argument in *Federalist 10* that conflict is inevitable, or at least that the costs of avoiding it far exceed the benefits, is rarely challenged. Since the fountainhead of conflict is inequality, only the most persistent and unlimited interposition could possibly extinguish it. But corporatism believes far less draconian measures can contain conflict. Pluralist theory speaks of governments' regulating conflict by establishing and enforcing general rules of appropriate conduct, by arranging compromises, balancing one interest against another, and by imposing settlements on the disputants. The traditional pluralist approach to "conflict management" has been one of advocating institutionalized channels between elites and masses and between competing elites. A political system with strong, cohesive parties and well-established interest groups makes conflict management a less onerous task than happens if parties are weak and groups obsessed and insecure.

CONFUCIANISM: THE ORGANIC STATISM OF HARMONY

Corporatism proposes a more active role for government. As government becomes more and more the domain of experts—

technocrats—it develops the ethical base for claiming an encompassing authority. Perhaps the most carefully constructed rationale for government by an intellectual elite is Confucianism, a form of corporatism pervasive in non-Western authoritarian and (although rarely since there are so few) democratic political systems.

Confucian thought uses the paradigm of the family to construct the ideal government. In traditional families, harmony occurs when all esteem the legitimate authority and superior moral position of the male head of the family. As Richard Solomon explains, "In the Confucian family tradition there is no behavior which is more likely to invoke swift punishment than a child's quarreling or fighting with siblings or neighborhood peers."[47] The governmental analogue to the father is the mandarin elite—the bureaucracy. Educated to rule—much as in the Platonic scheme—the mandarin class sought justification in acquiring an absolute monopoly on power. Confucianism is the ideology of the civil service.[48]

A class of administrators groomed for the position by education in Confucian ethics became the backbone of imperial China. The early appearance of a professionally trained civil service in China is pure Confucianism; the educated class rules not by force but because of superior training.[49] Confucianism makes a clear distinction between intellectual pursuits and expert knowledge. It is decidedly anti-expert, with civil servants trained generally in art, literature, and history. Much like the Oxford and Cambridge graduates who enlisted in the British Civil Service, Chinese civil servants were to be educated generalists, capable of developing the appropriate response to any contingency, but without any technical training in government or public administration. They were "amateurs in office . . . trained academically and . . . tested by written examinations, but they were not trained directly for tasks to be undertaken. . . . The higher degree holding members of the bureaucracy—the ruling class *par excellence*—were not identified with expertise."[50]

The mandarins became a class whose power supplanted that of the hereditary nobility. The ruling class was to consist of people of character and ability. Later Confucian thought recognized the legitimacy of replacing rulers when they were scoundrels, and Chinese society of course was but an approximation of the Confucian ideal.[51] But the exemplar was that of the organic state: "Just as the Confucian concept of the ideal government was an extension of the ideal family, so the prime tasks of government were the same as those of the family: to provide security, continuity, cohesion, and solidarity."[52] Superior people, educated in the classics and in traditional philosophy, were to guide the intercourse of the less worthy, but not necessarily to establish goals or ambitions for the government or the society. The Confucian ideal is one of a harmonious, conflict-free, organic whole. Its concerns are on process, not on substance. Whereas Marxism or fascism speaks to explicit wrongs to be righted and goals to be attained, Confucianism addresses only the question of technique. Political power flows hierarchically, from elites to masses, rather than being the prize awarded the victor in the competition between interest groups.

Confucian thought is best understood not so much from reading Confucius as from an examination of two much more articulate disciples, Mencius and Hsun-Tzu. Mencius argued for the overthrow of rulers who misused their "mandate from Heaven." Hsun-Tzu developed the idea of government by the enlightened few, believing that subjects are like children, given to self-indulgence and greed, and must be guided toward the collective good by experts. There is in Confucian thought a strong sense of consensus politics, rather than the conflict so central to pluralism. The emphasis is on *hierarchical* relationships. There is no need for balancing power between competing groups, since such groups were by definition usurpers of legitimate authority.

Much like Rousseau, Confucianism teaches that perfection is possible, but only if the state directs itself relentlessly toward the goal of cleansing the thoughts of its subjects. Conflict, which is derived from greed, will vanish if the rulers are wise. The explanation for conflict is not inequality, the Madisonian reason, or injustice, but rather an individual (not a societal) flaw. The conservative, authoritarian, character of Asian governments has deep roots in Confucianism.

Of course, even with a neutrally administered examination system in mandarin China, there was a strong link between social class and success in achieving an administrative career.[53] But the very fact that the bureaucracy became the occupation of choice for wealthier classes is of substantial importance in understanding how Confucian societies arrange relationships between government and economic interest groups.

Confucian Views of Political Economy

Confucian writings on economic matters reveal a belief that educated people ought not to learn commerce or the management of economic affairs. Just as the upper classes in England disdained the world of commerce, so did the mandarins. Moreover, the putative trappings of business (lavish consumption, extravagant behavior) are abhorrent to followers of the Confucian ethic. Consistent with the emphasis on harmony rather than conflict, the acquisitive urges required to succeed in business were believed to be unworthy of the mandarin class.[54] Hence, the bureaucracy stood in marked and superior contrast to practitioners of private enterprise, who followed the "crooked road," and to private coalitions such as commercial guilds, secret societies, or religious sects.

Such private associations were not, as is true of Western theories of organic statism and pluralism, central linkage mechanisms between people and governments. Rather, they were impediments to perfection. When interest groups are incorporated into the Confucian corporatist state, they are decidedly the junior partners. The obvious exception is Japan, whose modification of Confucianism encouraged aggressive, competitive skills and hence honored wealth, not for its own sake, but as an indication of proper upbringing. Lucian Pye draws a clear contrast between Chinese and Japanese Confucianism:

The differing roles of sons in China and Japan encouraged a passive approach to the outside world in China and an aggressive and activist approach in Japan. Chinese children were taught that they should do nothing that would bring shame to the family; in order to bring it honor, they were to excel in noneconomic pursuits by becoming scholar-officials. A Japanese, by contrast, could bring honor to his family by achieving material success.[55]

Confucian Organic Statism: Government and Family

The Confucian patterning of governments after families is consistent with a broader body of thought. In a sense the government *is* an extended family: Chinese believe they are part of an extended family; the pool of surnames is less than in Western society, and hence "families" are larger. Associations that are barriers to familial harmony (groups that practice self-aggrandizement) have to be made to understand that the social conflict endemic to their operation is ultimately likely to destroy the authority of the state and the family. Power is *relational,* as is the public good. The public good cannot be understood in absolute terms (as happens with the extreme Eastern religions) but rather should be seen as fair and equitable behavior of each person toward each "other" as defined in the outline of relationships. The son practices filial piety toward the father and faithfulness toward a friend.

Rulers too are obedient to the authority of their parents, and benevolent toward their loyal subjects. The ideal ruler of a people is the compliant offspring of a family.[56] Confucianism is thus organic statism of the most utopian sort. Its highest good is harmony, its most feared evil, conflict. In order to avoid conflict, a generally educated class of intellectuals must rule. To achieve the frictionless society, hierarchy must be respected. Government and society are merged into a seamless whole, with all subjects knowing their places.

The family thus becomes the microcosm for the entire, completely harmonious, arrangement. Good sons are docile; good subjects are obedient. Scholar-officials, selected because of their training, intelligence, and moral worth, are analogous to the father in the family.[57] Occasional current examples alert us to the centrality of the family and the reverence for paternal and maternal authority. Japanese psychiatrists use parental disapproval as a form of behavior modification. Japanese suffering from, say, alcoholism, are told that their parents would not approve of their behavior. The success rate for this form of treatment is impressive.

Cross-fertilization of Confucian and Western corporatist theories has never occurred. Admiration for Asian high-growth economies has led to popular infatuation with Confucianism but not to a synthesis at a more abstract level. It is not clear whether Confucianism is simply a euphemism for an amalgam of cultural tradition, historical accident, and formal theory suggesting a respect for hierarchy and an abhorrence of unconstrained political conflict. There are many examples of state corporatism without a trace of Confucius, as occurs in Latin America. But there is something uniquely Confucian about Asian polities. Lucian Pye explains:

In East Asian societies which were once infused with Confucian values political associations are themselves seen as being properly modeled after the family and clan, and hence participants are expected to act as though they were banded together in a blood relationship. This importance of belonging and of suppressing personal preferences in favor of the group's interests has other, secondary, consequences. The divide between friend and foe becomes exceedingly vivid and is not amenable to change. Conflicts take on the long range and uncompromising perspective of family feuds. There cannot be the kaleidoscopic realignments typical of the coalition politics of interest-oriented political systems.[58]

Whether Confucian thought is solely responsible for such broadly based cultural habits is not Pye's point; he uses "Confucian" to designate a way of life. Thus, when he argues that Taiwan, Japan, or South Korea "absorbed and refined Confucian values and concepts of authority," he does not intend to delineate a formal theory; nor does he suggest uniformity in the process of absorption and refinement.

Even such "apparent" aspects of Confucianism as the family/polity analog should be used with caution. Tu Wei-ming, perhaps the foremost proponent of Confucian ethics in the United States today, warns that, while the father-son dyad provides a hierarchical model for other relationships, each has a uniqueness. Of most direct interest to us is Tu's contention that the political relationship is not completely analogous to the father-son axis. The parent-child relationship, Tu reminds us, is a "primordial tie, absolutely binding and inescapably given." But the political relationship requires the ruler to be righteous in order to keep the claim on the mandate from heaven.[59] Misunderstanding of this point leads many to assign Confucianism a greater role in unresponsive, authoritarian government than it deserves. A brutal father is nevertheless still a father, while a compassionless ruler can be replaced. Tu concedes that Confucianism may have contributed to despotic government in premodern China, but insists that the essential component of key Confucian relationships "is not dependency but reciprocity."[60] Filial piety is reciprocated by compassion; wise rule is reciprocated by subject loyalty. The pervasiveness of reciprocity in Asian political systems, which we will consider in Chapters Six and Seven, finds its origins in the Confucian culture. But understanding reciprocity also enables us to acquit Confucianism of the charge that it is no more than a rationalization for tyranny. The Confucian Golden Rule—do not do to others what you would not want others to do to you—is, according to Tu, deliberately stated in the negative in order to convey a profound reluctance to impose a way of life on another.

Even though Confucianism is more easily applied to everyday life than more abstract or rigid ideologies, it is unlikely that the disparate ways of Asian political life are inspired by Mencius' Confucianism any more than that the government-business relationship in Austria is derived from the organic statism of medieval Catholic prelates. Ideas do not originate in intellectually pure vacuums. They reflect the culture of the time and place. *L'histoire des mentalités*, a form of historical writing made popular in France, has had its defenders in Mannheim and Durkheim and more recently has emerged with cultural history in the United States. Robert Darnton, one of its leading practitioners, uses the phrase "ethnographic history" to describe what he does:

While the historian of ideas traces the filtration of formal thought from philosopher, the ethnographic historian studies the way ordinary people made sense of the world. He attempts to uncover their cosmology, to show how they organized reality in their minds and expressed it in their behavior. He does not try to make a philosopher out of the man on the street but to see how street life called for a strategy. . . . Instead of deriving logical propositions, [ordinary people] think with things, or with anything else that their culture makes available to them, such as stories and ceremonies.[61]

Ordinary people in Asian societies are no more likely to read Confucius than ordinary people in the United States are to read Adam Smith. However, Confucian thought pervades the curriculum in Taiwan, while in mainland China, Mao tried to eliminate Confucian ethics by prohibiting the possession of Confucian literature, which he regarded as the vessel of unhealthy elitism.[62] He was not entirely successful. During the 1987 retreat from "bourgeois liberalism" in the People's Republic of China, a dismissed educator eschewed criticism of party leadership, pleading the Confucian tradition of obedience. That Mao believed Confucian thought worthy of proscription demonstrates both its significance and its durability.[63] Yet the Chinese version of Marxism has made it more Confucian, with emphases on self-cultivation, thought reform, opposition to purely technical expertise, the power of human will, and the primacy of managing interpersonal relations well. Other Confucian features, such as the importance of social hierarchies, have been internalized in practice even as they are condemned in theory.[64]

But families do not last forever, nor are they free of conflict. Divorces end traditional families more often than revolutions end governments. The quest for a conflict-free world, however, continues. Interest groups are symptomatic of flawed government in Confucian theory. Unregulated, fragmenting group conflict also connotes a malfunctioning government in corporatist theory. In both theories, the extent to which conflict is attenuated, constrained, or avoided altogether is the measure of success. In pluralism, such "evils" are either woven into the fabric of human nature or are fundamental to the governmental process.

Inferences About Organizations

Both pluralism and corporatism are culture-bound. Although more complex definitions with more empirically verifiable measures will be used later, it may be helpful to recapitulate the major differences between pluralism and corporatism, and between societal corporatism and state corporatism. Interest groups in pluralist theory are voluntary associations, free to organize and disband as they will and to gain influence in proportion to their political resources. The "governmental process" consists of the competition between interest groups, with government bureaucracies playing a major, but not necessarily dominant, role.

Under the decision rules of societal corporatism, interest groups are sanctioned by the government, excluding all but the "peak" associations (principally labor and business). Public economic policy, such as incomes legislation, is made by government bureaucracies in close and careful consultation with these "licensed" interest groups. Group influence in proposing and implementing policy is substantial.

State corporation goes one step further. The range of legitimate interests is defined unilaterally by the government. Economic associations are created and managed by the appropriate bureaucracy. While bureaucracies may find it prudent to listen to the views of interest groups, they are under no obligation to do so, and there are no implied or explicit power-sharing agreements.

The three modes of conflict resolution are not intended as pictures of reality. There are elements of each mode in all governments, with the nature of the times and the nature of the policy arena influencing the manner of decision making. They provide opportunities to expand our understanding of political organizations. The task of the remainder of the book is to explore the following ideas:

Is there evidence to support the hyper-pluralist belief that each person joins or withdraws from an organization based on a precise calculation of costs and benefits?

If so, are there variations according to the nature of the organization or the culture/value system of the society?

Since both the shared attitude and selective benefits theories of individual choice assume, at least tacitly, an open political environment, are there any variances in individual motive that are partially due to a more restrictive setting or to a less individualistic culture?

Does the mode of conflict resolution suggest different political outcomes? Are corporate political systems more durable, less conflictual, more humane, or more just?

Neither pluralism nor corporatism devote much attention to the problem of representation. If organizations provide selective benefits, do they also provide political unity for once disparate voices? Organizational leadership in corporatist settings enjoys the advantage of built-in access. Is this advantage reflected in individual choice?

These questions are explored in three types of political settings: the United States, surely the most pluralist, most aggressively individualist of the industrial democracies; Western Europe, where more collectivist, societal corporatist modes of conflict resolution are common; and the Asian state corporatist governments, especially Taiwan. Although the political cultures are dissimilar, the logic of the argument is to move from the least to the most corporate societies, hence from the United States to Asia. The in-depth analysis of Taiwan is intended as the Asian counterpart to the analysis of the United States.

The settings represent the extremes in the nontotalitarian political world. The questions also take into account the availability of information. To assess the impact of mode of conflict resolution on outcomes, comparative units with similarly measured variables are required; hence Western Europe is the logical choice. To put theories of individual choice to a comparative test, the Asian countries are ideal, as they stress the subordination of individual urges in their artistic, cultural, and political lives.

TWO

THE CREATION AND MAINTENANCE OF POLITICAL ORGANIZATIONS IN A PLURALIST SOCIETY

As important as individual choice is, the political reason for studying such choice is more crucial. Organizational creation and survival are more immediately related to macro-political events than are personal decisions. Individuals choose mates, careers, cars, movies, and organizations. Governments choose taxes, allies, wars, and constitutions. The private choice to join a group provides a resource to be used politically. Organizations convert nonpolitical decisions into political resources.

COMPETING THEORIES OF GROUP ORIGINS

We can presume that spontaneous combustion in response to a disturbance is not a reasonable explanation of how groups originate. The entrepreneur puts the pieces together. Using the same historical evidence as Truman about the rise of farm organizations, Robert Salisbury has shown that, without a person willing to work full time at organizing, shared attitudes will not coalesce into organizations.[1] An organization is not merely an institutionalization of shared attitudes; rather it is the consequence of intense organizational effort. But if Truman is wrong, so again is Olson.

There has been a surge of organizational growth in the United States, because of a variety of ingredients, such as the liberalization of campaign finance legislation, an explosion of federal economic regulations (beginning with the 1960's and lasting until the election of Reagan), and the development of computer-assisted communications. Many of the organizations so intimately involved with the growth of legislation do not dispense any selective benefits.[2] But there has always been a "patron"—either a foundation, an individual, a government agency, or another association—that supplies front money.

Examples of Entrepreneurial Activity

Two examples illustrate the role of entrepreneurs in organizational creation: Common Cause and the National Organization for Women.

John Gardner, long active in foundations (Carnegie) and government service (Lyndon Johnson's secretary of health, education, and welfare) founded Common Cause in 1970.[3] After leaving his government position, Gardner led the Urban Coalition. He sought to separate the lobbying arm of the Coalition, the Urban Coalition Action Council, from its parent organization because of tax legislation prohibiting foundations from financing lobbying organizations. Gardner sought to refinance through mass mailings, and changed the name to Common Cause. It was a propitious year for such an effort. Liberal elite discontent with government institutions and policy was high. The Cambodian invasion, the killing of protesting students at Kent State University, and the prevailing alienation from government made the times right.

There were similar, competitive, organizational efforts, but they failed. None had Gardner. He appealed successfully to people like him: educated professionals with discretionary income. The 1970's were years of economic growth, which freed the income of potential contributors. Right on the heels of the Cambodian fiasco, the country plunged into the spectacle of Watergate, making the writing of a check to an organization speaking for procedural reform and "good government" a convenient, painless way to "do something." The principal role of Gardner in tapping this resource cannot be overstated:

1970 conditions were ripe for the creation of a lobby such as Common Cause. But without John Gardner, that lobby would not have been as successful. It takes a rare person to launch successfully a general purpose public interest lobby. . . . [Other entrepreneurs] had a similar idea at about the same time as Gardner, but they were relieved to merge their effort with Gardner's. Ralph Nader did not think that a public subscription drive for members would succeed. Fred Harris in 1972 and George Romney in 1973 tried to start public interest lobbies but failed.[4]

His presence was good enough to raise ultimately more than 6 million dollars, some from foundations and wealthy patrons (the Rockefeller Foundation most prominently), but most from "well-educated professionals who, on an individual cost-benefit analysis, have nothing to gain by their contribution."[5]

Betty Friedan played the same role for the National Organization for Women.[6] In 1961, a Presidential Commission on the Status of Women was created, issuing its report two years later, the year that Friedan's *The Feminine Mystique* appeared. Most states created parallel agencies, and by 1967, every state had a commission on the status of women. These in turn formed a National Conference of State Commissions. The Presidential Commission report was less important for what it said than for creating the legitimacy of women as a constituency. Friedan's book, on the other hand, argued that the traditional family was an inherently repressive institution, and that the role of full-time housewife was crippling. The commercial success of *The Feminine Mystique* coincided with the creation of an Interdepartmental Committee on the Status of Women and a Citizens' Advisory Council on the Status of Women. Shortly thereafter, Title VII of the Civil Rights Act created the Equal Employment Opportunity Commission (EEOC).

As this legion of agencies began its various duties, "Betty Friedan was often in Washington conferring with interested women on what could be done to combat discrimination."[7] The source of dissatisfaction was the timid performance of the Equal Employment Opportunity Commission. The explicit organizational catalyst was the National Conference of State Commissions, funded by the Citizens' Advisory Council and the Interdepartmental Committee on the Status of Women. It was here that NOW was born. The particular spur was an EEOC reluctance to outlaw sex-segregated want ads. The National Conference of State Commissions would not accept a resolution opposing such ads, and this led to the formation of NOW, with Friedan as president.

Similarities and Contrasts

The similarities in these two accounts of organizational genesis are apparent: both Gardner and Friedan started from a strong base of contacts and friendship with existing bureaucracies. Both were well connected within the issue networks they intended to influence. In neither case did the founder participate in the birth of an organization for personal gain, and in neither case did membership appeals offer selective benefits. Yet both organizations are extant, while dozens of competitors are not. Because of the nature of the times— Truman's disturbances—these entrepreneurs were quickly and well funded. Start-up costs for any organization are substantial and the very technology that makes rapid membership growth possible is itself a major drain on resources:

> The key to success in these efforts is usually the ability of group organizers to secure both start up funds and reliable sources of continuing financial support from patrons of political action. . . . Most of the groups founded in the wake of the civil rights and peace movements that were to secure adequate patronage have disappeared.[8]

ORGANIZING THE PRIVATE SECTOR

Stable and substantial funding allows organizations to persist in spite of massive turnover in membership. Without selective benefits, organizations cannot hope for a long-term commitment, but rather must settle for a stable *total* membership. The problem of unstable membership—pervasive among interest groups—affects the ability of the organization to speak accurately for its membership. Rapid turnover is not necessarily a disadvantage, especially in the organization of private sector interest groups. Unlike those organizations that rose to prominence during the 1960's because of an increase in federal civil rights and social welfare legislation, organizations that aspire to speak for the private, profit-making, sector rarely enjoy government or foundation sponsorship.

Often, private sector organizations emerged in response to a perceived government threat rather than at the bidding of a governmental patron. Appeals are made for membership by stressing the persistent danger from traditionally hated evils: big labor, bureaucratic intervention, the menace of unbridled competition, the gobbling up of small businesses by corporations, the threat of foreign imports, and so on.

There have been episodic whiffs of corporatism in the history of American industrial relations, however. During the New Deal, the National Recovery Administration (NRA) authorized trade associations to develop fair trade codes that would have had the force of law. The opportunity to set prices for entire industries proved a major inducement for entrepreneurial activity. When the Supreme Court determined the NRA to be unconstitutional, more than five hundred trade associations—created to serve as auxiliary governments in establishing and maintaining rules of economic competition—were disbanded.[9]

During the 1960's, when the national government launched its "war on poverty," organizations were created explicitly to receive and disburse federal money. Legislation specified the creation of client groups ("Maximum feasible participation") with quasi-public status, much as happened in Europe when labor unions were designated as participants in incomes legislation. But like the trade associations established to implement New Deal legislation, the organizations spawned by the war on poverty disappeared once the official stimulus was removed.

The Group Business

A more typical pattern in pluralist systems is the response to a threat, coupled with the existence of an entrepreneur. Unlike the public sector entrepreneurs of the 1960's, the creators of business associations usually are in the business of associations. The resultant organizations are often the consequence of the initiative of a single entrepreneur who is merchandising a product in a competitive market. Since the profit motive drives businesses in a market economy, it is only reasonable to anticipate that the business organization entrepreneurs are Olsonian, establishing associations in the expectation of creating a profitable enterprise. The National Association of Manufacturers and the United States Chamber of

Commerce employ salespersons paid on a commission basis to recruit membership.

Perhaps the most entrepreneurial (in the traditional sense) are the various organizations representing small business. They are invariably the creation of a single entrepreneur, and they survive by using salespeople with regional territories, exactly like an individual firm. Since two or perhaps three canvassers will be in the same territory selling memberships, their appeals are also similar: each claims to be the only legitimate representative of small business.

As was true of civil rights associations, "public" interest groups, and women's organizations, the small business associations were given an initial push by the government: in 1938, President Roosevelt's Department of Commerce organized a small business conference to counter the opposition of large corporations to his policies. The conference was a dismal failure, but several small business organizations sprang up. An additional incentive was provided by the creation of the Small Business Administration in 1953. In recruiting new members, the competing organizations lay claim to access to this agency. Some of the businesses recruited are hardly small. One can find the gold National Federation of Independent Business plaque in Baskin and Robbins franchises, for example.[10]

The use of paid recruiters obviously contradicts the Truman shared attitude theory. If a door to door salesperson is needed to demonstrate shared attitudes, something is seriously wrong. However, both Truman and Olson neglect the problem of membership stability. The membership turnover in business organizations is horrendous, reaching 90 percent in some years. But the turnover rate lends support to Olson. There are few solidary benefits, and even fewer selective material benefits (see page 40). The initial surge of enthusiasm—fueled by a hard sell by recruiters—is likely to last only until the time for renewal of membership (Table 2-1).

Personal Motives and Organizational Goals

It is quite likely that turnover in groups that lack selective benefits is high. Group leaders are more politicized than group followers and sustain a consistently higher interest in politics. Without selective benefits the initial political reason for joining recedes, with noth-

TABLE 2-1
RENEWAL RATES IN FOUR U.S. INTEREST GROUPS

Type of group	% members renewing at the end of:*		
	1st year	2nd year	3rd year
Occupational			
Trade (n = 267)	30	42	54
General (n = 539)	12	38	46
Nonoccupational			
Citizens' (n = 301)	8	46	38
Single-issue (n = 124)	19	53	48

*Each percentage is computed on a base of the previous year; of the 30 percent in the trade association who renewed at the end of the first year, 42 percent renewed at the end of the second year, etc.

Source: These data are drawn from a mail survey of members of four organizations. The names were selected randomly from membership lists, and each person selected received one initial letter and two follow-ups. The return rate averaged 65 percent. In exchange for their cooperation, the request for anonymity was readily granted. The research was undertaken and completed in 1985. For Table 2-1, membership lists were searched by name for renewal rates.

ing to replace it. Most of the defection will take place in the first year of membership. Common Cause loses about half of its new recruits in their first year of membership, and this appears to be a higher than average retention rate.[11] The crucial period is at the end of the first year; in every kind of organization, the greatest attrition occurs then, as was true of other organizations for which we have data. The best renewal record is in the narrowly based trade associations and the single-issue groups, but even here the dropout rate is high. In the general occupational groups and nonoccupational groups, the turnover rate is even higher.

Political passions are transitory. A person might be moved by an anti-abortionist appeal or Gardner's condemnation of political action committees, write out a check, and feel assuaged. But a year or so passes, and the routines of life continue; other issues are given media attention, other groups compete for dollars. At the end of the first year, those who renew either are hooked by selective benefits or are sufficiently committed to the cause that the decision to renew is painless, even pleasurable.

Selective benefits are a better inducement than is commitment to a cause. Most people want to get through the tribulations of everyday life; if they join any organization, it will be an occupational group. Some people are political junkies, however, and they tend to gravitate toward those organizations with an ideology of participation, reform, and traditional citizen commitment. A fervent minority dedicate themselves to a cause, and for them the single-issue groups are an obvious entry—albeit temporary—into the world of political combat.

Rapid turnover is not necessarily a problem for an organization, since members are rarely involved in serious policy decisions. For the organization whose goal is to make a profit, membership turnover ironically can be an incentive to salespeople. They receive a higher commission on new membership than on renewals (as is true, for instance, of insurance salespeople). Turnover only becomes a problem when replacement cannot equal or exceed dropout rates.

Varieties of Entrepreneurial Behavior

Entrepreneurs, like joiners, have mixed reasons for doing what they do. A common typology of goods, which Olson's categorization augments, is one developed according to their substance. In this typology, goods are divided into material, solidary, and purposive categories.[12]

Material benefits, like selective ones, have calculable monetary value or can readily be converted into goods of equivalent monetary value. Solidary benefits, on the other hand, are intrinsic to people and have incalculable value:

They derive in the main from the act of associating and include such rewards as socializing, congeniality, the sense of group membership and identification, the status resulting from membership, fun and conviviality, the maintenance of social distinctions, and so on. Their common characteristic is that they tend to be independent of the precise ends of the association.[13]

Solidary benefits are obvious inducements to join existing organizations, such as the various veterans' groups that provide at least as much fun and companionship as they do lobbying either for abstract causes such as patriotic fervor or for explicit, material benefits.[14]

But solidary gains also can be motives for entrepreneurs, who usually derive great personal satisfaction out of their association with like-minded activists. The intense pleasure associated with some forms of entrepreneurial activity—the development of tight interpersonal networks—is quite important.[15] Personal gratification plays a major role in the formation and maintenance especially of organizations with a deeply felt mission, such as the civil rights organizations of the 1960's:

Eating, sleeping, working side by side day after day, SNCC activists created a way of life more than a set of ideas. . . . Out of such experiences the SNCC staff developed a deep sense of kinship. Even today those who were once at the center of the SNCC experience feel bound to each other, although their political beliefs and personal lives have since diverged widely.[16]

The strength of personal loyalties is enhanced when people believe the fledgling organization is promoting an unpopular cause, one that is likely to encourage opposition, repression, or even violence from other groups or from governments. Since most emergent organizations produce and distribute the rhetoric of the apocalypse, opportunities for solidary payoffs are substantial.

But the opportunities for such rewards—and indeed the opportunities for purposive benefits—are more attractive to politicized, active people. Usually these opportunities are important enough for them to forego any selective returns on investment. Passion, commitment to a cause, unswerving belief in the goals of the organization, possibly to the point of obsession, will keep entrepreneurs faithful for a lifetime. But for the person weighing a decision to join, such solidary and purposive benefits are not apparent. Enthusiasm for the cause might be enough for the initial decision to join, but can it sustain loyalty indefinitely? Apparently enthusiasm alone cannot, since membership turnover is quite high. As Salisbury argues:

For most people the act of joining an expressive group . . . is a marginal act. The benefits derived from value expression are seldom of great intrinsic worth. Generally, even if civil liberties remain equally endangered, a slight change in the member's resources or social pressures may lead to his failure to renew his membership.[17]

A very few groups will have the opportunity to provide selective benefits. Professional or occupational associations and trade associations based upon a narrow definition of membership (interstate trucking companies, import-export companies, for example) are most likely to provide selective benefits (insurance, the dissemination of technical information, and job opportunity networks are often cited). But most other groups do not have the resources for such expensive services; nor do they have a membership definition that would allow them to provide selective benefits. It is just these sorts of groups—those unable to offer selective goods and thus appealing for membership on the strength of a cause or ideology— that have contributed the most to the growth of interest groups in the last two decades in the United States. Most of the occupational groups were in place by World War II, but the majority of the citizens' groups, consumer groups, various single-issue groups (pro-abortion, anti-abortion, and the like) date from the 1960's at the earliest.[18] They have both a higher turnover rate and a shorter lifespan than do those organizations that provide selective benefits.

THE QUESTION OF SIZE

The larger the potential group, the more difficult it will be to provide even a collective good upon which most can agree most of the time. Size—traditionally valued in pluralist group theory—can be a debilitating handicap in Olson's reformulation. Pluralists recognize that size can impede cohesion, and they know that size is a major influence upon organizational goals, as large groups reduce the precision of their demands in order to prevent the destruction of fragile member-coalitions. Curiously, one of pluralism's most prominent champions treats the problem of size in a cursory manner, although his general theory fits well. Speaking of polities, Robert Dahl (with Edward Tufte) proposes and defends the view that, as size increases, the opportunities for participation decrease, as does leaders' ability to comprehend and represent the views of followers. With regard to interest groups, he makes two points: larger, more complex polities are not likely to be faced with the trauma of a single dominant interest; and, while there is an upper threshold for effective "span of control" (representation), there is also a lower threshold below which the probability of an interest group being formed is remote.[19]

Truman writes of the threat to cohesion posed by "overlapping membership."[20] Olson is therefore not completely justified when he observes:

In so far as the traditional theory draws any distinction at all between small and large groups, it is apparently with respect to the scale of the function they perform, not the extent they succeed in performing [it]. . . . It assumes that small and large groups differ in degree, but not in kind.[21]

True, Truman did not come to understand that larger groups are inherently vulnerable to overlapping affiliations pulling members in different directions, but the inference is clear. Additionally, Murray Edelman, whose work Olson does not consider, is, if not a pluralist, certainly a "traditional" theorist, since he grounds much of his writing in the idea of politics as a struggle among groups.[22] Edelman writes of two types of group activity:

Pattern A: a relatively high degree of organization—rational, cognitive procedures—precise information—an effective interest in specifically identified, tangible resources—a favorably perceived strategic position with respect to reference groups—*relatively small numbers.*
Pattern B: shared interest in the improvement of status through activity—an unfavorably perceived strategic position with respect to reference groups—distorted, stereotyped, inexact information and perception—response to symbols connoting suppression of threats—relative ineffectiveness in securing tangible resources through political activity—little organization for purposeful action—quiescence—*relatively large numbers.*[23]

Size and Strategy

Beyond determining the nature of its appeals, size has much to do with determining the type and the amount of resources available to the group. Resources, in turn, affect the tactical options open to groups in their pursuit of policy goals. Large groups wish to rely on advantages associated with voting and majorities, since they aspire to deliver, or to withhold, their members' votes. This is an exceedingly difficult course of action. The appeal of an organization to a large number of potential supporters will require a wider range of benefits than would be true if it were to limit its solicitation to a smaller public, and the group must adopt a more ambiguous, more rhetorical appeal. Obscuring the clarity of focus on a single central issue may result in expanded membership; however, the cost of such obfuscation is considerable. The original members might be alienated without attracting appreciable numbers of replacements.

The student movements—particularly those organized in opposition to the war in Vietnam in the 1960's and 1970's—provide instructive evidence of the perils of goal expansion. Originally created to pursue a single goal—ending the United States' involvement in the war—they attracted patrons and participants from beyond universities. The only characteristic these diverse elements had in common was opposition to the war, and even that goal generated a variety of factional disputes (between philosophical pacifists and those who objected to the war as an unwise instrument of foreign policy, for example). The Vietnam Moratorium, a holding company for various emergent anti-war movements, soon sought to expand its membership and to create a stable organization by enlarging the scope of its interest. At each subsequent demonstration, the scope was enlarged. The second Moratorium-organized march included striking union members and speakers who condemned police harassment of minorities.

As a result, original members of the organization defected, reasoning that the initial commitment of the organization had expanded beyond their initial interests. By introducing a larger set of goals, the organization fostered cleavages along different socioeconomic axes. Although protest continued throughout the duration of the war, the Moratorium went out of business; thus no organizations emerged from the obvious "disturbance" of the Vietnam war, except for veterans' associations, whose shaky structure lasted for a while.

The decision of Moratorium leaders to expand represents a fatal entrepreneurial error. If the "spontaneous combustion" theory were credible, it would take more than inept leadership to destroy an organization. Largely inexperienced and unconnected, Moratorium leaders had no patron and no working arrangement with government bureaucracies, in vivid contrast to NOW and Common Cause. They assumed wrongly that issue expansion would ensure a wider membership base, when the reverse effect was more likely. If the multiple issues are compatible—that is, if they create parallel cleavages within a group or an organization—it is likely that they will attract more members than if the various issue positions clash. But potential entrepreneurs are more likely to have a set of constrained, compatible, complementary goals. Potential *members* are more likely to have fragmented, unconstrained value systems. Thus there is a strong probability that entrepreneurs will misperceive how potential group members will react to a given set of issues.

Youthful organizations with "angels" can indulge in trial and error, but most entrepreneurs spend more time raising money than conducting market research; hence the decision to try for a broader audience is rarely successful. The greater risk is that initial supporters will withdraw support. The final collapse of the various student organizations that flowered during the 1960's can be attributed largely to inept entrepreneurs. Jack Walker's description of the demise of the Students for Democratic Society is a classic illustration of inexperienced leadership. As SDS moved from student organization to revolutionary vanguard, its patron, the United Automobile Workers, withdrew its support, leaving the Weathermen the job of raising money, a task they accomplished by robbing banks.[24]

Size and the Logic of Individual Choice

The clear implication is that enlarging the issue agenda requires an expansion of selective benefits in order to counteract the danger of membership loss because of crosscutting cleavages (the "overlapping membership" of Truman's theory).[25] Ironically, it is the large, symbolically oriented groups that cannot provide such benefits. The tactical options that become available as the policy menu expands are illustrated graphically in Figure 2-1. Let the area inside the rectangle represent a policy. The area inside the circle (Issue A) represents that subset of persons who have an interest in Issue A.

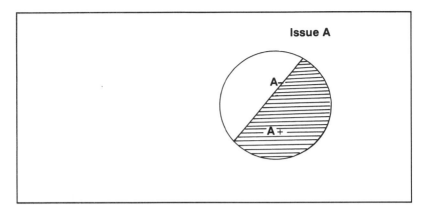

Figure 2-1. Choice and Issue Salience

The diagonal line cutting through Issue A separates those who favor Issue A (the subset A+) from those who oppose it (A-). Assume that an entrepreneur has formed an interest group that has as its sole objective the adoption of Issue A. Suppose again that no selective benefits are offered; hence the potential membership of the interest group is the complete set of those persons who fall into the A+ sector of the circle. Since the A+ sector is larger than the A- sector, pluralist theory presumes that Issue A will be enacted.

Of course pluralist theory makes this inference solely as a model. It is correct only if (1) policies were made exclusively by those directly interested in the issues at stake, and (2) if numerical superiority were the most important resource in a political contest. Neither of these conditions is uniformly true in democratic polities. Citizens rarely have the opportunity to determine public policy directly. Moreover, their representatives are generally likely to be persuaded by many more circumstances than the number of people actively supporting or opposing an issue. In societies in which responsiveness is not a valued resource, the size of the competing groups is even less consequential.

Presuming a high value of responsiveness, let us imagine an interest group composed of all those persons who fall into the A+ sector. Suppose this group decides to expand its scope of involvement and to take a position on a second issue, Issue B. Such a decision might be based upon a desire to expand membership, on moral or ideological grounds, or on other tactical or material considerations. The results of issue expansion in terms of membership support will depend upon several factors. Four distinct types of situations will result.

Figure 2-2 illustrates the first condition. Issue B is salient to a totally different set of people than is Issue A. Our hypothetical interest group has taken a position favorable to Issue B (vertical shading) in addition to its pro-A stance. Thus, although the A+ people have little in common with the B+'s, they can unite for purposes of mutual benefit. Such a group could be called a "confederated" interest group. The A+'s lend their support to the B+'s, in whose issue they have no intrinsic interest. Such coalitions are common *between* organizations since they are temporary marriages of convenience.

Occasionally the alliance unites normally antagonistic groups. The unions representing restaurant and hotel workers and trade associations representing the "hospitality" industry couple to oppose reduction in tax deductions for entertainment. Fundamentalist New Right organizations and some feminist groups cooperate in efforts to control pornography. Once these issues are resolved, such

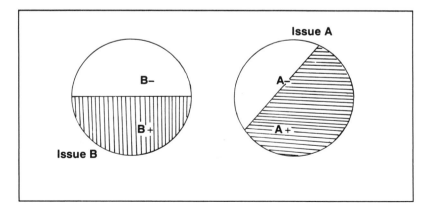

Figure 2-2. Individual Preference on Two Issues

coalitions disintegrate. If the policy goals are likely to require a sustained struggle, coalitions can become more stable through the device of umbrella associations that allow the component groups to continue their antagonism and yet institutionalize their coalition through the notion of confederation.

Figure 2-3 shows a different type of circumstance that may result from the group's expansion of issues. Issue A and Issue B are important to the same subset of people. However, in this example, the lines of cleavage are crosscutting; that is, they bisect the group along different axes. Therefore the result is four sectors rather than two. Those who oppose both issues fall in the northern sector, in the south are those who favor both, and in the east and west are those who favor one but oppose the other. Only the southern cross-hatched sector, composed of A+'s and B+'s, contains persons whose interests are congruent with the avowed position of the interest group. Some people who are either A+/B-'s or A-/B+'s may be attracted to the group if they place a greater weight on the issue on which they agree with the group's position than on the one on which they disagree. But such persons, even if they retain membership in the group, are marginal members, for their commitment to the goals of the group is less than absolute, and they may easily

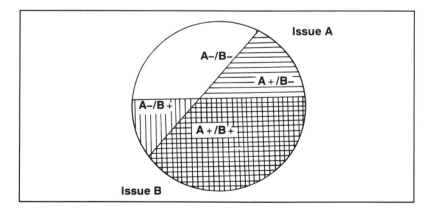

Figure 2-3. Crosscutting Cleavages

withdraw their support without greatly violating their own self-interest.

This is an obvious example of how groups can decrease their support by expanding their scope of interests. It is a "crosscutting" case, as opposed to the "logrolling" case involving coalitions. The coalition is an effort to minimize membership loss, since it is a temporary alliance committing only a portion of the group's resources.

Figure 2-4 represents a special type of the crosscutting situation. The sole difference between Figures 2-3 and 2-4 is that the axis along which the Issue B cleavage occurs has been rotated so that it is parallel to that of Issue A. Both issues are important to a coincident set of people, but instead of four distinct subsets, parallel cleavage results in only three. Once again, those in the cross-hatched A+/B+ subset find the positions of the group consistent with their own interests, while those in the A–/B– subset find the group positions wholly at odds with their own. The A+/B–'s will be divided into nonsupporters and marginal supporters.

The situations represented here are rather pure abstractions of what may occur in the existential world. Figure 2-5 is more likely to describe actual group phenomena. In the problem represented in Figure 2-5, Issues A and B are critical for distinct but overlapping

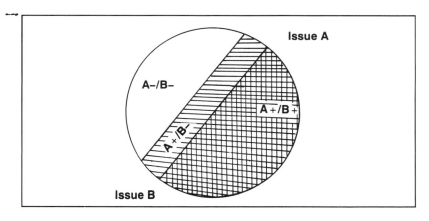

Figure 2–4. Parallel Cleavages

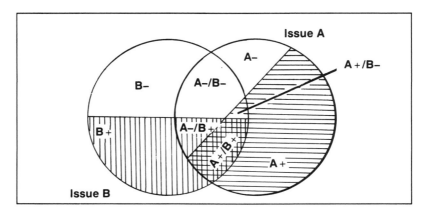

Figure 2-5. An Approximation of "Real" Choice

sets of people. Those persons who are favorably disposed toward one issue and who have no interest in the others (the A+'s and the B+'s) should react to the group as did their counterparts in Figure 2-2. That is, for them the group functions as an umbrella under which interests are confederated for mutual advantage. Group membership for such persons takes on the quality of logrolling for tactical benefit.

Within the intersection of the two subsets, however, the situation is reminiscent of Figure 2-3, for four distinct orderings of issue orientation occur within the area of overlap. The A+/B+ subset is unequivocal in its agreement with the group goals, just as the A-/B- subset is in disagreement. The organization can expect support from the former and opposition from the latter. As was true of Figure 2-3, those who are either A+/B-, or A-/B+ will be only marginal members at best.

In each of these cases, the effects of multiple issues on group membership can be analyzed in terms of the following factors:

—The number of issues on which the group adopts a position.
—The population (size of the set) for which each issue is important.
—The size of the respective pro and con subsets within each issue set.
—The extent of overlap when two or more issue sets intersect.

—The relative angles between the lines of cleavage in intersecting issue sets.

The closer the lines of severance are to congruence, the more compatible are the issues. When cleavage lines are not congruent, the closer they become to being parallel, the more compatible the issues are. The more nearly the angles between the lines of dissection approach 90 degrees, the more pronounced will be the conflicting cross-pressures felt by potential members.

Much of the above revolves around size. Expanding a coalition generally involves more costs than benefits. William Riker's "law" of minimum coalitions predicts just this sort of problem. Huge majorities are unmanageable; hence smaller majorities are preferable. Large organizations are unmanageable; hence smaller ones are preferable.[26]

The growth of single-issue groups in the United States illustrates the advantages of small size, providing support for the Edelman notion of size as a contributor to the seeking of tangible benefits.[27] Unlike governments (in democratic societies), interest groups have no mechanism to ensure *public* accountability. But rarely is there much assessment of the ability (or willingness) of interest group leaders—lobbyists, elected organization officials, and staff—faithfully to reflect *members'* opinions.

THE PROBLEM OF MISREPRESENTATION

Interest group leaders argue that a thousand voices together have more impact than a single one alone. But suppose if, in the combining of voices, the message is so garbled that it is unintelligible? Misrepresentation is the clear message of Roberto Michels' "iron law of oligarchy." The very fact of organization implies oligarchy. Entrepreneurs have different interests and skills from those who join later. As entrepreneurs are replaced—as the organization develops a bureaucracy—those new to staff or leadership positions will inevitably be more politically sensitive to other elites and more attuned to the nuances of elite political dialogue.[28] They will spend most of their time talking to others active in policy formation, while their image of "the membership" will become clouded.

It is imperative to remember the difference between the *effects* of group goals and benefits and the *origins* of these goals and benefits. Evaluations of group goals and benefits need not make much of a distinction between leaders and followers, for both are in a sense "prior to" the enunciation of goals and the provision of goods. The process whereby such articulation and provision are conducted is leadership originated and executed. Since organizational leadership, as do all political elites, imputes attitudes to passive followers, its estimate is likely to be inaccurate. Erroneous perception of members' values is not necessarily improved by many of the devices used by interest groups to convey a democratic image. Most organizations recognize the need for some form of communication between leaders and followers. The largest and most affluent hold national conventions, supplemented by member surveys, some of which are haphazard but others of which are quite carefully undertaken. There are examples of organizational leadership abandoning a proposed plan of lobbying activity because of negative response to organizationally conducted member surveys. Such examples are rare, but impressive in that they tend to occur in organizations lacking any sort of selective benefits.[29]

The Fragile Nature of Participation

In such organizations, ordinarily afflicted with unstable membership in any case, a serious and continuing disagreement between leaders and followers can often result in a loss of membership. But keep in mind that collective goods are the only product offered by such organizations. People join because they believe in the organization's aspirations, for the most part, and would surely leave if the association were to alter them. Common Cause leadership wanted to expand the agenda to include efforts toward a moratorium on the construction of nuclear reactors, but was dissuaded from doing so because of the opposition of a persistent minority as revealed in member surveys. This outcome caused Andrew McFarland to conclude that "the exit option is an important limit to the oligarchical tendencies within interest group organizations."[30]

But the generalization is too great. Like most groups that offer only a commitment to abstract goals, Common Cause does not provide many of even the collective benefits that Olson believes are singly inadequate to sustain membership. Members join because they want to "do good," because they hunger to become involved in government, but the fruits of their labor will not appreciably improve their personal financial status. Collective benefits really only refer to the rational person who abstains, believing that his or her minimal investment in an organization is too costly, especially when the realization of group goals will provide the same benefits as would be available had they joined. But the goals of Common Cause have only the most distant connection with a member's calculus of probable financial outcomes. Lobbying for limitation, regulation, and monitoring of the activities of political action committees, for example, will do nothing for or against the income of a Common Cause member. People join because they are joiners: comparatively wealthy, highly educated reformers. To expect them to sit idly by while Common Cause leadership stakes out an independent course of action is unrealistic.

As Table 2-2 shows, the percentage aware of an explicit lobbying effort varies with the nature of the organization, as does the percentage of those aware who agree with the position of the organization. In the single-issue groups and the narrowly based trade associations, most of the membership is aware and in agreement.

TABLE 2-2
PERCENTAGE OF MEMBERS AWARE OF AN EXPLICIT
LOBBYING EFFORT DURING THE PAST TWO YEARS

Type of group	*% aware*	*% agreeing (of those aware)*
Occupational		
Trade (n = 267)	53	70
General (n = 539)	38	52
Nonoccupational		
Citizens' (n = 301)	40	61
Single-issue (n = 124)	72	86

This relatively alert membership is probably a supporting case for Edelman's idea of the consequence of size.

Narrowly based trade associations such as those for truckers or software companies have limited goals of presumably immediate and tangible consequence. An example again is the trade associations representing used car dealers that lobbied successfully against legislation mandating the display of defects on the window of the car. The proposed bill would have required dealers to inspect cars and either rectify the flaws or inform the buyer. Lobbyists opposed to the law argued solely on the contention of increased cost to consumers (adding the obvious probability that the price increase would be passed along), but in truth the consequences of the legislation would have had a more immediate impact on the lobbyists' clients, the car dealers, than on the potential end users.

In clear contrast to such a narrow mandate stands the Sierra Club membership. In the middle 1970's, implementation of the 1972 Water Pollution Control Act established explicit compliance guidelines, an effort that Sierra Club lobbyists strongly supported. Although the Sierra Club provided unwavering support for the federal legislation, its members admitted that they knew very little about it. Of all the groups active in support of, or in opposition to, enforcement of the legislation, Sierra Club members ranked lowest in information, but very high in their disagreement with the statement that water pollution was so complex that it should be left in the hands of professionals.[31]

Size and Stability

The larger organizations with less homogeneous membership are less successful in establishing a policy connection to members. However, there is not much evidence that this failure is fatal (see Table 2-3). For the more narrowly focused organizations, awareness of, and agreement with, lobbying goals has a modest positive effect on renewal rates, but for the larger groups no clear pattern emerges.

Smaller groups apparently have a more politically attentive membership, leaving leadership with less room to bargain. In no organization, however, is the membership hanging on every decision, waiting to exercise the exit option when organizational policy

TABLE 2-3
RENEWAL RATES FOR MEMBERS AND AWARENESS
OF LOBBYING GOALS: PERCENTAGE RENEWING

Type of group	% unaware	% aware	% in agreement
Occupational			
Trade (n = 267)	22	41	43
General (n = 539)	13	10	11
Nonoccupational			
Citizens' (n = 391)	13	9	10
Single-issue (n = 124)	14	29	42

veers away from individual preference. The decision to renew is more political in the narrowly focused organizations, but never can we conclude that policy differences between leaders and followers are a major cause of membership turnover. This analysis of the decision to renew differs from Moe's work on the decision to join, but the conclusions are similar.[32]

Another political activity, campaign contributions, reinforces these suggestions (see Table 2–4). No one needs a refresher course on the meteoric rise of the political action committees as major contributors to campaigns, especially congressional ones. Much of this growth is accounted for by corporate PAC's, trade association PAC's, and, to a lesser extent, ideological PAC's. All told, 42 percent of the money raised and spent by winners in the 1986 congressional elections came from PAC's.[33] As a result, they have captured a major portion of the attention afforded to such elections by popular commentaries, many of which allege that PAC's can buy success. Less is known about how they organize, but they are of at least two varieties: those affiliated with an established group, such as AMPAC with the American Medical Association, and those operating without such organizational arrangements.[34]

Not all interest groups have formed PAC's. Among the organizations in this study, the citizens' group not only did not have a PAC but made no campaign contributions. The single-issue group joined forces with several others of similar persuasion to fund a

TABLE 2-4
PERCENTAGE OF MEMBERS AWARE OF AT LEAST ONE
CAMPAIGN CONTRIBUTION, PERCENTAGE AGREEING,
PERCENTAGE DISAGREEING, AND PERCENTAGE INDIFFERENT

	% aware	% agreeing*	% disagreeing*	% indifferent*
Occupational				
Trade (n = 267)	40	30	14	44
General (n = 539)	36	20	19	61
Nonoccupational				
Single-issue (n = 124)	56	79	4	19

*All percentages use the first column (percentage aware) as the base. Among nonoccupational groups, only the single-issue group appears here, as the citizens' group does not make campaign contributions.

PAC, and both the general occupational group and the trade association created fully subordinate PAC's. Given this variety of institutional arrangements, it would be a minor miracle if there were much member awareness of, and control over, campaign contributions.

In some kinds of organizations, principally those with a narrow mandate, the membership is more politicized than is the case for the larger, more symbolically oriented organizations. Thus the trade association membership is more politically aware, and less indifferent, than the general organization membership, and neither is as politicized as is the membership of the single-issue group. Aptly named, this kind of organization attracts members because of the urgency of only one issue. There is only one reason to join, and no reason at all to be insouciant about the organization's campaign activities.

There are of course other explanations for the comparatively unpoliticized behavior of the members of the remaining organizations. Many people know very little about congressional activity; turnout in congressional campaigns is generally 15 to 20 percentage points lower than in presidential elections, and only about half of the population in a given congressional district can name the representative and his or her party. The media are largely indifferent. The single-issue groups, those despised enemies of compromise, make the greatest contribution to the enlightened electorate. More of their members know where the money goes, and are happy with the choice. The larger organizations are less successful in propagandizing their members, and they also suffer from high turnover in membership. The notion of single-issue groups as champions of democracy is an idea unlikely to win much favor among reformers.

THE COMPETITION AND THE MARKET

Ironically, it is the larger organizations that find the provision of selective benefits most difficult, as there are others in the market with more attractive offerings. Business organizations have a tough time in offering services that trade associations cannot match or exceed. Information is a valuable resource in business, but the most highly prized information is so technical that it is beyond the scope of the general association. The Chamber of Commerce of the United States, for example, has a membership of such diversity that its largest component, manufacturing, accounts for only 22 percent.[35] An analysis of business associations by Claus Offe concludes that, even though the "central life interests" of members do not regularly appear on a business association's agenda, there is less of a "disincentive to join." Unlike unions, business associations do not impede members' economic decision making.[36] Perhaps businesspeople answer the question "why join?" with "why not?"

Under such circumstances, an association's appeals are inevitably more in the nature of solidary benefits, as when local chapters offer elbow-rubbing opportunities. But because of the fragility of interests common to "business," trade associations play a larger role in providing the explicit information required by various kinds of business. The American Horse Council and the American Petroleum Institute probably do not exchange memos very often.

Ideologically, general membership organizations are vague and symbolic; they believe in free enterprise, distrust bureaucrats, and hate Communists. Increasingly, symbolic appeals seem to be largely unconnected to the intricate struggles surrounding federal regulation, deregulation, taxing, and trade policies.

Because of their strident and archaic pronunciamentos, the Chamber and the National Association of Manufacturers (NAM) were largely displaced in the market by the pragmatic, prestigious Business Roundtable. The Roundtable was "to have a very different style, stressing the technocratic competence of its officials rather than the conservative dogma stressed by the Chamber of Commerce and the NAM."[37] Observe, however, that the Roundtable limits its membership to the chief executive officers of the two hundred largest corporations, each of which pays annual dues of $50,000. Graham Wilson believes that the Chamber of Commerce has begun to rebound from its stigma, an assessment shared by Thomas Edsall.[38]

Trade associations are more pragmatic and more successful in offering truly valued selected utilities. Raymond Bauer, Ithiel de Sola Poole, and Lewis A. Dexter painted a dismal picture of trade associations in the 1950's and 1960's, one in which businesses regarded them as receptacles for failed business entrepreneurs.[39] Today, however, partially because of the rapid increase in the electoral activities of political action committees, trade associations have become much more respected in the business community. In fact, much of the current growth in organizational membership is a consequence of trade association expansion.

The staffs of the trade associations are often professionally trained in the substance of their association's interest and in law or economics. Services provided for members are generally of high quality and informational rather than preachy. A few provide insurance, charter flights, and other nonprofessional opportunities, but find the market flooded. Besides slick publications, some of the more successful trade associations conduct workshops, arrange small conferences, and provide referral services. Of course they all lobby, but often there is nothing much happening of any great import. Much like war, in which only a handful of soldiers actually face genuine combat, a fair amount of trade association lobbying is hurrying up to wait. Citizens' groups, general occupational groups, and single-issue groups have a fuller lobbying schedule.

The Supply and Demand of Goods

We should look upon the interaction between leaders and followers as an economic exchange. In this "market," membership trades support, or at least compliance, for leadership-provided goods. Support—whether it is expressed simply by renewing membership or by acquiescence in the decisions and activities of leaders—is the essence of a continuing relationship between the active few and the passive many. Whether a leader realizes a "profit" as an organizational entrepreneur depends upon several considerations, foremost of which are market competition, the cost of providing benefits, and the demand curves of members and potential members. Leaders must figure out what sorts of products are attractive; they must know their market.

Salisbury differentiates between the kinds of commodities offered by leaders to members (purposive, solidary, or material) and traces the implications of each. He recognizes that leaders will not usually deal exclusively in one type of benefit, although he treats exchanges as if they were conducted in a single currency for purposes of analytic clarity.[40] He discounts solidary benefits since groups based solely on them have little politically relevant content. Groups in which members exchange solidary benefits, and which are political, are so only by virtue of some other material or purposive benefits offered as supplements to the solidary ones. However, such benefits can coexist with other kinds of inducements. Purposive or expressive goods are cheap to acquire. Causes can be promoted, ideology can be articulated, and rhetoric can be disseminated without much capital outlay. Leaders who offer such commodities to their members do so without much material cost to themselves or their organizations.

Depending on the conditions of the exchange, it is easy to see how leaders of largely purposive or symbolic groups could realize a substantial profit from their enterprise. Such profits may be largely in the form of money earned by the entrepreneur. People do get rich from espousing causes, and the woods are full of entrepreneurs who convert political passion and moral outrage into hard currency. Profits may also take the form of permissiveness, allowing entrepreneurs the opportunity to use group-supported media for expressive gratification. In so doing, leaders also provide cost-free expressive benefits to followers merely by staying in the news. Newsletters, group meetings at which rhetorical diatribes are delivered, and public demonstrations are examples of an inexpensive means of providing expressive benefits. Furthermore, once a capital investment has been made for disseminating such goods, an increase in the intensity of evocative content can result in greater value of benefits at no increase in dissemination costs.

We know that such groups are very unstable, in terms of both membership turnover and organizational survival, but it is also likely that the profit potential is high. Just as in business, when the opportunity for profits is good, especially with a minimal initial outlay, competition will increase. Once an issue area is targeted as marketable, new entrepreneurs will compete for the same limited pool of potential members. We see scrambling for members especially among the various organizations serving the New Right. In response to increased competition, Jerry Falwell's Moral Majority changed its name to the Liberty Federation in order to gain a market advantage (the old name had allegedly become shopworn).

On the other hand, material benefits are more expensive to provide, but once established, the organizations that provide them are not likely to face serious competition, for the cost of entering the market discourages opportunistic speculation. Few organizations offer material, selective benefits. They are very rare in nonoccupationally based groups. Walker estimates that 15 percent of citizens' groups offer insurance, even fewer offer discounts on consumer goods, and about one third sponsor trips for their members. The American Association of Retired People, which runs (in association with Hartford) a full-service insurance company for people over fifty-one years old and employs James Whitmore to sell its wares on television, and the National Rifle Association, which has a comparable program, are glaring exceptions.[41]

Demand Curves

Demand curves determine the amount of benefit a person requires before he or she is willing to incur a given cost. Figure 2-6 is a graphic representation of a demand curve. The price per unit to the "buyer" of the inducements in question is measured along the y-axis. The quantity of units is measured along the x-axis. The curve represents the amount of the good that person A will demand at each price level. It is readily apparent from Figure 2-6 that, if the

Figure 2-6. A Demand Curve

good were offered at a price of "3," person A will buy ten units but no more. Alternatively, if the price were "1," person A would buy twenty units.

Each buyer has a unique demand curve for any conceivable product. Some may not want a particular commodity at any price (in which case their curves would be lines congruent with the y-axis); others may strongly value a good and have sufficient resources at their disposal so that their demand curves are offset to the right of that of person A, curve less sharply downward, or both. Curves such as A's, which are almost vertical, are said to be *inelastic*; comparatively horizontal curves, such as B's, are regarded as *elastic* (see Figure 2-7). Inelastic demands are usually stable and are less sensitive to price differences than are elastic demands, which may fluctuate wildly as prices rise and fall and personal needs are adjusted in response.

The shapes of the demand curves of group members substantially affect the character of the transactions among leaders, followers, and potential members. Leaders must be careful in establishing an acceptable balance of price, quantity of induce-

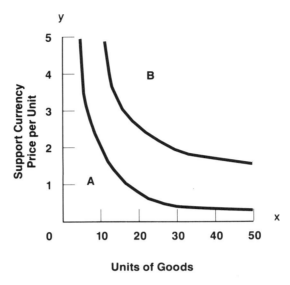

Figure 2-7. Elastic and Inelastic Curves

ments offered, and the demand characteristics of followers. The problem is in estimating demand curves, for leaders generally project their own needs and values on followers.

Since leaders are politically involved and ideologically committed, they believe followers to be equally so. Political decision makers routinely make the same assumption, thinking that those who represent an interest do so without much distortion or loss of information. Misrepresentation is unavoidable, even with the polling of members that some of the more affluent organizations undertake.[42]

The different worlds of leaders and followers account for some of the variance. Labor leaders, sensitive to the potential impacts of Reaganomics, were major contributors to Walter Mondale's campaign, yet union members were just about as likely to vote for Reagan. Feminist leaders, angered by what they believed to be rampant sexism in the Reagan administration, urged women to vote against the incumbent, but a majority of women did not.[43]

Part of the problem, however, is in the elasticity of demands. As the group member continues his or her participation, motivations present at the initial decision to join may be modified or replaced. Demands for political service may replace demands for political activity, and entrepreneurs cannot predict the demand accurately from a single temporal reference point.

Using the categories devised by Moe,[44] we notice the frequent elasticity of demands. In narrowly focused occupational groups, demands for lobbying decline, demands for services remain constant, a sense of obligation vanishes, and the most important demand among those who renew more than once is for social interaction— an inexpensive solidary benefit. In the more general occupational group, demands for services increase while demands for lobbying decrease. In the citizens' group, a need to fulfill social obligations— of trivial value to members of occupational groups—starts strong and finishes stronger, becoming by far the most important reason given by renewing members. The expectations of group members are compatible with the willingness and ability of leaders to supply a variety of inducements. Jeffrey Berry concludes that lobbyists for citizens' groups, women's organizations, and similar organizations are much more dedicated to an ideology than are the more pragmatic lobbyists for trade associations.[45] Along with the members of single-issue groups; those of the citizens' organization rank and file display the most inelastic demands, due presumably to their sense of commitment (see Table 2-5).

The mix of goods offered by leaders thus depends to some extent on turnover rates and on the combination of new and renewing members. It is instructive to record that the two most narrowly focused organizations, the trade association (with substantial selective benefits) and the single-issue group (with none), have the highest first-time renewal rates. The data strongly support Moe and his corevisionists. Even with elasticity of demands, selective benefits are more important in trade and occupational associations, and collective benefits are more important in citizens' organizations and single-issue groups. Information about organizational maintenance thus augments what we know about the initial decision to join.

So the evidence supports a synthesis: both selective and collective goods are important, depending on the organization. Taking into account rates of retention, the extent to which an organiza-

TABLE 2-5
MAIN REASONS FOR INITIALLY
JOINING AND RENEWING MEMBERSHIP: PERCENTAGES

Type of group	% initially	% 1st renewal	% 2nd renewal
Occupational			
Trade (n = 267)			
Lobbying	35	22	20
Services	20	18	21
Sense of obligation	19	12	8
Social interaction	26	48	51
General (n = 539)			
Lobbying	24	29	19
Services	31	41	44
Sense of obligation	11	5	6
Social interaction	34	25	31
Nonoccupational			
Citizens' (n = 301)			
Lobbying	19	21	11
Services	9	7	5
Sense of obligation	45	41	53
Social interaction	24	31	31
Single-issue (n = 124)			
Lobbying	51	61	60
Services	2	1	2
Sense of obligation	38	36	38
Social interaction	9	2	—

tion addresses broad or narrow goals is significant. Additionally, personal motives are not constant; as people remain in the organization, there is a shift from collective to selective inducements. Olson set out to show that selective benefits refuted the assumptions of pluralism. If people were induced to join because of selective benefits, they would know or care very little about the political objectives of the organization.

But the real world is more complex than is the world produced by inductive logic. Some organizations do maintain membership with collective benefits, especially when the goal is one that excites passion. The single-issue groups are, ironically, quite responsive to their membership; it is just such groups that anger pluralists because of their refusal to wheel and deal. But Olson's point is well taken: as the initial surge of enthusiasm wears off, selective benefits become more important. We should keep in mind the difference between entrepreneurial activity and joining an existing group. There is more passion, more commitment, among entrepreneurs than is true among people making the far less costly decision to join. These caveats aside, pluralism's major empirical component, that people join organizations to achieve political goals, is not refuted by Olson's work.

It is typical of the culture of pluralism that so much of the research of the last three decades has concerned the individual. Organizations must tease out what people want and devise a plan for giving it to them cheaper than the competition. The idea of the common good is ridiculed as utopian; what "really" matters is personal self-actualization. Corporatism is not troubled by thoughts of declining membership, of selective goods, and of organizational renewal. Its central point of departure is the collectivity.

THREE

GROUP BEHAVIOR AND GOVERNMENT PERFORMANCE IN SOCIETAL CORPORATIST SETTINGS

We will now consider what corporatism "does," both as a process whereby interest group conflict is regulated and contained and as an independent variable predicting policy outputs. Although the availability of output data is impressive, we are interested solely in measures of policy for which claims for (or against) corporatism have been made. These are economic growth, income equality, budget priorities (and thus regime ideology), and fiscal "responsibility."

Concerning processes, the obvious starting point is the relation between government bureaucracies and interest groups. This relationship is explored in a variety of ways. Does corporatism matter *procedurally?* That is, do interest groups and government bureaucracies have an institutional alliance cemented by the bonds of self-interest? Does corporatism matter *substantively?* Do corporatist states have different budget priorities than pluralist ones? Is income or wealth more equally distributed? Do corporatist states enjoy more sustained economic growth?

We begin with an examination of interest group behavior. Virtually everyone writing about pluralism and corporatism correctly points to the absence of systematic assessments of the consequences of corporatism.[1] Corporatism invites definition, modification, redefinition, recapitulation. Schmitter, who certainly should know, laments:

On the one hand, it has become such a vaguely bounded phenomenon that . . . it can be found everywhere and, hence, is nowhere very distinctive; on the other hand, it has been so narrowly attached to a single political culture, regime-type or macrosocietal configuration that it becomes, at best, uniquely descriptive rather than comparatively analytic.[2]

There are two problems: the decision rules for deciding whether a country is corporatist or pluralist, or a little bit of both, are subjective; and the comparative data base is limited.[3] Donald Share, as he begins to "tease out" propositions from a disparate literature, remarks that corporatism's proponents rarely distinguish between its effect on economic outputs and its impact on political processes. For example, he responds with skepticism to Schmitter's oft-cited claim that corporatism leads to "governability," and accuses corporatism of being responsible for high levels of economic inequality.[4] Economic inequality *may* be related to governability, but it addresses a quite different problem: income distribution is the (partial) output of a political-economic system, while governability is not.

COSTS AND BENEFITS OF CORPORATISM

More cautious observers worry that corporatism, even if it does prove valuable as a guide for the economy, is so depersonalized, so committed to consensus politics, and so confining that political parties decline in influence, as alienation and apathy drive participation down.[5] But many of these lamentations condemn a state of affairs equally prevalent in the most pluralist of societies, the United States. No one questions the decline of political parties, the rise of alienation, the erosion of confidence, the loss of interest in politics that occurred between, say, 1963 and 1980. It is these events, plus terrorism, that Share uses as examples of the costs of corporatism, thus questioning the belief that it makes nations more governable.[6] The criticism of corporatism is not without ideological baggage; the traditional left attacks corporatism because it excludes much of the clientele of protest politics, while the right objects to its statism.

If corporatism's consensus politics deprives populations of a level of conflict harsh enough to make politics interesting for the masses, the cost might be acceptable if a healthy economy is the exchange. But another set of critics, especially Charles Lindblom, believe that business easily gains the upper hand in industrial democracies, whether corporatist or not.[7] Although the practices that offend Lindblom (the granting of quasi-governmental status to business organizations or their representatives) are the essence of corporatism, they occur in all developed countries.

Lindblom's criticism is in the tradition of Lowi, discussed earlier. It condemns all developed non-Communist countries, pluralist or corporatist, for allowing public policy to become a consequence of the conflict between competing interest groups. Since corporatism is more deliberate in its cooptation of business and labor, it is more likely to trade influence for compliance. Britain, not a strong corporatist country, shifted responsibility for economic planning "from Parliament to another body in which representatives of the country's major economic organizations deliberate in secret and bargain with one another."[8] The shift occurred not because of deliberate scheming but because any attempt at economic planning, no matter how minimalist, involves accepting some degree of corporatism.

The problem is in the extent to which bargains struck by government and a business-labor coalition are insulated from the *political* process. We shall see, in describing state corporatism, that such insulation is viewed as necessary for economic growth; reflect now on the fact that that insulation is possibly almost as severe in societal corporatism.

Corporatism requires of each interest group that it at least suspend, if not eliminate, commitment to its own well-being in favor of a more public good. When economic planning fails, the failure is often said to be because of the participating interest groups' inability to look beyond their own short-term interest. Lamenting the failure of economic planning in Britain, France, and Italy, Michael Watson concludes:

Coordination and concerted action aim at establishing consistency and rationality of decisions of economic actors, public and private. This involves the assumption by each of them of some of the general responsibility that the government has for the performance of the whole system. . . . This has not happened. Industrialists, financiers, trade unions, and government departments have continued to devote their single-minded attention to the pursuit of their own specific aims.[9]

A Mask for Inequality?

Viewed from Lindblom's perspective, it makes little difference how a government engages in interest group intermediation; the result is the same: corporations and their representatives dominate the policy-making process. Thus even the societal corporatism of the Northern European countries is, in Share's apt phrase, a "mask for inequality."[10] Madison's argument (that conflict was a consequence of unequal distribution of wealth), the ideology of socialist and communist political systems, and the emergence of the modern welfare state are merely the more apparent manifestations of the centrality of wealth distribution in the scheme of politics.

Income distribution is implicitly at the center of corporatist theory, and the implementation of corporatism addresses distribution either directly or indirectly. Again, the left believes corporatism perpetuates inequality; but the implementation of an incomes policy, a fundamental criterion of the definition of societal corporatism, strongly suggests that corporatism is not a "mask for inequality" (especially in its Austrian and Northern European forms).[11]

John Kenneth Galbraith rightly regards income distribution as "one of the major debates in the nonsocialist world."[12] He argues that socialist ideology no longer debates the notion of public ownership of property and hence as much leveling as possible has already occurred. Thus the nonsocialist world is the only arena for debating equality. Inequality remains a major focus of classical political theory and its modern practitioners, such as John Rawls.[13]

Among the critics of corporatism, the tendency is to explore the political role of the participating organizations, rather than the actual distribution of income. Thus, Leo Panitch argues that labor unions, the core of the corporatist confederation, in reality are instruments of oppression. He is especially anxious to have proponents of corporatism lay bare their ideological bias, and calls our attention to the incompatibility of corporatism (which assumes the existence of cooperation between groups) and Marxism (which assumes perpetual antagonism).[14] Unions must be able to assure business and government that their members will comply with the terms of the "social contract."[15]

Societal corporatism, then, is distinguished from state corporatism in the extent and severity of its sanctions; the distinction is one of degree, not kind. Phrased less compassionately, societal corporatism is state corporatism without the will to coerce.

It is in the spirit of the presumed association between corporatism and the oppression of the working class that Panitch, in a general attack on the hidden class bias of corporatism, makes a distinction between state and societal corporatism based solely on the degree of success. Noting the inability of corporatist governments to cope with a newly hostile labor force, he concludes:

The reason for the new state coercive measures in this area is to be found in the contradictions they pose to liberal democracy itself. To meet the challenge of a working class united against the operation of laws that contradict the freedom of their indigenous class organizations, coercive measures have to go far beyond the immediate field of industrial relations. To have made these laws operable, the extensive use of police powers would likely have been necessary, and probably would involve limiting the rights to mobilize opposition through free speech and assembly.[16]

The process he describes fits well with Asian authoritarian, state corporatist governments, which will be examined beginning in Chapter Five.

Finally, inequality has commanded the attention of those who believe it is a cause of violence, and its reduction a fundamental purpose of governments.[17]

But much of this rancorous debate avoids the question. Even if societal corporatism "uses" interest groups to gain compliance, does the resulting policy operate to the disadvantage of the clients of the organizations? Does the working class, once again a victim of false consciousness, give away freedom in exchange for fair income distribution only to discover that it has been once more betrayed?

Interest Intermediation

As explained earlier, it is unlikely that *any* interest group, in either pluralist or corporatist settings, can transmit accurately the views and aspirations of its membership. If the working class is betrayed by corporatism, so are the business organizations, for the problem of misrepresentation is ubiquitous. The conundrum persists even when associations make sincere efforts to assemble and interpret reliable summaries of opinion. In corporatist settings, where the "licensed" economic groups have legitimate monopolies on the representative function, they do not necessarily represent opinions any better or worse than political parties.

Moreover, the monopolizing of representation might make organizations in corporatist habitats lazy. With no competition, and a stable membership assured, why should organizations bother with improving the accuracy of their representation? For that matter, interest groups in authoritarian political systems may be as representative as those in more open settings. In societal corporatism, selected organizations may be equal partners with bureaucracies in policy making and implementation, but they nevertheless may act against the preferences of their members. In state corporatism, interest groups may be more dependent upon bureaucracies in forming or implementing policy, but reliable in representing their members' views.

THE LEGITIMATE PARTICIPANTS IN CORPORATIST ARENAS

Different as they are, the variants of corporatism have in common the groups that are incorporated: labor and business, not the various single-issue, citizens', and protest groups that scatter themselves across the landscapes of pluralist democracies. Corporatism embraces only those organizations that the economic division of labor creates; some students of corporatist societies virtually define corporatism in terms of the bargain struck with organized labor:

In the case of societal corporatism, it is primarily the labor movement, or a sector of it, that is acting through the state—or, more specifically, extracting concessions from the state or winning concessions by allying with other actors in the state or associated with it. With state corporatism, and in those cases which involve a complex mix of initiative from above and mobilization from below, a variety of economic and political interests may come into play.[18]

Although the dominance of labor in societal corporatism is an overstatement, the claim that corporatism is largely an arrangement between economic interest groups is not.[19] Its inability or unwillingness to incorporate emergent groups built on different cleavages is corporatism's greatest theoretical weakness as an alternative to traditional representation or pluralism.

Charges of exclusion pervade the prescriptive analyses of both pluralism and corporatism. Attackers and defenders find it difficult to separate normative from empirical theory. Thus the language is sprinkled with statements of value *and* fact, and words such as "flawed" are used to describe both an unsatisfactory system from a normative perspective and a weakness in empirical theory. The claim that corporatism arose because of the failure of political parties to represent *functional* interest groups, for example, assumes that the representative responsibility is a limited one.[20] Although most scholars argue, with Lowi, that pluralist systems are moving toward corporatism, Schmitter believes that corporatism may have outlived its usefulness.[21]

The Pivotal Role of Labor

If labor does not cooperate, corporatism is unlikely to succeed. A major finding by Brian Barry is in accord with this view.[22] He believes that the incorporation of unions into the policy process causes them to act contrary to the intentions that guided their origins; that is, they cooperate in the preservation of a stable, rather than inflationary, economy. Unions in corporatist systems are allies with industry in the cause of wage restraint. This notion requires that workers either are unable to ascertain their best interest or that they believe their best interest lies in collaborative rather than competitive behavior. Walter Korpi, who rejects Marxism, believes nonetheless that unions in corporatist settings can increase their power.[23] The cooperation of corporatism may be coerced, or achieved by cooptation, but an unruly labor force is not compatible with corporatism. From the Marxist perspective discussed earlier, the task of corporatism is the cooptation of the working class. Corporatism's theoretical development, irrespective of which strand one selects, invariably addresses the political and economic conditions of the working class. The bargain proffered is the same for labor as for other invited participants; protection for deference.

One of the principal concerns of corporatist theorists was the position of the working class under capitalism. Such a concern was double-sided; on the one side the conditions of poverty and alienation from society endured by the proletariat made it impossible to talk of a harmonious society; on the other, there was fear that such conditions combined with democracy or revolutionary agitation would lead inevitably to socialism. . . . Under corporatism the worker would enjoy a degree of material protection, but in return he had to accept his position in the social hierarchy.[24]

In Western industrial corporatist democracies, the method of achieving a docile labor force is the direct incorporation of union leadership into the policy process. In Asia, "corporatism without labor" has shown that peak associations representing most workers are not necessary. The substitution of strong cultural expectations of loyalty and obedience, or the willingness to oppress labor, are efficient alternatives.[25]

It is not surprising that the most explicit empirical operationalization of corporatism, by Manfred Schmidt, is based (procedurally and substantively) principally on labor-management relations (see below). Those who bemoan the loss of America's international economic competitive edge attribute our decline to, among other things, a strike-prone labor force. The comparison is, of course, with Japan, Taiwan, Singapore, or South Korea, where corporatist (authoritarian, except for Japan) regimes have avoided extremes of conflict between labor and management, and with the European corporatist democracies.

One should not misinterpret these comparisons. In authoritarian Asian countries, unions are severely constrained, and potential organizers are sometimes jailed or harassed. Working conditions are rarely evaluated, and political pressure to keep wages low, although not always successful, is common. But, while unions are legal in

Japan, this democratic country cracked down on radical unions and encouraged compliant ones.[26]

Robert Reich argues that the inability of the United States to integrate labor into a decision-making consensus is destroying the "foundation of economic community," while Ezra Vogel's ebullient praise of Japan stems largely from his admiration for the degree of consensus between groups that are routinely at each other's throats in pluralist systems.[27] These conclusions are not in accord with the reality of labor-management relations in Asia. These claims and counterclaims simply bolster the conclusion that labor is at the heart of corporatism, and pluralism's inability to channel or constrain labor demands receives the blame for economic stagnation. As we will see, these conjectures are overstated.

Olson's Rise and Decline

By far the most curious position about labor is Olson's.[28] He concludes that narrowly concentrated interest groups, as opposed to "encompassing" ones, inhibit economic growth. His measure of interest group strength is the proportion of the economically active population that belongs to unions, organizations that he believes to be capable of enhancing or impeding economic growth. Thus he believes that unions are especially egregious examples of the "narrow distributional coalitions" that "reduce efficiency and aggregate income in the societies in which they operate and make political life more divisive."[29]

Although Olson is not interested in discussing corporatism, his condemnation of interest groups as self-seeking distributional coalitions sounds very much like a description of a malady for which corporatism promises a cure. Thus his assessment of the causes of economic stagnation (narrow distributional coalitions) could easily fit into the debate about the merits of corporatism. If self-interest, which according to *The Logic of Collective Action* motivates us all, cannot be arrested in its institutional form, the "public interest" suffers. Olson thus strikes at the heart of corporatism, for he has little faith in a government's ability to act dispassionately. Like most of the proponents of "public choice," he argues that government is out of control *because* the bureaucracy, the grand orchestrator of corporatism, is no longer accountable to elected bodies.[30] In this fear they form an odd alliance with the corporatism's critics from the left, who believe as does Olson that government is the captive of interest groups.

Unions could be "encompassing" if they were to include most of the labor force, and therefore would have an incentive to engage in cooperative behavior. Olson is not very precise about the discriminating traits of encompassing organizations. "Encompassing" means, judging by his use of the word, a commitment to the public interest, or common good, even at the expense of group demands. If so, how does Olson justify his conclusion that the higher the proportion of the labor force belonging to a union, the slower will be economic growth? He generally reserves the term for those organizations that have enrolled most of the potential members. But as unions become encompassing in numbers, presumably they do not become encompassing in behavior. Two recent essays on Sweden suggest that this is the case.[31]

So Olson, against his will, ends up in the camp of the corporatist theorists, even though he presumably would be hostile to the statism that corporatism implies. In a corrective, he sets forth his mistrust of interventionist theories, remarking, "Perhaps it is no accident that so many of the early corporatists were also fascists." Olson's plea for the encompassing organization does *not* include a belief that the state is the best guarantor of encompassing behavior.[32]

Olson's *The Rise and Decline of Nations* tries to build from the logic of his earlier work. He asserts that the micro theory that he used to study individual choice, and thus to refute traditional group theorists, can be extended to macro theory and thus applied to states.[33] But the argument, while logically appealing, seems a bit strained. Students of corporatism rarely address matters concerned with individual choice. The pivotal problem for pluralist group theory, the individual's reason for joining or withdrawing from a group, is of no concern when the group environment is so different. Corporatism legitimates its peak associations by conferring quasi-official status on them. They participate in policy formation as invited equals, not as grubby seekers of "access."[34] The preferences of members receive scant attention, and the question most often posed is "so what?" Does the mode of conflict resolution lead to certain unique patterns in the content of policy? Can the extent of corporatism predict policy outcomes better than, say, party strength or wealth? The issues in corporatism are macroeconomic; attention is not directed toward the individual but toward the collectivity.

DOES CORPORATISM MATTER?

The only way to decide whether a country has a strongly corporatist political system is to examine certain agreed-on criteria and impose a judgment (see Tables 3-1 and 3-2). Truly comparative research awaits such an effort, but in the meantime we are fortunate to have Manfred Schmidt's classification.[35]

TABLE 3-1
A CLASSIFICATION OF COUNTRIES

Countries	Corporatism	GNP/PC (1984)	GNP growth (1968–1982)	GOVINDEX*
U.S.A.	L	13,160	2.2	23.4
France	L	11,680	3.0	42.1
Italy	L	6,840	2.2	47.3
Canada	L	11,320	2.9	23.3
Ireland	L	5,150	2.9	51.7
United Kingdom	L	9,660	1.9	40.8
Luxembourg	M	14,510	3.5	43.0
Finland	M	10,870	2.2	22.9
Iceland	M	11,330	2.8	22.0
Germany	M	12,460	2.6	31.0
Australia	M	11,140	1.4	24.6
New Zealand	M	7,920	1.5	39.6
Belgium	M	10,760	2.9	55.8
Netherlands	M	10,930	2.2	55.5
Denmark	M	12,470	2.1	43.8
Israel	M	4,500	1.6	78.4
Austria	H	9,880	3.5	39.4
Japan	H	10,080	3.9	19.0
Norway	H	14,280	3.7	38.9
Sweden	H	11,320	2.9	43.1
Switzerland	H	17,010	1.0	18.3

*Government expenditure as proportion of GNP.

TABLE 3-2
POLITICAL CHARACTERISTICS OF COUNTRIES

Country	Corporatism	Left/right*	% unions
U.S.A.	L	5	23
France	L	4	17
Italy	L	4	20
Canada	L	5	27
Ireland	L	4	36
United Kingdom	L	3	40
Luxembourg	M	3	45
Finland	M	3	60
Iceland	M	4	60
Germany	M	3	31
Australia	M	3	44
New Zealand	M	3	52
Belgium	M	4	48
Netherlands	M	4	33
Denmark	M	3	65
Israel	M	3	90
Austria	H	1	66
Japan	H	5	35
Norway	H	3	60
Sweden	H	3	75
Switzerland	H	4	20

*1 = strong left; 5 = strong right.

Schmidt regards "strong corporatism" as requiring trade union leadership and employers' associations that are committed to a "social partnership" ideology, unions and management that actually cooperate, a low strike volume, and no "authoritarian" incomes policy.[36] "Weak corporatism" describes political systems without much labor-management cooperation (measured by frequent strikes), strong socialist or Communist activity within the labor movement, and weak industrial democracy.[37] Schmidt's classification of capitalist democracies is thus explicitly based on the notion of resolving conflict without resorting to the authoritarian mode (characteristic of state corporatism) or the competitive (e.g., pluralist) style.[38]

Schmidt's use of the relative absence of strikes as a measure of corporatism, with 1974–1978 as a base, works nicely with 1980 data. The correlation between corporatism and the ratio of days lost because of strikes to civilian employment is −.40 (sig. = .05), controlling for percentage of the labor force in unions and GNP per capita. Perhaps we should be astonished that the correlation is not almost perfect. But the correlation allows one to argue that the components of the definition are not invariably reductionist.

Kerry Schott offers useful addendum to the relationship between corporatism and strikes. Using Schmidt's classification, he proposes an additional variable: the proportion of GNP invested in capital formation. Corporatist countries invest more than noncorporatist ones, and they also have lower strike activity.[39] He believes that rate of investment is more important than corporatism, and he is right. The partial correlation between investment and strike activity (controlling for corporatism) is significant, while the reverse correlation is not.

Predictors of Policy Outputs

In order to appraise the role of corporatism in public policy I have used as control variables the ideology of the ruling party, the proportion of the work force in unions, wealth (measured as GNP per capita), and government expenditures. Each has its defenders.

The ideology of the governing party is the variable in which most of us would put the least hope, given the generally low impact that parties are believed to have on American public policy.[40] Theories of corporatism can easily do without political parties. After all, the essence of corporatism is consensus. If a corporatist system is successful, all political parties would adhere to this consensus, honoring access agreements with peak associations. But European political parties offer more of a choice than do American ones. The United States, the most thoroughly pluralist country, presents voters with a less clear cut option.[41] The generally greater difference between parties in Europe has led some, as we shall see, to argue for a causal relationship.

Those who believe that the ideological disposition of the governing party is not linked to policy outputs generally settle on economic variables as more significant. The foundation for such reasoning is Thomas R. Dye's *Politics, Economics, and the Public*[42] and Gabriel Almond and Bingham Powell's *Comparative Politics: A Developmental Approach*.[43] Each stresses the strong correlation between politics and economics, with Dye concluding that political institutions are minor compared with economic structure in explaining policy. Marxist scholarship has always argued for the preeminence of economics, and "studies of dependency theory, multinational corporations, corporatism, political development, and the distribution of wealth, all build on this orientation."[44] The lack of clarity concerning the assessment of the role of political parties is well illustrated in Francis Castles' volume of essays on European parties.[45] Castles remarks that bivariate analysis, which his volume uses with rare exception, cannot reveal the complexities of the relationship between "the party system and the development of international trade patterns, or between corporatist forms of social organizations and the goals of political parties."[46] Attempts to assess the role of parties in the setting of European economic policy have had mixed results. Bivariate correlations do not hold up well under controls. The most fruitful approach is one of devising more complex measures of political-economic coalitions, a process that does not support an independent role for political parties.

Government expenditures estimate the role of the state in the economy. Pluralism generally has regarded the state as either a neutral referee (initially) or at best an advantaged competitor (in more recent versions). This indicator is far from ideal as a measure of governmental intervention, for control can be established with very little capital outlay. Economists are developing measures of "market distortion" but as yet have not prepared a comprehensive list. Corporatism sees a much more positive role for the state, either as orchestrator of group conflict or as the most powerful actor in the policy formation process.

Finally, the proportion of the labor force in unions speaks directly to Olson, who uses this variable to measure interest group strength. The approach here is to use it for what it is: the measure of the numerical strength of one of the interest groups central to the functioning of the corporatist state. The countries are arrayed on these variables.

Corporatism and Its Related Characteristics

Because corporatism and pluralism mirror to some extent the cultures in which they originated, and are not truly independent of the larger economic and social setting in their development and style, some understanding of what corporatist political systems look like is helpful (Table 3-3).[47] These data are not meant to construe *anything* about the "causes" of corporatism; nor do they argue for a mystical "culture of corporatism." Schmitter is surely correct when he castigates those who find corporatism to be an "exclusive part" of a political culture. He writes: "[Cultural explanations] fail completely to explain why similar configurations and behavior in interest politics have emerged and persist in a great variety of cultural settings, stretching from Northern Europe, across the Mediterranean to such exotic places as Turkey, Iran, Thailand, Indonesia and Taiwan."[48] But it is instructive to locate other variables that associate themselves with corporatism, especially those derived from the components of its definition.

Corporatist systems are strongly correlated, as we might suspect, with the proportion of the working population belonging to unions. The clear exceptions are Japan and Switzerland, which in spite of seemingly massive cultural differences appear similar in their brand of corporatism. Corporatist countries are, as we discovered, wealthier than the noncorporatist ones. The two corporatist countries with the largest negative residuals are Japan and Austria, with Switzerland having the largest positive residuals.

Among the pluralist countries, Ireland and the United States are conspicuous at the extremes. Still, the per capita GNP of the noncorporatist countries is $9,636, compared with $11,048 for the corporatist ones; the proportion of the work force belonging to unions is 27 for the noncorporatist countries and 51 for the corpo-

TABLE 3-3
THE CORRELATES OF CORPORATISM (53%)*

Correlation	r	T†	β
Left/right	−.40‡	.270	.25
% labor	.47‡	2.104‡	.46‡
Wealth	.40‡	3.061§	.60§

*Variance explained.
†Student's T.
‡Sig. = .05.
§Sig. = .01.

ratist ones. Do not conclude, however, that wealth and unionism are themselves positively correlated, as this is not the case; on the contrary, they are significantly *negatively* associated.

The culture of corporatism is linked to some extent with cultural and linguistic homogeneity.[49] Corporatist governments rule more homogeneous nations (except, of course, for Switzerland), while the less homogeneous populations (except for Ireland and Italy) provide the settings for the relative anarchy of pluralism.

Political ideology is a less apparent accompaniment to the mode of interest group intermediation. Corporatist countries are marginally more left than pluralist ones, but the corporatist cluster also contains Switzerland and Japan, consistently right. However, there is virtually no leftism among the noncorporatist nations, the closest being the United Kingdom's "balanced" score. Those who believe that corporatism is a right-wing answer to socialism or left-wing radicalism will find little support in these data.

Corporatism and Growth

Neither corporatism nor either of the labor-related measures have any appreciable impact on economic growth (Table 3-4).[50] Schmidt's early data found no relationship between corporatism and growth; the lack of association using more recent data and partial correlation is even more apparent. There is an irony here, since both the detractors of labor and the defenders of corporatism assume that each is inextricably intertwined with growth. True, the

TABLE 3-4
CORPORATISM AND GNP GROWTH (11%)*

Correlation	r	T†	β
Corporatism	.13	1.00	.26
Left/right	.11	.15	-.17
% labor	-.19	-1.03	.26
Wealth	.10	-.38	.10
GOVINDEX	-.26	-.49	.10

*Variance explained.
†Student's T.

high flyers are the most corporately organized, and Sweden (which had a negative GNP growth from 1974 through 1978, the period covered by Schmidt) drags down the performance of this group.[51] The corporatism-equals-growth hypothesis is given added support since the least corporatist political systems have nothing in the same range as Norway, Austria, and Japan, suggesting the possibility that if more countries were classified the relationship might strengthen. Nevertheless, the general assessment is one that does not support corporatism as a growth-inducing management style.[52]

Additionally, the influence of wealth should be taken into account. The fastest-growing economies in the world are to be found among the rapidly developing Pacific Rim authoritarian governments: South Korea, Singapore, and Taiwan, none of which has a per capita income in the same league as Japan. Olson attributes this growth to the antipathy of Chinese culture toward narrow distributional coalitions, to its preference for encompassing modes of interest representation, and to historical circumstances suppressing the growth of interest groups (all were colonies of industrial countries until recently.[53] The hostility toward narrow distributional coalitions is very much a part of Confucian ethics.

Olson may well be right, but it is equally possible that developed countries do not have the room to maintain the level of economic growth common in the Pacific Rim. Economically developed countries do not grow as rapidly as developing ones, irrespective of their role of interest aggregation. For instance, Japan's former colonies, South Korea and Taiwan, averaged about twice the growth of the mother country from 1960 through 1982, with about one-third of Japan's gross national product per capita.

There are some grounds, however, for supporting Olson's thesis. Corporatism has nothing to do with growth, but government spending is (weakly) negatively associated with growth. Since corporatism generally is taken to imply a strong government presence, the negative correlation between growth and spending operates to corporatism's disadvantage. If we compute the ratio of government expenditures (as a proportion of GNP) to GNP per capita, we can make an estimate of the actual contribution of public expenditures to the total economy (Table 3-5).[54] Those countries with the least visible government impact achieve the better growth. But the

TABLE 3-5
CORPORATISM AND THE RATIO OF
GOVERNMENT EXPENDITURES TO GNP (64%)*

Correlation	r	T†	β
Corporatism	−.24	−1.600	−.41‡
Left/right	−.15	.640	.31
% labor	.49§	2.773§	.61§
Wealth	−.66§	−2.140‡	−.46‡

*Variance explained.
†Student's T.
‡Sig. = .05.
§Sig. = .01.

weakness of the correlation (controlling for wealth and corporatism reduces it substantially) is apparent. Indeed, corporatism and the ratio are *negatively* associated. Wealthy countries are frugal.

But corporatism does not necessarily mean that the central government is the major participant in economic life, merely that it coordinates the activities of the private sector. Examples of every conceivable combination of corporatism, growth, and government spending can be found: exceedingly corporatist Switzerland's government is almost invisible, as is its growth; extremely corporatist Japan's government is equally reticent but its growth the best of the corporatist countries. The opposite pattern is illustrated by Sweden, which spends the most and grows the least, thus supplying ammunition for the governmental minimalists.[55] Among the pluralist countries, Canada spends a little and grows a lot, while Ireland spends a lot and grows a lot. There is, neither anecdotally nor by use of regression, any data to support the belief that corporatism contributes to economic growth.

If labor is not the *bête noire* Olson believes it to be, there is at least some solace in the correlation between unionism and big spending. The problem is that neither big spending nor unionism can be said to have a clear, independent, unequivocal impact on growth. Growth is an illusive variable; for all its putative merits, corporatism does not contribute to it.

WEALTH AND GOVERNMENT   Corporatism is negatively associated with high levels of government spending, and high levels of public spending are strongly, negatively, associated with wealth (Table 3-6). There is a lesser negative relationship between days lost to strikes and wealth. The strongest correlation, one that holds up well under controls, is that between government spending and wealth.

It may seem unusual to use wealth as a dependent variable, but the invitation is from Olson, commenting on the stability of Austrian corporatism:

In Austria neo-corporatist arrangements appear . . . to be relatively stable. . . . The real per-capita income in Austria is, however, significantly below the level of per-capita income in neighboring countries of West Germany and Switzerland, and behind that of several other comparable West European countries, so that it is open to question whether Austrian economic policy has been very successful.[56]

Ironically, Austria refutes the point Olson wishes to make: it is not a big spender, yet it is relatively poor. The residuals reveal just how far away from the predicted relationship between spending and wealth Austria is; New Zealand is a more convincing example (Table 3-7). The fact of the matter is that the corporatism that Olson believes has caused Austria to remain poorer than her neighbors is a less compelling explanation than he might have thought, since the relationship between corporatism and wealth is less than that between government spending and wealth, and is reduced substantially by controlling for spending.

TABLE 3-6
CORPORATISM AND WEALTH (45%)*

Correlation	r	T†	β
Corporatism	.40‡	2.050‡	.40‡
Left/right	.05	−.184	.04
% labor	.19	−1.830‡	−.14
GOVINDEX	.55§	−1.663	−.40‡

*Variance explained.
†Student's T.
‡Sig. = .05.
§Sig. = .01.

TABLE 3-7
ACTUAL AND ESTIMATED WEALTH VALUES

Country	Observed	Expected	Residual
Australia	11,140	12,197.33	−1,057.33
Austria	9,880	12,349.25	−2,469.25
Belgium	10,760	9,535.78	1,224.22
Canada	11,320	10,807.70	512.30
Denmark	12,470	9,807.81	2,662.19
Finland	10,870	11,599.83	−729.83
France	11,680	9,995.84	1,684.16
Germany	12,460	12,306.88	153.12
Iceland	11,330	11,523.92	−193.92
Ireland	5,150	8,416.01	−3,266.01
Israel	4,500	6,083.55	−1,583.55
Italy	14,510	10,773.79	3,736.21
Japan	6,840	9,470.43	−2,630.43
Luxembourg	10,080	14,708.39	−4,628.39
Netherlands	10,930	10,237.79	692.21
New Zealand	7,920	10,711.34	−2,791.34
Norway	14,280	12,371.87	1,908.13
Sweden	14,040	11,332.79	2,707.21
Switzerland	17,010	15,583.69	1,426.31
United Kingdom	9,660	9,194.58	465.42
U.S.A.	13,160	10,981.42	2,178.58

LABOR, WEALTH, AND GROWTH   Labor unions are not in themselves likely to impede economic growth; nor are any of the other interest groups that Olson evaluates. Any organization that is unlikely to become encompassing would pose a threat to economic health. Olson singles out Austria, Sweden, and Norway as examples of encompassing labor organizations (in contrast to those of Britain and the United States).[57] The distinction he makes is an important one for his theory, for there is no significant correlation between the proportion of the work force in the unions and growth.

He would argue, presumably, that the extent of union membership does not predict growth, but might lead to encompassing behavior. If we can agree that encompassing behavior is, if not synonymous with, at least similar to, corporatism, Olson's argument is better tested, not by the extent of union membership, but rather by the number of days lost to strikes.[58] Both measures are negatively correlated with economic growth, but not significantly so. We turn next to indicators presumed to be more "in the grasp" of governments, especially those related to fiscal and economic management.

FOUR

CORPORATISM AND
THE SHAPE OF POLICY

"Neo-corporatist systems have aroused the interest and envy of other states for some years now," says Graham Wilson. "Their success in securing above-average incomes and economic growth with lower than average inflation has fueled both admiration and envy. . . . The neo-corporatist systems have provided their inhabitants with 30 years of high employment, low inflation, and considerable economic growth."[1] A more straightforward endorsement is difficult to imagine. In addition, Wilson endorses Schmitter's conclusion that corporatist societies are less fiscally irresponsible and suffer fewer problems with citizen unrest.[2]

We know that, while there is more corporatism among the wealthy democracies, there is a stronger linkage between central government expenditures (or the absence thereof) and wealth. We know also that corporatism does not have much of an independent effect on growth. Schmidt, in addition to those authors discussed in Chapter Three, was suspicious of the benevolent effects of corporatism. Unlike them, however, he was more concerned with growth than equality or oppression.[3]

The question is part of a more basic problem: does *government* matter? Do things happen when socialist governments win that are substantially different from events that occur when conservative governments win? Certainly we think so; otherwise why vote (indeed!). But the evidence is far from unidimensional. In Castles' volume, the answer is generally that parties make a difference in budget priorities, but not necessarily in an actual change in income growth or its distribution.[4] Richard Rose[5] and Peter Hall[6] argue, however, that political parties are not truly independent sources of policy initiation: "Much of a party's record in office will be stamped upon it by forces outside its control."[7] Thus bivariate analysis is unlikely to get at the problem.

Students of policy in the United States have never reached consensus on the extent to which political variables matter, and comparative policy has not established clear, universal connections between a government's structure, process, or ideology and the policy outcomes attributed to it.[8]

THE INDEPENDENT EFFECTS OF CORPORATISM: INFLATION, UNEMPLOYMENT, AND EQUITY

Inflation and unemployment are problems that corporatist countries have consistently been able to solve with more reliability and consistency than have the pluralist ones. Corporatist countries are not necessarily committed to any economic ideology, but the balancing of demands from potentially competing groups is believed to work exceptionally well. There is a strong positive independent correlation between the proportion of the work force in unions and the rate of inflation, but only a weak negative independent relationship between the degree of corporatism and inflation.

Corporatism and Inflation

Notice (Table 4-1) that the percentage of the labor force belonging to unions, a characteristic of the Western corporatist societies, is itself the best independent predictor of inflation. The greater the percentage belonging to unions, the higher the inflation, irrespective of the extent of corporatism. Olson's premise is given unqualified support, but only if we assume that labor, as it increases its membership, becomes less encompassing, a point about which he is unclear. But when we add the degree of corporatism, the inflationary impact of labor declines. Corporatism's commitment to unionism compromises its ability to control inflation.

TABLE 4-1
CORPORATISM AND INFLATION (69%)*

Correlation	r	T†	β
Corporatism	−.15	−2.604‡	.55‡
Left/right	.49‡	1.966§	.44§
% labor	−.009	3.757‡	.69‡
Wealth	−.51‡	−1.507	.33
Unemployment	−.14	−2.604‡	.56‡

*Variance explained.
†Student's T.
‡Sig. = .01.
§Sig. = .05.

Nevertheless, the record of the corporatist countries is good. Switzerland, Japan, and Austria have inflation rates among the lowest in the world. Japan's and Switzerland's low rates of unionism should not be ignored, but neither should the high unionization of Austria's work force.

Corporatism and Unemployment

Inflation and unemployment do vary together in the way Phillips curves suggest: declining inflation means rising unemployment. However, the corporatist governments are better at coping with unemployment, just as they manage inflation with more success. The rate of inflation in corporatist countries, 7.5 percent, is substantially lower than that of the pluralist countries; but it is in the control of unemployment (Table 4-2) that the corporatist nations appear in their most dramatic contrast. There is virtually *no* unemployment, even in Sweden, a country that, as we have seen, has lost some of its cohesion and suffers from the highest inflation rate among the corporatist countries. Control of unemployment is not a consequence of the political ideology of the government, as the most and least conservative governments have equally low rates of unemployment.

The independent effect of corporatism—and the absence of any independent effect of political ideology—is not exactly what Schmidt predicts. He believes that left-wing and Social-Democratic

TABLE 4-2
CORPORATISM AND UNEMPLOYMENT (67%)*

Correlation	r	T†	β
Corporatism	−.73‡	−4.157‡	.72‡
Left/right	.26	.889	.24
% labor	−.32	1.649	.39
Wealth	−.31	−.798	.14
Inflation	−.14	−2.604‡	.57‡

*Variance explained.
†Student's T.
‡Sig. = .01.

governments are more attuned to unemployment and more success-ful in reducing it. Schmidt observes:

> The presence of a strong corporatist mode of conflict regulation and the presence of a strong left-wing milieu increase the salience of unemploy-ment as a political issue. Both political factors tend to put indirect pres-sure on the policy choice and restrict the government's capacity to shift the burden of the economic crisis, in its entirety, to labour.[9]

But the independent effect of the ideology of the government is not significant. Concerning the conditions of labor's "contract" (see Chapter One) with corporatism, David Cameron concludes that a *combination* of Social Democratic control and corporatism is the best guarantor of union quiescence, but that corporatism is the stronger contributor to the combination.[10] This view, consistent with Schmidt's, is also in keeping with my emphasis on *combina-tions* of variables.

For example, Switzerland and Japan have right-wing govern-ments and moribund labor movements, but they both have low inflation and low unemployment. Corporatist income policies are favorable to capital accumulation, and corporatist conflict regula-tion operates to soften the impact of the business cycle, as Schmidt correctly maintains. But whether the government is symbolically identified with an ideology is unimportant.

Perhaps we should interpret the irrelevance of ideology as an indication of cohesion. Ideology may be the enemy of corporatism, if the ideology identifies an interest group as evil, or dangerous. But if all participants are in fundamental accord, that the left or right is in a majority is of little consequence. No Austrian or Swedish government would disenfranchise labor or interrupt the flow of bargaining and compromise over which it has traditionally presided. Even as inflation dogged Sweden's economy, its rate of unemployment was not affected.

Corporatism and Budget Priorities

Corporatist countries are rich, but the *distribution* of wealth is another matter. It is after all required of corporatist states that they have adopted an incomes policy in a nonauthoritarian manner; the question is not whether a government has an incomes policy, understood here as "voluntary or compulsory limits on the rate of growth of wages and, to a lesser extent, prices."[11] Most governments have, at one time or another, used one or the other. Rather the question is what such policies accomplish. Traditionally, one assesses incomes policies according to the degree of equity achieved by them. But the distribution of wealth, and the putative political consequences of varieties of distribution patterns, has always been nestled at the center of political debate.

But is there, among the nonsocialist countries, a corporatist or pluralist ideology that addresses income distribution? Presumably there is not; Switzerland and Japan do not puruse income transfers with the vigor of the Scandinavian countries or Austria. There is not much to separate the corporatist from the pluralist countries on their priorities of spending or taxing.

We are left with less of a conclusion than we might have expected. Corporatism and pluralism do yield different policy outcomes, but not consistently and not always in the predicted direction. For example, corporatist governments tax *less* (measured as a percentage of total revenue) than pluralist ones, irrespective of whether we compare individual or corporate taxes. We would hardly expect corporatism to impose less of a tax burden than pluralism, given the belief that corporatism requires a strong government presence. But government participation in the economy does not require a heavy-handed bureaucracy. When we recall that corporatism means lower levels of government spending, the pattern becomes consistent. Corporatism's image is tarnished further because of taxing policies. The tax burden falls more heavily on *individuals* in corporatist countries and more heavily on *corporations* in pluralist ones. Corporatism does lead to a more favorable treatment of corporations, a view consistent with those, most notably Robert Reich, who argue that Japan and most of Europe understand the business culture, but the United States does not. He writes:

The industrialized countries of Europe (with the exception of Great Britain) and Japan took paths to industrialization radically different from America's. While the United States began its development with an almost empty continent, these other nations began with the remnants of a feudal system. . . . The Japanese and these Europeans draw no sharp distinction between their business and civic cultures.[12]

Given this cozy arrangement, taxing yourself hardly makes sense. Reich's use of the feudal past to explain corporatism, however, runs counter to Olson's belief that older nations, whose history does not include a major upheaval, develop intractable networks of interest groups and hence do not experience good economic growth.[13] Disputes aside, corporatism is responsive in its taxing policy to the interest groups snuggled comfortably in the policy network.

Should the mode of interest group intermediation affect spending priorities? If pluralism's ancestor and cultural companion is individualism, then perhaps there should be a difference. Individualist countries should spend less on health or welfare, leaving everyone to sink or swim. In aggressive individualist cultures, guns should be more important than butter since individualism imagines a minimal role for the state in the domestic economy. Corporatist, more collective, cultures should spend more on health and welfare.

Corporatist countries *do* spend less for defense but not less in comparison with their social welfare expenditures (Tables 4-3 and 4-4). The ratio of defense to health and welfare is more favorable to domestic nondefense spending in the pluralist countries. Even so, one is hard pressed to find evidence of corporatist governments neglecting the needs of their citizens in favor of ever-increasing defense expenditures.

TABLE 4-3
CORPORATISM AND DEFENSE EXPENDITURES (46%)*

Correlation	r	T†	β
Corporatism	−.05	.048	.001
Left/right	−.10	.731	.20
% labor	.46‡	.940	.14
Wealth	.44‡	−.376	−.14
GOVINDEX	.64§	1.383	.33

*Variance explained.
†Student's T.
‡Sig. = .05.
§Sig. = .01.

TABLE 4-4
RATIO: DEFENSE/HEALTH AND WELFARE*

Correlation	r	T†	Ratio
Corporatism	−.19	−1.537	−.31
Left/right	−.05	.161	.00
% labor	.10	.568	.31
Wealth	−.19	.896	.17
GOVINDEX	−.03	−1.755‡	−.41‡

*Variance explained.
†Student's T.
‡Sig. = .05.

Richard J. Estes and John Morgan[14] seek to capture the essence of the direction of policy with a composite Index of Social progress. Unfortunately, they do not include data for Iceland and Luxembourg. Had the size of the sample been larger, the usual substitution for missing data would have been appropriate. The index, which is composed of many of the measures used here, does suggest a greater commitment of the corporatist governments to various forms of social progress, but the difference (89.5 for pluralist governments and 92.5 for corporatist ones) is not very great, and the correlation (performed with the missing data adjustment) is only .11. The Estes-Morgan Index is in agreement with the data presented here.

THE PAYOFF: INCOME DISTRIBUTION

The test of incomes policies is income distribution. Although income distribution is traditionally measured by either the Gini index or some derivation thereof, Michael Don Ward has made a compelling case for the use of a more inclusive index.[15] There is no appreciable relationship between level of corporatism and income distribution, nor is there any obvious connection between the *mode* of corporatism and economic equity (Table 4-5). Ward's equality values show that, except for Ireland, all countries have good equality indexes (negative numbers indicate greater equality).

The Swiss and Japanese mode ("private" corporatism and business group dominance) is not appreciably different from the Austrian mode (a major economic role for the government and the near hegemony of labor). Thus it is hardly surprising that no independent association between corporatism and income distribution

TABLE 4-5
EQUALITY SCORES

Country	Score
Australia	–93
Austria	–108
Belgium	–108
Canada	–95
Denmark	–85
Finland	–87
France	–87
Germany	–97
Iceland	–6
Ireland	7
Israel	–88
Italy	–122
Japan	–50
Luxembourg	–106
Netherlands	–92
New Zealand	–81
Norway	–62
Sweden	–69
Switzerland	–165
United Kingdom	–97
U.S.A.	–138

can be established (Table 4-6).

Switzerland, with a business-dominated corporatist system like Japan's, does not address equity issues openly:

Switzerland is a bastion of private business and the home of an electorate that defends personal liberty and property energetically through the institution of direct democracy. Because Switzerland's trade unions and Social Democratic left have failed in mounting a substantial offensive against this strong coalition defending the status quo, social distribution is not an issue seriously debated or acted upon by the Swiss state."[16]

Switzerland resembles the United States, which has a less impressive equality index but still a noteworthy one in comparison with the pluralist countries.

Recall the original discussion of corporatism as a "mask for inequality." Corporatism does not address the issue directly, and perhaps this is the root of the disappointment. Panitch sees betrayal in that "the guarantee of legal and political equality for functional groups makes the 'social contract' appear as an exchange between equals despite vast inequalities between the groups in power and distributional terms."[17] But he is addressing the wrongs of the labor- and socialist-dominated corporatist states, not the right-wing ones.

Is there nothing governments can do about equality?[18] Ward argues that the centrally planned socialist economies are no more successful than the market economies in redistributing wealth.[19]

TABLE 4-6
CORPORATISM AND EQUALITY (55%)*

Correlation	r	T†	β
Corporatism	−.02	1.11	.28
Left/right	.04	1.474	.36
% labor	.32	.403	.14
Wealth	−.39‡	−.885	.24
GOVINDEX	.33	.784	.20
Def. ratio	.55§	2.818§	.60§

*Variance explained.
†Student's T.
‡Sig. = .05.
§Sig. = .01.

However, Ward's measure does not measure *wealth*, a person's total assets. It is probable that, while different results might be forthcoming, wealth would prove to be as unpliable as income. Among the market economies, neither the corporatist nor the pluralist countries have shown much ability to intervene in the cause of equity.[20] Nor have the most draconian efforts met with much success.

One might be tempted to argue that leaving it alone is a good start. Austria, with a good equality index and a strong socialist tradition, is no more deliberate in its incomes policy than is Switzerland. An informal collaboration between unions and business was institutionalized in 1957 as the Joint Commission on Prices and Wages. Labor representation to the Commission is from the Austrian Federation of Trade Unions and from the Chambers of Labor. The Federal Chamber of Business and the Conference of Presidents of the Chambers of Agriculture represent business.

The Austrian government merely provides the structure for interest group bargaining and ratifies the decisions reached by the participating interest groups. A decision to strike, for example, cannot be made by an individual union acting unilaterally, but only after a protracted and complex set of negotiations among the peak associations.[21] But with so much planning, the Austrians do not address income distribution. The unions eschew the ideologically loaded subject of inequality in exchange for maximum influence ("access") "at the very highest levels in the arenas of economic and social policy most critical to Austria's strategy in the world economy"; labor as a force for conservatism is of course not unique to Austria."[22]

So corporatism and income distribution are unrelated, perhaps disappointing both the left and the right. But we should know more about the mode of corporatism. The left has in mind Iberian corporatism rather than Northern European or Asian corporatism.[23]

The best predictor of income distribution is the ratio between welfare and defense spending. Those countries with the lowest ratio, those whose spending priorities are heavily tilted away from defense, have the most impressive equality indexes. These, as we know, are not the corporatist countries.

Studies of pluralist countries have shown the same thing: income distribution has little to do with the ideology of ruling elites.

In the United States, where much popular ink has been spilled over the presumed widening income gap during the Reagan years, Lester Thurow writes:

Sometimes the Reagan administration's tax and social-welfare policies are given the chief responsibility for the growing inequality, but this ignores the fact that this movement toward inequality began before the president was elected. . . . Most of the four million people added to [the poverty roll] were not forced into poverty by the Administration's social welfare policies; they were added *by much more fundamental economic forces*.[24]

If a deliberate *laissez faire* attitude toward inequality makes no difference, neither does a conscious effort to narrow the gap. Rose, noting the British Labour Party's "professed egalitarian outlook," and thus wondering if perhaps Labour could reduce inequality, concludes that "the distribution of income tended to narrow, whichever party was in office."[25] We should not be surprised; if the centrally planned East European economies are unable to make much of a dent in income inequality, the pallid efforts of welfare states could not be expected to do so. Inequality is apparently intractable.

ARE CORPORATIST SYSTEMS MORE FISCALLY SOUND?

With national deficits now firmly established as a major focus of international economics, the putative ability of corporatist governmental systems to avoid the trap of excessive debt are much praised.[26] Corporatist governments—especially the right-wing ones such as Switzerland and Japan—are more fiscally responsible than the pluralist nations (Tables 4-7 and 4-8). The most stable and significant correlation, however, is between the extent of central government spending and debt. Big spenders are likely to incur more debt.

Remember that there is a negative correlation between corporatism and level of spending. Corporatism keeps the industrial democracies on the fiscal straight and narrow because the corporatist governments are less extravagant. Those countries with a unionized

TABLE 4-7
CORPORATISM AND THE RATIO OF DEBT TO GNP (72%)*

Correlation	r	T†	β
Corporatism	.40‡	1.950‡	.44‡
Left/right	.25	2.195‡	.48‡
% labor	.24	.646	.001
Wealth	.25	−1.587	.35
GOVINDEX	−.73§	−3.764§	−.69§

*Variance explained.
†Student's T.
‡Sig. = .05.
§Sig. = .01.

TABLE 4-8
RATIO OF DEBT TO GNP WITH CORPORATISM
AND IDEOLOGY COMBINED (68%)*

Correlation	r	T†	β
Corporatism/ideology	.87‡	2.412§	.54‡
GOVINDEX	−.73‡	−4.109‡	.72‡

*Variance explained.
†Student's T.
‡Sig. = .01.
§Sig. = .05.

corporatism and labor operates in the opposite direction. The up-
shot is that, while the proportion of the work force in unions has
no independent effect on level of debt, a unionized work force is
strongly associated with level of spending, which, in turn, is
strongly correlated with extent of debt. Simple as it may seem, if
governments would spend less they would have a more favorable
ratio of debt to GNP. The almost unbelievable ratio, +26.6 for
Japan, sets the example. Its ratio is miles ahead of any Western
nation.

Those seeking another answer can take solace in Norway (a big
spending country) with the best debt to GNP ratio among Western
industrial democracies and no clear tilt to left or right. But the
thrust of the linkage between corporatism and fiscal responsibility

is in the opposite direction. Right-wing corporatist governments manage debt exceptionally well.

Among the many claims advanced for corporatism, managing debt is justifiably listed; however, it is a less impressive claim than appears at first glance because corporatism needs an ideological gradient to the right in order to be a good predictor of debt ratio. Given the general presumption that forms of government do not matter, corporatism's performance is impressive, although limited. Its putative association with strong economic sanity growth is confirmed.

Corporatism's real strength is in those areas on which its advocates lay the greatest stress: unemployment and, to a lesser extent, inflation. Unemployment is less unyielding than income distribution. These conclusions are in accord with Schott's interpretation of similar data. He construes his data to mean:

In the case of both unemployment and inflation it is clear that strong corporatism is associated with better economic performance. In all countries where strong corporatist arrangements were in force the unemployment rate was low. . . . Furthermore this low unemployment rate was accompanied by relatively low inflation rates. On the other hand, where corporatism was not practiced . . . it is clear that unemployment was severe and that inflation was a relatively more serious concern. . . . However . . . the connections between economic growth and political arrangements [extent of corporatism] are less obvious. . . . Investment and growth outcomes do not appear to be as obviously related to corporatism as unemployment and inflation outcomes.[27]

Classifying rates of growth, inflation, and unemployment numerically (1 = poor, 2 = medium, 3 = good), Schott's conclusions, and my own, are provided with strong support. With regard to growth, strong corporatist countries average 2.4, compared to a nearly identical 2.1 for the weak corporatist ones; concerning inflation, the respective averages are 2.6 and 1.1; and with respect to unemployment the difference (3.0 to 1.0) is even more striking.

Although unrelated to political ideology measured by the traditional left/right continuum, corporatism is itself an ideology, but not one so easily classified. It is a doctrine of unity, cooperation, and the common good. Compared with others, corporatism is an *effective* ideology. In five cases, mode of conflict resolution is the best independent predictor of policy, followed by percentage in unions (3), left/right ideology (2), and wealth (1).

The fact that corporatism "works" in ways unrelated to economic growth is a point Olson might do well to consider. Economic growth is certainly the engine of political stability, especially when coupled with an equitable income distribution. But, although Olson infers that corporatism—presumably in ways akin to central planning in socialist economies—stifles or impedes economic growth, this is not the case. Corporatism manages conflict well, although it excludes large segments of the potential organizational environment.

The correct belief that corporatism leads to a set of policy outputs different from those of pluralism is quite unlike the complaints about *process*. The point now becomes one of contrasting the constrained conflict of corporatism with the free market basis of pluralism. The normative and the empirical are blurred, as proponents of corporatism as a preferred method of interest group intermediation believe it to be a superior form of political process. There are costs—for example, its exclusive nature—but the argument that benefits exceed these costs is hard to refute. We do not know whether people who join organizations in corporatist settings do so for the same or similar reasons as do people in pluralist settings. It is reasonable to assume that they do not. Those organizations admitted as participants can claim more consistent influence than is true of even the most powerful organizations in pluralist settings. It might be suggested that such permanent access, coupled with a somewhat higher rate of political participation and interest in European industrial democracies, yields a less fickle membership. It is time for these proposals to be tested. A synthesis of Olson's study of organizations with his study of economic growth might produce more definitive answers.

Encompassing Organizations

Examination of selected countries does offer support for Olson's argument and, given the small sample, is a useful contribution. The three countries he cites as encompassing—Austria, Norway, and Sweden—have also been regarded as thoroughly corporatist governmental cultures. But the economic performance of these countries, as well as the behavior and size of their union membership, varies greatly. Sweden has the highest proportion of union members, the least favorable proportion of strike days to economically active population, and the lowest rate of growth. Austria has a somewhat smaller union membership, but the least strike-prone work force and a healthy rate of growth, as does Norway.

It is ironic that Olson selects Sweden as a special case to prove his point. He argues that Sweden is an example of a dynamic, healthy economy not because it has few interest groups but because it has an encompassing ideology. But he is wrong. As we see, Sweden has not done nearly so well economically as Olson believed, but this may well be because his *theory is supported.* There is less corporatism in Sweden than Olson supposed, and the general inability of government to balance, to regulate labor-employer relations (as shown by the high strike ratio), contributes to Sweden's economic decline.[28]

Cooperation is hindered because the largest employer association, the Swedish Employers' Association, is less in command of its territory than is the Swedish Trade Union Confederation. It has a membership of 40,000, but these members employ only one-third of the Swedish labor force.[29] Labor and management are more confrontational than the corporatist model suggests, arguably because the most active employers' group has lost its public corporation membership at a time during which public sector employment has been growing substantially.

The same sort of fragmentation applies to the Swedish Trade Union Confederation, which does not represent those employed in the public sector. Add to this the growth of the white-collar work force (which either bargains separately or is likely to do so in the future), and the great increase in the number of women working (largely in the public sector), and the ability of any organization to claim legitimacy is doubtful. Lash concludes that "the Swedish labour markets are in a process of fragmentation. . . . This . . . will . . . lead to a long term devolution of Swedish industrial relations."[30]

The Response to Fragmentation

Western societal corporatism, unlike its Confucian manifestations, does not suggest the absence of conflict. On the contrary, the Western brand of corporatism recognizes that fragmentation is likely to accelerate as the distinction between public and private becomes less apparent. Schmitter uses the gradual erosion of corporatism as a refutation of those who argue that corporatism is solely the result of cultural and historical traditions, and encourages the view of corporatism as varied and at least partially a consequence of deliberate government policy. Sweden's fragmentation illustrates this point well.[31] Styles of conflict resolution change, although dramatic change is unlikely.

Whether the disintegration of the corporatist consensus is characteristic of all Western industrial democracies is not at issue; open societies can hardly be expected to relish any form of democratic centralism. Narrow distributional coalitions surely impose a more reasonable demand on human nature than do the encompassing organizations so desired by those who regard traditional groups as barriers to effective government management. But in the response to diversity, pluralism and corporatism diverge. Pluralism assumes that the group process is self-regulating. Truman's belief that organization breeds counterorganization implies a natural balancing. There are occasional and incremental adjustments—regulating the flow of PAC money and so on—but the individualism so apparent in pluralism, and the free association associated with its ideology, does not leave much of an intermediary role for the state. Schmitter, pointing to certain similarities between corporatism and pluralism, nevertheless concludes that the response to fragmentation is quite distinct: "Pluralists place their faith in the shifting balance of mechanically intersecting forces; corporatists appeal to the functional adjustment of an organically interdependent whole."[32]

Sweden may well be the precursor of more fragmentation in other corporatist cultures. There is little doubt that Sweden's corporatist consensus is shattered, as its increase in strikes illustrates well.[33] Hugh Heclo and Henrik Madsen carry the argument further. They believe that the erosion of Swedish corporatism began well before the onset of the economic troubles discussed here, and that the events of the 1970's and 1980's were not resolved according to the corporatist mode. They conclude that corporatism "offers an incomplete and often distorted interpretation of how Swedish politics and policies actually work."[34]

CORPORATISM AND CULTURE

But it is unlikely that Sweden's response to fragmentation will be to abandon its corporatist mechanisms of conflict resolution. Labor's well-established and institutionalized role in policy formation and implementation is not likely to be reduced substantially. In response to its declining economy, both the previous nonsocialist and the present socialist governments have cut back on public spending and have phased out industrial subsidies.[35] But the policy *structure* was not touched. Corporatism and pluralism are not easily interchangeable, as they are rooted in political culture. Other corporatist cultures (notably Austria, Norway, and Japan) are durable even as some fragmentation appears.

Change and Stability: Spain and Japan

Evidence of the fragmentation of corporatist systems requires a more systematic analysis of a major "process" variable: governability. Although some corporatist systems may be bending, perhaps breaking, moving perhaps toward a more pluralistic mode of conflict resolution, what can we say of the stability of either? Examples of the replacement of state corporatism by societal corporatism (rather than its deterioration and subsequent replacement by pluralism) give us some clues to stability. Two examples, Spain and Japan, serve to illustrate these changes.

Share establishes that Spain did not develop a powerful interest group system, even during the Second Republic. Labor unions, a crucial peak association, were (and are) weak, paralyzed by factional disputes. Other potential interest groups were underdeveloped due to the delay in Spain of a capitalist economy, possibly because the alliance among the aristocracy, the church, and the middle classes was intolerant of independent interest groups.[36] Unlike the European societal corporatist states, the Spanish work force is un-unionized and conservative, somewhat like Japan's.[37]

The Spanish church, which owned about one-third of Spanish national wealth, was the only clear example of a peak association.[38] The Franco period, although authoritarian, did little to incorporate diverse segments of the economy into the implementation process, as is usually done in state corporatism. Spain's smooth transition to democracy, beginning with the liberalization and modernization of the economy in 1958 and culminating with the death of Franco, is justifiably admired as an example of a rare phenomenon; however, the electoral process quickly became almost the exclusive property of the Spanish Socialist Workers Party, which appears destined to establish a *de facto* one-party system like Japan's. The move to societal corporatism, however, has been retarded by the same problems that plagued earlier regimes; in particular, Spain has not institutionalized a working relationship with interest groups.[39]

Spain thus appears to have paused short of a societal corporatist system. The political coalition is probably in place indefinitely; the next steps would be the control of labor, the creation and cooptation of business associations, and the cultivation of a strong and honored bureaucracy. The result is a curious one: weak interest groups and a powerful, authoritarian socialist party that gives every indication of staying in power indefinitely, yet without the integration of societal corporatism.

Japan's transition from authoritarian to corporatism (whether state or societal is a much-disputed point) also resulted in a *de facto* one-party system. But Japan already had the bureaucratic-business link. During the Meiji revolution (1867–1868), capitalism replaced feudalism, and a market economy was the result. Although we are accustomed to thinking of the modern Japanese state as rising from the ashes of World War II, the Meiji period was a forerunner, almost a duplicate, of the development of postwar Japanese corporatism. A massive industrialization effort was begun, culminating in the defeat of the Russians in the Russo-Japanese War in 1905. Interest groups were encouraged, sometimes created where none existed, by the state. Interest group leaders were usually former bureaucrats (a pattern duplicated today in Taiwan). As Takeshi Ishida explains, "The conduct of their activities was very often governed by a need to help spread and develop the policies of the government, while the original function of interest articulation was more or less suppressed."[40]

Political parties then, as now, were not truly competitive. Between 1892 and 1937, the party in power was *never* replaced by election.[41] Leadership replacement occurred when senior Japanese politicians, deciding it was time for a change, chose new prime ministers and used elections to ratify their choice. Japan's current political system inherited the corporatism of the past, accepted a few of the demands of the occupation government for more democracy, but reverted to a more comfortable style in reality.

Spain and Japan also can be compared on the dimension of the influence of their respective religions. As we know, Confucianism is not a formally established religion as is Roman Catholicism, but is rather a "secular ideology."[42] The role of the Spanish church was more partisan, since its tenets were more explicitly linked to policy, and hence it was a major participant in serious religious-political conflicts. In Meiji Japan, the various governments actually promoted Confucian studies, as a way of combating Western influence. Since Confucianism is not a religion, it is compatible with Shintoism and Buddhism, and it could avoid religious disputes easily. Confucianism in Japan was more of a glue holding the fabric of society together than was the church in Spain. As Michio Morishima concludes:

The fact that the whole nation was trained in the Confucianist way of thought throughout this more than 200 year period of isolation should not be undervalued. In fact, since the Japanese, though ethical, is nonreligious by nature, we can at once understand that it was of immense significance. During that period, the Japanese were brainwashed and molded into a specific type of person by their Confucianist education."[43]

These examples raise the issue of corporatism and "governability." Is corporatism, and hence governability, merely an artifact of a broader pattern of culture? Or is corporatism, irrespective of its host political culture, likely to be more "governable" because it channels conflict, even though it cannot always impede the development of social and political conflict?

Corporatism and Governability

Corporatism can claim an independent effect on a variety of policies—not as pervasive an impact as its partisans suppose, but more than such moderate variations in mode of governance as degree of party competition, or the ideology of ruling elites. While not primarily responsible for economic growth, corporatism does make a major contribution toward the control of inflation and unemployment. The failure to redistribute wealth may be due as much to lack of interest by the peak organizations as to any inherent "failure of corporatism." If Ward is right, it would take a radical incomes policy—presumably more extreme than that adopted by the East European socialist countries—to achieve any substantial reallocation of wealth.

Given these healthy and prosperous economies, are corporatist states truly more "governable"? For Schmitter, there is no question: "Those countries previously 'fortunate' enough to have developed a pluralist mode of interest intermediation with its multiple, overlapping, spontaneously formed, voluntaristically supported, easily abandoned, and politically autonomous associations, are likely to find it a serious impediment to governability in the post-liberal, advanced capitalist state."[44] The Olsonian critics of pluralism argue that "interest group liberalism" spells the decline of public authority and the inability of the state to meet its obligations. The counterargument is that the strength of interest groups—and the increase in demands (system overload)—that occurs as a consequence is not necessarily debilitating. Rather, it is the *process* that pluralist or corporatist systems adopt in order to respond to demands that makes the difference. *Unregulated* interest group systems may well lead to governments unable to develop sound fiscal policy, unable to cope with political instability.

But the corporatist system, based on the integration of private and public goods, is better suited to cope:

Polities in which interests are processed through formal associations that cover the widest variety of potential interests with national networks of representation, that have the highest proportion of those potentially affected as members, and whose pattern of interaction with the state is monopolistic, specialized, hierarchical, and mutually collusive should be more orderly, stable, and effective.[45]

Aside from his reliance on Truman's spontaneous combustion theory as an example of pluralist views of group origins, a theory we know to be discredited, Schmitter makes a compelling case.

Whether governability and stability are desirable depends on whether one wins or loses with a particular configuration of interests and policies. Instability may mean responsiveness or it may mean a weakening of the bonds of authority. The revolving door governments of pre-Fifth Republic France generated demands for a more stable constitution. The durability of dictators, however, is generally regarded as artificially imposed by state violence or repression. Surely in industrial democracies, frequent turnover of top-ranking government personnel is an early warning of deeply felt divisions. Corporatism is indeed associated with stability, but not as directly as its proponents might think (Tables 4-9 and 4-10).

There is not much *independent* correlation between corporatism and the extent of turnover in executive personnel, a measure of stability.[46] There is, however, a strong independent correlation between the level of protest and the extent of executive turnover. More protest contributes to more instability. In turn, the two best predictors of protest are extent of corporatism and level of unemployment. However, degree of inequality is not a good predictor of protest, in spite of its centrality to political theory.

One might have supposed that extremes of wealth and poverty, if not directly related to the intensity of political protest, would at

TABLE 4-9
CORPORATISM AND GOVERNMENT STABILITY (37%)*

Correlation	r	T[†]	β
Corporatism	−.45[‡]	.877	.22
Left/right	.27	.804	.19
% labor	−.30	−.033	−.001
Wealth	.15	−.781	.20
Unemployment	.56[§]	1.026	.24
Civil disorder	.76[§]	3.435[§]	.67[§]

*Variance explained.
[†]Student's T.
[‡]Sig. = .05.
[§]Sig. = .01.

TABLE 4-10
CORPORATISM/IDEOLOGY AND GOVERNMENT STABILITY (65%)

Correlation	r	T†	β
Corporatism/unemployment	.60‡	2.375§	.51§
Left/right	.28	−.451	.001
% labor	−.30	.215	.001
Wealth	−.16	.016	.000

*Variance explained.
†Student's T.
‡Sig. = .01.
§Sig. = .05.

least provide a filter for other variables. Of course, using only a universe of comparatively well-off countries dilutes the empirical test substantially. Ward finds that the European nations have low levels of inequality irrespective of economic or political organization. A less homogeneous sample is needed before rejecting out of hand the idea that inequality contributes to protest. After all, to Madison, inequality was the root of political conflict.[47]

Since corporatist systems are especially adept at controlling unemployment, but no better than pluralist ones at eliminating income inequalities, it is not surprising that they are less likely to fall victim to protest and civil disobedience. Merging degree of corporatism with extent of unemployment creates a powerful variable. Consensus politics is exactly what the phrase suggests.

Corporatism and Stability: The Explanatory Chain

Since corporatism, unemployment, and protest are associated in opposite ways (Table 4-11), neither is as impressive singly. But the combined contribution of both is clear and unequivocal. Corporatism is better at controlling the mischief of faction. The explanatory chain runs as follows: corporatism contributes to a low level of unemployment, which yields less civil disobedience. Less civil disobedience produces more stability. Certainly the integration of public policy and private interests that define corporatism does all that its proponents claim. The integration promoted by corporatism accomplishes more than do political parties. The independent effect

TABLE 4-11
CORPORATISM/UNEMPLOYMENT AND CIVIL DISORDER (54%)

Correlation	r	T†	β
Corporatism/unemployment	.60‡	2.564§	.53‡
Left/right	.21	−.358	.30
% labor	.36	−.723	.17
Wealth	−.05	.434	.14

*Variance explained.
†Student's T.
‡Sig. = .01.
§Sig. = .05.

of the political values of a government are trivial compared with the extent of corporatism. Whether the nature of the political regime is associated with economic outputs, as Douglas Hibbs claims, or is not, as James Payne contends, there is no independent correlation between political ideology and governability.[48] The contribution of corporatism becomes even more significant, given the failure of more traditional distinctions in government ideology. Pragmatic corporatism is a good guarantor of stability.

Stability does not necessarily mean ossification, as Schmitter believes.[49] It suggests that economic and social change can be accomplished without the upheavals so often associated with anything greater than incremental change in pluralist countries. Both the conflict-oriented, open political systems of the most pluralist countries and the consensus-oriented corporatist ones are, as is true of all established polities, disinclined to undertake more radical changes, since they disturb the networks of communication. In response to economic changes, corporatist countries seem either remarkably capable of easing the stress that accompanies new ways of living (as Japan's sunset and sunrise industry concept illustrates) or almost as haphazard as pluralist countries (as Sweden's hesitant adjustment to changes in the work force demonstrates). As Colin Crouch concludes:

There does seem to be a case for taking seriously the argument that, once economic actors have become organized, the sociopolitical context most likely to be consistent with relative freedom from economic distortion will be one that encourages coordination of action and centralization of organization, rather than one that tries to reproduce among organized interest situations analogous to a free market.[50]

Varieties of Corporatism

Corporatism is hardly a "pure" concept or even a unidimensional description of a government. Sweden, Austria, and Japan are all corporatist governments. What do they have in common? Austria and Switzerland, neighbors, share only corporatism:

Austria exemplifies democratic socialism, Switzerland liberal capitalism. The strongest political force in Austria is the labor movement, in Switzerland the business community. The Swiss state enjoys restricted power in society, the Austrian state far-reaching ones. These differences notwithstanding, both countries are small and prosperous.[51]

If Switzerland and Austria are so dissimilar, what of Japan in comparison with its Western corporatist brethren? Its corporatism is paternalistic and more private than Western corporatist states. Much of the corporatism in Japan is achieved through the political power of the business community, while the long tradition of cooperation between business and government is responsible for coordination and planning. Hence private corporations are the encompassing organizations.

A Classification of Corporatism

There is so much disagreement over the varieties of corporatism that it is almost criminal to propose another.[52] Hall, noting that the literature of corporatism is "replete with competing definitions," is troubled by the tendency to think in dichotomies: either a nation is, or is not, corporatist. He rightly points out that most governments appear to be corporatist at one time or another, and argues for an exploration of the *varieties* of corporatism.[53]

Irrespective of the various ways corporatist governments orchestrate group conflict, there are some common features. All corporatist systems posit an active role for the state, and all assume at least a shared role for the economic market. Partial reliance upon the

market supposes private property. Hence, centrally planned economies, even those no more authoritarian than Yugoslavia, Poland,
or Hungary are excluded.[54] All corporatist systems offer a monopoly
in functional representation to peak associations and exclude competitors from the political exchange.[55] However, the granting of a
monopoly in a given policy arena need not spill over into another
policy network. It is possible, then, for a state to edge toward
pluralism in one set of political exchanges and to veer toward corporatism in others.[56]

Given these similarities, some quite clear distinctions do
emerge. First, within the interest group sector, does labor or business dominate, or is there a balance? The extremes are Austria
(labor) and Switzerland and Japan (business). Second, where does
the initiative for policy lie? In the government bureaucracy or with
the interest groups?[57] This scheme is far less complex than most,
and it is also more easily adjusted as circumstances change. It is
quite similar to Hall's classification. In his analysis of France and
Britain, he distinguishes them on the degree of centralization, the
frequency of bargaining, the "inclusiveness" of the system (he finds
labor more "included" in Britain, capital in France), the role of
the state, the scope of the bargains, and their durability.[58] Both of
these approaches are less concerned with ideal typical corporatist
arrangements; they are more descriptive.

Eric Nordlinger believes that the bureaucracy in corporatist systems has an advantage, but that interest groups' control over "critical economic resources" can constrict the bureaucratic advantage.[59]
An example of Nordlinger's proposal is Australia, where the concentration of population in two major cities has given labor a stran-
gle hold on the economy. Forty percent of the country's population
lives in Sydney or Melbourne (compared with, for example, 16
percent of the U.S. population living in New York or Los Angeles).
Critical economic resources are more vulnerable when there are
fewer points of access. The four largest industrial firms account for
50 percent of industrial employment, further augmenting the strategic economic position of labor.[60] Bureaucracy, in turn, can limit
the substance of group demands, excluding those that deviate too
much from its preferences. Corporatism minimizes the "Australian
problem" by cooptation and control. Recall that strong corporatism

and unruly labor unions are incompatible, as Australia, with an appalling strike ratio and little inclination by labor to behave other than according to the dictates of narrow distributional coalitions, shows.[61]

The extremes of the policy initiation dimension are Austria and Switzerland (interest groups) and Japan (balance). The Japanese "balance," however, does not reflect the pluralist notion of an equilibrium of power. The line between private business and public management is indistinct, but public bureaucracies are major initiators of public policy, albeit in close collaboration with businesses. T. J. Pempel estimates that 90 percent of all successful legislation is bureaucratically drafted.[62] Graham Wilson also rejects the simplistic notion that business "runs" Japan.[63]

There are no examples of an independent bureaucracy, but quite possibly such examples are rare even in the pluralist countries. We must turn to the "state corporatist" systems of Latin America and Asia, in which the governments are able to maintain a posi-

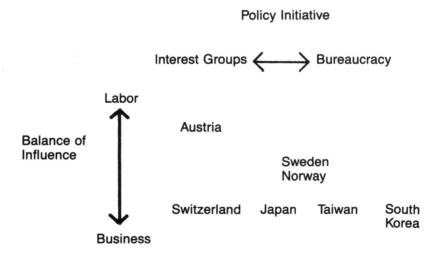

Figure 4-1

tion of supremacy (or at least more of one than is true of the industrial democracies) for examples of bureaucracies capturing their clientele rather than the reverse. Even these authoritarian governments, in a more advantageous position than corporatist ones, are not totally free of interest group constraint. Ruth and David Collier's scheme of classification is conceptually quite close to these ideas. They write of the ratio of inducements to constraints. State corporatism is high in both, and social corporatism, as found in Europe, is high on inducements but low on constraints. The combination of inducements and constraints may vary not only from country to country but also from time to time in the same country. But the combination of both inducements and constraints can be found only in authoritarian governments. (Low inducements and high constraints characterize more repressive regimes.)[64]

The nature of the distinction I propose is consistent with Williamson's distinction between "authoritarian licensed" and "contract" forms of corporatism. In the former, the state achieves control by restricting the freedom of action of interest groups; in the latter the state attains dominance by securing advantages through bargaining. Yet noncorporatist countries restrict the freedom of action of some groups. In the United States, the National Labor Relations Board sets forth the terms of union elections, as does Britain's recent industrial relations legislation. Nonetheless, both are at the weakest end of the corporatism-pluralism continuum. The continuum notion is given even stronger support by the most recent incarnation of corporatist classifications, *meso-corporatism*—that is, corporatism in some policy areas but not in others.

The essential idea is that corporatism and pluralism are not exclusive or rigid categories. In the next chapter, we will examine state corporatism. Although the difference between societal and state corporatism is greater than the difference between societal corporatism and pluralism, the continuum notion still holds. State corporatism generally occurs in less affluent countries, authoritarian countries. They are different from the stable democracies in many ways not connected directly to the themes of this book. The levels of political and civil liberties are lower than in democracies, and opposition political parties are scarce. Yet when we consider the essential ingredients of corporatism, bureaucratic encounters with peak associations, many striking similarities appear.

FIVE

STATE CORPORATISM
IN ASIAN SOCIETY

State corporatism is a characteristic of Asian and Latin American authoritarian governments, in particular, but is found in a variety of authoritarian regimes (Turkey, Iran before the revolution). The forms such state corporatism takes are quite different both between Asia and Latin America and within Asia. The corporatism literature has concentrated on Western Europe and, to a slightly lesser degree, Latin America. But, except for an occasional piece in one of the many collections of essays on corporatism, Asia has been neglected.[1] Perhaps those specializing in Asian area studies have found models developed by European corporatism specialists unpersuasive. Or perhaps the European corporatism specialists have not regarded the East as theoretically productive.[2]

The Asian form of state corporatism is often called Confucian; however, to speak of Asia as "Confucian" is not the same as to describe a country, say Austria, as Roman Catholic. As we have noted, Confucianism is not a religion, although it was the state-sanctioned belief system of the Han dynasty (136 B.C.).[3] There are a few Confucian temples in Taiwan and in the People's Republic of China, and a steady stream of enthusiasts visits them. But these edifices are centers of study and meditation rather than of religious commitment (much like the shrines of the more arcane Taoists). There are almost no formal Confucians in Japan, and about 2 percent of South Korea's and Singapore's population claims to be Confucian. In these four countries, religious life is varied, with Buddhism being more popular. About 12 percent of the entire ulation claims Confucianism as a religion. (By contrast, 93 percent of Latin America's population is Roman Catholic.) Since one may be a Buddhist, Shintoist, Taoist, and Confucian simultaneously, data are not very meaningful. Wu Teh-yao, who heads a national committee on Confucian ethics at the Institute of East Asian Philosophies in Singapore, explains, "I am a Christian and a Presbyterian elder, but I am also a Confucian disciple."[4]

The compatibility of Confucianism with formal religions and political philosophies is fundamental to understanding why Asian countries can be shaped by it. For example, even though Confucianism structures interpersonal relations by status, it was very popular during the European Enlightenment, having been touted by Jesuit missionaries. At the time, "neo-Confucianism" was dominant in China, and, since this manifestation was more despotic than the original, Chinese philosophy fell into disrepute. Nevertheless, Enlightenment thinking was influenced by the earlier, "pure" Confucianism, an influence widely reported at the time by, among others, Voltaire.[5] Sun Yat-sen, intellectual leader of the Nationalist rebellion against the dynasty, was influenced by Confucius, but also by Montesquieu and Marx. Above all, Confucianism is easily absorbed and transformed. Mao's attack on Confucianism (coupled, as is common, with an attack on a contemporary, such as Lin Piao, who was said to be a believer) derived from his belief that it was a relic of the past. In a similar way, among modern scholars, Confucianism became a code word for hierarchy and repression. Yet it is possible to read Confucian philosophy as a defense of representative democracy. How repressive does this interpretation of Confucius sound?

Several important rules of political democracy are deduced [from Confucianism]. They are: (1) in the conduct of state affairs, public opinion must be respected; (2) the government should exist by the consent of the governed; (3) the kind may be deposed on the ground of tyranny, and revolution for such a purpose is justified; (4) government should operate for the welfare of the people; and (5) liberty, equality, and impartiality should be maintained."[6]

Small wonder Confucianism was well received during the Enlightenment.

Since we cannot be sure what Confucianism is, it is not surprising that we do not know how many "practicing" Confucians there are. Since Confucianism, unlike Christianity, believes that humans are fundamentally good and rational (it has no doctrine of original sin), it is a kind of secular humanism. Since it argues against superstition, it might offend fundamental Christians.[7] Still, Pye writes of the "Confucian cultural region" and James Hsiung addresses human rights in China, Korea, and Japan since they "share a cultural tradition known as Confucian."[8] Herman Kahn is even more explicit: "The *Neo-Confucian* cultures have many strengths and few weaknesses. Japan, South Korea, Taiwan, Hong Kong, Singapore, and the ethnic Chinese minorities in Malaysia and Thailand seem more adept at industrialization than the West."[9] Kahn actually writes of the "properly trained member of a Confucian Culture,"[10] implying some manner of Berlitz course in Confucianism, perhaps with Cliffs Notes and cassettes for home study.

The proponents of this line of thought should remember that, from the days of Max Weber's *The Religion of China*,[11] a strong case has been made for Confucianism as an impediment to capitalism and economic growth. After all, the original Confucian ideal of the educated, culturally enlightened civil service denigrated economic activity. It was thought to be unbecoming for educated people to understand economics.[12] However relevant this sort of belief system was in its day, the current interpretations of Confucianism are unlikely to encourage ascetic star-gazing. An important reinterpretation, by Roderick MacFarquhar, restates Confucianism as a "cause" of industrial accomplishments:

Confucianism has been the ideology par excellence of state cohesion, and it is that cohesion which makes post-Confucian states particularly formidable. . . . Comet-like they trail an incandescent tail of post-Confucian East Asians: Koreans from South Korea, Chinese from Taiwan, Singapore, and Hong Kong. . . . The significant coincidence is culture, the shared heritage of centuries of inculcation with Confucianism. The tenets of Confucianism still provide an inner compass to most east Asians. . . . All east Asian peoples, however they met the challenge of the west, benefitted from their Confucian heritage. Since Confucianism was essentially an agnostic ideology, concerned with the management of the visible world, the post-Confucians experienced little of the spiritual angst that afflicted Hindus, Moslems and indeed Christians in their collision with the "materialism" of the industrial revolution."[13]

It would be unlikely that we would read of the threat of Cuban and Soviet military involvement in "Roman Catholic Latin America." Peter Berger explains that the type of Confucianism that permeates Asian politics "is not that of the Mandarins of Imperial China, but Confucian derived (or at least Confucian legitimated) values motivating very ordinary and unlearned people—petty entrepreneurs in Taipei, say, or bank clerks in Manila (or for that matter, San Francisco)."[14]

The most sophisticated analysis of everyday Confucianism is Solomon's interviews with ninety-one mainland-born Chinese. He believes:

The values inculcated as part of the "great [Confucian] tradition," spread beyond those who received formal training in the Confucian classics. The social outlook and values of that portion of our sample who had only elementary schooling or who were educated decades after the abolition of the Confucian educational system are very similar to those of the elderly respondents who had been educated before the turn of the last century in Confucian schools.

Most important, Solomon argues for a strong link—surely stronger than in Western societies—between elite articulation of cultural traditions and mass acceptance of them, because "the formal logic of Confucianism and the life style of the scholar-official represented an *elaboration* and ideological justification of the peasant cultural pattern rather than being divorced from it."[15]

Nevertheless, Taiwanese education includes compulsory courses in Confucian ideology, and when Prime Minister Lee Kuan-yew of Singapore felt that his country was slipping into degeneracy (the opposition had elected one legislator), he called for a reinstitution of Confucian values, the "rhetoric expected of a Confucian statesman."[16] Efforts to emulate Taiwan's curriculum ensued.

As a cultural tradition, Confucianism is as varied as are the politics, economics, and history of Austria and Mexico, both "Roman Catholic." The Asian countries have their "separate versions of Confucianism, which increasingly diverged as each country followed a different path to political modernization."[17] The description of the different paths depends on who is describing them. Hsiung writes that, "compared with China, both Korea and Japan were incompletely Confucianized." Pye, more judiciously, concludes that "the evolution of Confucianism . . . produced . . . distinct political cultures, each with a unique approach to the concept of power."[18] Confucianism, then, is a shorthand way of referring to the broader notion of political culture. Hung Chao-tai explains that "Confucianism as we now know it has absorbed ingredients of Taoism and Buddhism."[19] An apt analogy is the Protestant Reformation. Just as Protestantism revoked some of the more dogmatic aspects of Catholicism without renouncing Christianity, so did Japan develop substantial modifications in the doctrinal teachings of Confucianism without eliminating its essence.[20]

THE CONFUCIAN POLITICAL CULTURE

Confucianism has absorbed more than just some disparate religions; it has also assimilated traditional Asian authoritarianism. What are the essential components of this culture? We have seen that Confucian thought stresses group loyalty and obedience. The Confucian political culture encourages a consensual style, eluding direct confrontation. When politics becomes adversarial, which happens rarely, it is usually because the stakes are very high (as was the case in South Korea in 1987). Political systems that avoid conflict are not well equipped to channel or regulate conflict when it occurs. Concerning the corporatist mode of group legitimation or cooptation, Asian state corporatism typically establishes the bureaucracy as the agent of incorporation. Negotiations are usually undertaken without much notice by those attending the *political* process, either electorally or in the various semi-autonomous legislatures of the region.

This common cultural precept does not mean that all Confucian systems operate much the same. We shall discuss substantial differences among Japan, South Korea, and Taiwan concerning the regulation of business and its attendant interest groups. But a fundamental difference can be observed in the response to political opposition. As the culture stresses consensual decision making, the existence of a formal opposition party is more indicative of systemic pathology than is true of industrial democracies.

Japan is the most open of the Asian corporatist countries. Opposition parties are unfettered. Yet the Liberal Democrats have not lost an election in three decades. Few question the commitment of Japan to consensus politics, and some, such as Chalmers Johnson, believe that the Japanese "disguise and ameliorate their *soft authoritarianism* through many common, as well as some unusual, political devices."[21] Among the more common forms of deception, Johnson mentions a democratic constitution, indirect elections, and party factionalism. Still, opposition parties are not constrained.

Pye writes of the "aggressive Confucianism" of Taiwan and South Korea.[22] He believes that South Korea, unlike Taiwan and Japan, has been unable to establish the legitimacy of the ruling elite. Hence, South Korean opposition is more vociferous, and more cruelly repressed, than in Taiwan. It has an abominable human rights record in comparison with Taiwan's. Although government-organized phony "opposition groups" are common in both countries, the level of cynicism is higher in South Korea. But somewhat as Japanese youth go through the ritual period of rebellion before settling into middle-class life, South Korean opposition may be exaggerated by those not familiar with the rules of the game. There is a crisis of authority in South Korea. *Seriously enforced* martial law has been in effect since 1972. The opposition—alternately jailed and released—is challenging the authoritarian government with pressure toward more democratization. Assassinations and coups abound, and the degree of repression seems coordinated with the rage of the opposition. Yet even this comparatively unstable authoritarian government can be described as Confucian. Ilpyong Kim, conceding unrest, argues the Confucian conviction that the emperor's "mandate from heaven" could be judged to have been withdrawn, justifying rebellion.[23]

Taiwan's Confucianism is less coercive. Nevertheless, it has not disguised its authoritarianism. Upon the death of Chiang Kai-shek, his son, Chiang Ching-kuo, inherited his job. Since lineal descent is not normally a characteristic of competitive democratic party systems, Taiwan's transfer of power was correctly regarded as independent of any expression of popular sentiment. There was no opposition or protest of any serious nature to this process. Taiwanese are no more addicted to democracy than are the other Asian populations. Hu Fu, an empirically oriented political scientist at Taiwan National University, has conducted frequent surveys regarding college students' attitudes about democracy. He concludes that Taiwanese students prefer the rule of wise leaders to a government of laws, centralization of political authority, and "uniformity of thought to divergence of thought."[24]

Opposition candidates could not, until 1986, form an opposition organization, yet they have been able to compete *individually* (with a success rate of about 20 percent) for seats in the Legislative Yuan. Riots accompanying the U.S. decision to withdraw diplomatic recognition in 1979, coupled with some Taiwan independence activity, led to the arrest and conviction of demonstrators, and earlier Taiwanese independence agitation resulted in longer terms of imprisonment. But the decision to revoke martial law and to allow opposition leaders to organize that occurred in 1987 was the institutionalization of a gradual easing of restraints.[25] The 1979 rioters are no longer in jail; their relatives in some cases have been elected to the legislature.

Taiwan's relatively relaxed attitude toward its opposition was possible because the party leadership was able to "accept the idea that their initially superior political position did not give them the traditional Confucian claim to authority in all areas of life."[26] Such a peaceful downgrading of authority has not occurred in the People's Republic, or South Korea, or Singapore.[27] The agreement in South Korea to allow opposition parties to contest elections, made after weeks of hard, confrontational, media-saturated demonstrations, is just about the same as that made in Taiwan without more than an occasional demonstration. Several reasons for this uncharacteristic turn of events will become apparent as the book explores government-business relations. They are: the decline in social distance and antagonism between native Taiwanese and mainlanders, the continued growth of the economy, and the humiliation of the defeat suffered by the Nationalists in 1949.

Singapore has been more rigid: "The Chinese are in the dominant, majority position, and the consequence is a politics of consensus in which opposition as trivial as the loss of a single seat by the People's Action Party (PAP) is treated as a major, and personally insulting, threat to the regime."[28] Opposition candidates claim that Singapore's tough Internal Security Act is used against their members, and even some venerable Chicago-style "neutral" bureaucratic pressure is evident (securing the required permits for office space often proves to be impossible). When *two* opposition candidates won in 1984, reflecting a decline in the PAP's share of 13 percent, the party was "shocked."[29] PAP leaders spoke of "flaws" in the democratic design of politics. Complaining of the responsiveness of competitive democracies to whims of public opinion, a PAP leader offered an impeccable definition of the Confucian, state corporatist encompassing organization, one that could apply well to Taiwan's Kuomintang: "I think a stable system is one where there is a mainstream political party representing a broad range of the population. Then you can have a few other parties on the periphery, very serious minded parties. They are unable to have wider views but they nevertheless represent sectional interests. And the mainstream is returned all the time."[30]

With these differences in mind, we address some of the similarities in the political structure and process of the state corporatist political systems, Confucian variety.

The Encompassing Organization

The major characteristics of such systems are the more assertive role of government and the relative impotence of labor in the design and execution of public policy. State corporatist countries are typically authoritarian and there is usually a genuinely encompassing organization to provide continuity and legitimacy to the policy formation process. Often the formation of interest groups—and the individual's opportunity to join them—is constrained and prohibited by the government. Typically individual firms are required to join, and the government—to a degree greater than Walker and Wilson have argued happens in the United States—creates its own captive organizations.[31]

It is also normal for the government to infiltrate groups. Usually the bureaucracy, rather than the organization or its members, appoints its director.[32] Politically authoritarian countries, although relying heavily on bureaucratic initiative in economic planning, do not generally resort to the stifling central planning of the East

European socialist economies. To the contrary, often market incentives become the essential control mechanisms in encounters between bureaucracies and interest groups.[33]

Perhaps the least compelling argument in Olson's body of thought is the idea of the encompassing organization. He provides three examples: a labor union that includes most of the manual workers in a country, a lobbying organization that includes all the major firms in an industrialized country, and a disciplined political party.[34] Because they are numerically encompassing, such organizations have an incentive to work for the adoption of public policies that are "rewarding for the society as a whole."[35] Increased productivity is in Olson's view the foremost example of the public good; efforts to reallocate wealth or income to the members of the encompassing organization will result in lower productivity, and less wealth. Hence no rational leadership would propose them.

But why should numerical superiority cause an organization to place the growth of national wealth above its distribution? Granted that there can be no equity without growth and wealth, why should encompassing organizations be exempt from the universal law of interest group politics: what's good for my organization is good for the country; hence my group is not a "special interest" group (although my opponents' organizations are).[36] Numerical superiority might have just the opposite effect. Surely the encompassing political party of the Philippines, the new Society Movement, and the encompassing organization of Mexico, the Institutional Revolutionary Party, have found plunder and graft more rewarding than GNP growth, and the only income distribution for which they can claim credit is the billions diverted to the ruling elite.

It is more probable that the willingness of people and organizations to suspend belief in the merits of their own causes is at least partially a consequence of the culture in which they live.

Encompassing Organizations in Confucian Societies

Confucianism is one of many ideologies that speaks unambiguously about the desirability of negating the human error of individualism. When combined with the cultural collectivism of Asian societies, it offers a strong opportunity for encompassing organizations that do (at least theoretically) argue that the public good and the good of the group are not necessarily identical and, when they are incompatible, the public good should prevail.

Pye believes that Confucian cultures promote a more unidimensional image of the public good not only because of the stress on authority and discipline but also because of the view of government as a natural extension of the family.[37] With the government playing the role of father (a role stressed by the Confucian reverence for legal authority), nongovernmental organizations would quite reasonably be regarded as legitimate only within the confines of state-sanctioned activity. More than occurs in the European corporatist governments, Confucian systems fix legitimate authority solely upon the formal, legal government. But Confucianism was adapted to the unique cultural patterns of Asian countries, so that Japanese, South Korean, Singaporean, and Taiwanese governments are all Confucian in culture but with major differences (Tables 5-1–5-5).

Japan is democratic and open, while the others are authoritarian. As we would expect, the executive turnover in Japan is twice

TABLE 5-1
CHARACTERISTICS OF ASIAN GOVERNMENTS:
EXTENT OF GOVERNMENT ECONOMIC ACTIVITY,
RACIAL HOMOGENEITY, AND CIVIL DISOBEDIENCE

Country	GOVINDEX (1984)*	Homogeneity (1984)	Civil disobedience (1948–1977)[†]
Japan	.12	99	524
Taiwan	.07	58	475
South Korea	.06	100	629
Singapore	.30	58	124

*Government expenditures as proportion of gross national product.
[†]Total incidents.
Sources: GOVINDEX: World Bank (International Bank for Reconstruction and Development). *World Development Report, 1986* (Washington, D.C.: World Bank, 1987), pp. 270–271; Charles Lewis Taylor and David A. Jodice, *World Handbook of Political and Social Indicators* (3rd ed.; New Haven, Conn.: Yale University Press, 1983), pp. 5–8. Homogeneity: George Thomas Kurian, *The New Book of World Rankings* (New York: Facts on File, 1984), p. 48. Civil disobedience: Taylor and Jodice, *World Handbook*, vol. 2, pp. 22–44.

TABLE 5-2
CHARACTERISTICS OF ASIAN GOVERNMENTS:
SPENDING PRIORITIES AND QUALITY OF LIFE

Country	Ratio defense/health (1984)	Physical quality of life (1984)*	Index of social progress (1984)[†]
Japan	.9	96	91.75
Taiwan	6.5	86	57.75
South Korea	9.7	82	49
Singapore	5.1	82	61.67

*A composite index made by averaging life expectancy, infant mortality, and literacy.

[†]High = more for education, etc.

Sources: Physical quality of life: George Thomas Kurian, *The New Book of World Rankings* (New York: Facts on File, 1984), pp. 331–332. Index of social progress: Richard J. Estes and John Morgan, *The Social Progress of Nations* (New York: Praeger, 1984), pp. 199–208.

TABLE 5-3
CHARACTERISTICS OF ASIAN
GOVERNMENTS: ECONOMIC PERFORMANCE

Country	Inflation (1973–1984)	Ratio debt/GNP (1984)	GNP/per capita (1984)	GNP growth (1968–1983)	Equality (1978)
Japan	4.5	26.1	10,600	3.9	−50
Taiwan	3.0	3.57	3,700	8.3	−15
South Korea	17.6	1.51	2,100	8.4	8
Singapore	3.1	1.26	7,260	7.4	−1

Sources: Inflation: World Bank (International Bank for Reconstruction and Development). *World Development Report, 1986* (Washington, D.C.: World Bank, 1986), pp. 180–181. Ratio debt/GNP: George Thomas Kurian, *The New Book of World Rankings* (New York: Facts on File, 1984), p. 48. GNP/per capita: World Bank, *World Development Report, 1986,* pp. 180–181. GNP growth: World Bank, *World Development Report, 1986,* pp. 180–181. Equality: Michael Don Ward, *The Political Economy of Distribution* (New York: Elsevier, 1978), p. 43.

as high as its nearest competitor, South Korea. Singapore and Taiwan are stable, while South Korea is ruptured by assassinations, protests, and coups. Additionally, South Korea is less equitable in income distribution than Japan, Taiwan, or Singapore. Finally,

TABLE 5-4
CHARACTERISTICS OF ASIAN GOVERNMENTS:
CONDITIONS IN THE WORKFORCE

Country	Unemployment (1984)	% of workers in unions (1984)	Days lost to strikes (1984)
Japan	2.2	22	.010
Taiwan	1.3	18	.003
South Korea	4.6	13	.004
Singapore	3.1	23	.009

Sources: Unemployment: International Labour Office, 1986 Yearbook of Labour Statistics (Geneva: ILO, 1986), pp. 22, 528–529. % of workers in unions: George Thomas Kurian, New Book of World Rankings (New York: Facts on File Publications, 1984), p. 255; Republic of China, Executive Yuan, Directorate-General of Budget, Accounting, and Statistics, Yearbook of Labor Statistics, 1985 (Taipei, 1986), pp. 26, 875. Days lost to strikes: Kurian, New Book of World Rankings, p. 256.

TABLE 5-5
CHARACTERISTICS OF ASIAN GOVERNMENTS:
PARTICIPATION AND LEGAL RIGHTS FOR WOMEN

Country	Political participation (1984)*	Women's status index (1984)†
Japan	1.07	1.33
Taiwan	54.11	4.00
South Korea	66.13	47.11
Singapore	48.10	47.11

*Low scores mean fewer violations of political and civil rights.
†Low = greater rights.
Sources: Political participation: Richard J. Estes and John Morgan, The Social Progress of Nations (New York: Praeger, 1984), pp. 199–208. Women's status index: Estes and Morgan, Social Progress, pp. 106–108.

South Korea and Japan are ethnically homogeneous, while Singapore and Taiwan, the objects of major migrations, are less so.

Taiwanese authoritarianism leaves all but the most overtly political matters alone, as does Singapore's. The mechanism for a more aggressive authoritarianism is certainly there, and it is used on occasion. There have been two political murders in the last half-dozen years in Taiwan (or planned from Taiwan), and none in Singapore. South Korea is more brutal than either.

Like Taiwan's former martial law, Singapore's Internal Security Act eliminated civil liberty. Citizens could be arrested for unspecified charges and held for two years without trial. But the trial is by a hand-picked board whose opinions are not binding. Once this procedure is completed, a prisoner can be detained indefinitely. In June, 1987, twelve people accused of involvement in a "Marxist conspiracy to subvert the existing social and political system" were held without trial for one year (one for two years). Mass arrests of union leaders, and the creation of a government-endorsed union, ended the possibility of union influence, since the official union— unlike the labor partners in European corporatism—had no bargaining leverage. When youths were conscripted into construction brigades, the union offered no opposition.[38] Examples of how unsavory each can be are the death of Henry Liu (author of an unflattering biography of Taiwan president Chiang Ching-kuo), killed in San Francisco by thugs engaged by high-ranking officials in the intelligence apparatus on Taiwan, and Singapore's harassment of *Time* for its reports on efforts to stifle opposition.

Singapore's reaction to press criticism is typical of the mixed and often contradictory behavior of these authoritarian countries. It has restricted circulation of foreign and domestic newspapers and magazines judged to be hostile to the government. Yet Singapore has more international magazines available than Taiwan, and it has many satellite dishes available for private use, thus making its crackdowns somewhat pointless.

Singapore and Taiwan are internationally frugal, borrowing as little as possible, while South Korea borrows up to the hilt for extravagant industrial expansion. Partially as a consequence, South Korea's rate of inflation is exceptionally high by any standards, and unthinkable by Pacific Rim standards.[39] South Korea also has a higher than average unemployment rate. Its government has adopted an economic policy only superficially comparable with Taiwan's, which thrives with less borrowing and more emphasis on stability and on increasing the rate of savings.[40]

Taiwan does not tamper very much with the structure of the economy, while South Korea imposes mergers. Taiwan relies on incentives, whereas South Korea combines "incentive and command devices."[41] In Collier and Collier's scheme, Taiwan uses more inducements and South Korea more restraints.[42]

But these differences aside, the Asian Confucian governments have many of the characteristics of corporatist political systems. They have almost no strikes, and the proportion of the work force in unions is very low. Taiwan does not prohibit strikes; rather it establishes an elaborate and cumbersome method for calling them.[43] Because the government stresses equality more than South Korea does (see Table 5-1), it has viewed the tiny, family-owned firm with satisfaction and pride. Until 1987 South Korea outlawed strikes; when rules were relaxed after the protests, large-scale strike activity increased sharply. Singapore still forbids them. Unions have a more secure role in Japanese politics because the U.S.-written constitution sought the creation of free, non-Communist labor organizations.[44] Yet work stoppages rarely occur in any of these countries, whether because of prohibition or disinclination.[45] They have low unemployment and low inflation, and they have high GNP growth. As we have seen, high growth does not characterize the European corporatist countries. The Asian authoritarian governments have the growth characteristics attributed, erroneously, to European corporatist countries.

The high growth of the Asian economies has been attributed to Confucianism as often as to corporatism, or, specifically, to the absence of distributional coalitions. Pye remarks that fascination with Confucianism as a "compelling force," driving its adherents to high achievement, began with Marco Polo and continues with the extravagant praise of Vogel. Even the above-average achievement of Asian children in American schools is credited to the Confucian respect for authority and stress on filial piety.[46] The example of the Philippines, a Christian country, can only serve to strengthen the enthusiasm of the pro-Confucians.[47]

As tempting as single-cause theories are—and certainly the Taiwanese in particular are willing to give the credit to Confucius—successful economic policies are as much a consequence of a high rate of saving (except in South Korea), a well-trained bureaucracy, which limits corruption to "honest graft," and the consensual style of decision making that creates "interlocking directorates as between government and business."[48] Berger believes that the government-business "symbiosis" is "specifically East Asian."[49] This symbiosis, of all the claims for Confucianism, seems reasonably well founded; the consensual model of political decision making, derived from Chinese Confucian culture, prescribes such a paradigm. Yet there are other examples of a government-business symbiosis that do not yield the high growth of the Asian governments. Mexico's one-party system, with a powerful bureaucracy coopting business, is an obvious case. But Mexico's economic performance has been dismal, and the hemorrhaging of the consensus managed by the Institutional Revolutionary Party seems to have begun in 1986.

Other aspects of the development of Taiwan, Singapore, and South Korea are unrelated to any tenets of Confucianism. The Confucian ideology, and the ensuing Confucian culture, says nothing about equity; indeed, the hierarchical structure of authority argues against such matters. In Singapore and Taiwan the Gini index has been declining as (until recently) GNP growth continues to increase consistently.

The zest with which these countries pursue economic success, and the enthusiasm of the business community, hardly reflect the original Confucian aversion to economic activity. Indeed Berger, drawing on Weber, describes a value system that promotes, almost requires, a commitment to economic success: "A highly developed sense of practicality or pragmatism, an active rather than a contemplative orientation to life, great interest in material things (emphatically including a positive valuation of wealth)."[50] Coupled, however, with these "Western" cultural traditions are typically Confucian ones: respect for the family and willingness to delay gratification.

The danger in thinking of Confucianism as a coherent ideology is in disregarding other complementary factors and events that made Asia economically and politically what it is today. One reason that they have similar economies is their shared Confucian tradition. But the region has had a history as a single economic unit, brought together first under Japanese imperialism, and since World War II integrated by Japanese economic imperialism. The role of foreign investment, especially in Taiwan, cannot be discounted. Bruce Cumings argues that Japan, South Korea, and Taiwan are actually a regional political-economic system, which he calls "bureaucratic-authoritarian industrializing regimes." The distinguishing characteristics of such regimes are relative state autonomy, central coordination, bureaucratic short- and long-range planning, high flexibility in moving in and out of industrial sectors, private concentration in big conglomerates (except in Taiwan), low expenditures on social welfare, exploitation of women, exclusion of labor, and military and authoritarian repression (in pre-war Japan, and in South Korea more than in Taiwan in the 1980's). Additionally, all three were recipients of major United States aid and tutelage.[51] The connection of these characteristics to Confucianism is obscure at best.

THE COMMITMENT TO A SINGLE PARTY

The most distinguishing political characteristic of the Asian Confucian cultures has been their recognition of a single political party as the vessel of the accumulated wisdom of the country. The Japanese Liberal Democratic Party (LDP), the Kuomintang, (KMT) of Taiwan, the People's Action Party of Singapore, and South Korea's Democratic Justice Party all, with varying degrees of success, lay claim to the mantle of keeper of the faith. The Liberal Democratic Party has been in power for three decades and is probably more stable than the Democratic Justice Party, in spite of South Korea's sometimes rigid authoritarianism.

Asian politics is a politics of respect and consensus, a tradition that appears more important than the form of government. These political patterns stress harmony and hierarchy, and thus are part of the Confucian culture.[52] Had the Japanese not lost World War II and as a result had a democratic constitution imposed on them, it is doubtful if they would have installed a parliamentary democracy. Ward concludes:

The terms of political competition and decision-making in postwar Japan have altered substantially since the 1932–1945 period, that these changes are democratic in tendency, that they have been stimulated in important degree by the efforts of SCAP [Supreme Commander for the Allied Powers], and that they would not have achieved anything very closely resembling their present status were it not for those efforts. . . . Too much of what occurred was due wholly or largely to SCAP initiatives and pressures, while the relatively few cases of official Japanese initiative were decidedly modest in terms of the political changes involved."[53]

The Japan Socialist Party can count on about 20 percent of the vote, a figure comparable to the opposition vote in Taiwan; the legal opposition in 1987 received about the same percentage of votes as the disparate anti-Kuomintang candidates in previous elections, a one-party authoritarian state.[54] Pye describes the comparability of the Kuomintang and the Liberal Democratic Party: "During the late 1970's and early 1980's, the Taiwanese electorate became quite clearly divided, with 70 percent favoring the KMT and 30 percent the various *dang-wai* [opposition] candidates. As a consequence people both within and outside the KMT came to believe that Taiwan was moving toward a modified Japanese party system, with the KMT performing the role of the LDP, even to the point of having factions, and the *dang-wai* being the equivalent of the Japanese opposition parties."[55]

The similarity of outcome should not obscure the obvious truth that Japan imposes no restrictions on opponents of the Liberal Democratic Party, whereas Taiwan curbs opposition parties. But the similarities remain. Pempel, noting the troubles of the Japanese Liberal Democrats, calls our attention to the loss of control in local elections.[56] Yet Taiwanese opposition candidates, running as independents, were able to defeat the Kuomintang occasionally in small cities and rural areas, sometimes in larger cities, and even in Taipei *before* the legalization of opposition parties in 1987.[57] In the first election under the new rules, Taiwan's KMT received about 75 percent of the vote, far more than Japan's Liberal Democratic Party, which has not received an absolute majority vote since 1963. When electoral competition becomes more routine in Taiwan, a comparison with the Liberal Democratic Party will be appropriate.

Thus the best examples of the Olsonian encompassing organization are Asian one-party governments. Generally the single dominant party forges an alliance with the most active interest groups, merging them into a structure of authority. Since labor is impotent in Asian politics, business organizations—single-industry trade associations, more generally based organizations resembling chambers of commerce, and single industries—are brought into the decision-making process.

But it is not the interest groups on whom the burden of encompassing attitudes falls. We may assume that they are at least equally interested in advancing their own cause. Political parties are the encompassing organizations. Since the same political parties have always been in power, there is little opportunity for hostile interest groups to develop a working coalition with an opposition party, as usually happens in Europe. There is less incentive to be "encompassing" when there is a realistic possibility of electoral defeat.[58]

Taiwan's Kuomintang

Among the Asian one-party political systems, Taiwan's Kuomintang is the oldest in the grand tradition of revolutionary parties. (The mainland's Communists split away from this parent organization.) To overthrow the Manchu monarchy, Sun Yat-sen founded the two precursors of the Kuomintang, the Sinchu Hui (Society for the Rebuilding of China) in Honolulu in 1894 and the Tung Ming Hui (Society for the Common Cause) in Tokyo in 1905. At the time of the overthrow of the monarchy (1912) the two organizations merged to become the Kuomintang (KMT), which began the first of its many revolutionary endeavors, the launching of the Northern Expedition against Manchu-sympathetic warlords. Then came the war with Japan, followed by the civil war. When the Nationalist government retreated to Taiwan in 1949, conceding the mainland to the Communists, it was merely the latest episode in the violent history of the party.

Presumably because of the nature of the times, the Kuomintang was always an authoritarian, militarily dominated, political organization. The Nationalist armies faced a major rebellion in 1947 and repressed it brutally, a bit of history that neither the Kuomintang nor the Taiwanese are likely to forget (Taiwanese are those who immigrated from the mainland, generally from Fukien province, in the nineteenth century).[59] Upon its arrival in Taiwan in 1949, the

KMT continued to crush opposition from native Taiwanese ruth-
lessly. Since Taiwan had been a Japanese colony until the end of
World War II, the Kuomintang assumed the Taiwanese to have
been collaborators.

The Taiwanese had not participated in the civil war, and certainly did not identify with either Mao or Chiang Kai-shek.
Kuomintang loyalists believe even now that Taiwanese, especially
the upper classes, were happy with the Japanese occupation. The
residual use of Japanese as a second language by older members of
the Taiwanese upper classes continues to rankle. About 70 percent
of native Taiwanese were literate in Japanese at the end of World
War II. Taiwanese, the first language, is unintelligible to a Mandarin speaker.[60]

There was no major outbreak of violence from 1949 until 1979,
when frustration over American withdrawal of diplomatic recognition triggered another outbreak of Taiwanese riots; this time, however, the government merely arrested and jailed the rioters. The
brutal repression of the early days was no longer possible.[61]

THE INITIAL DIRECTION: LAND REFORM   From an inauspicious debut,
the Kuomintang has evolved into a less authoritarian organization
than the ruling party in either South Korea or Singapore. The land
reforms of 1949–1950 are responsible for the reversal of the
Kuomintang's fortunes, transforming it from an army of occupation
to something a good deal less ominous.[62]

In these reforms Taiwanese landholders were given government
bonds in exchange for land, which was then distributed to the
former tenants. An American-designed agrarian-aid program was
established, much like the farm programs of the 1930's begun by
the Department of Agriculture. The "land to the tiller" program
was a conspicuous success. By Asian standards applied to developing nations and in comparison with developed nations, the income
distribution of Taiwan is unusually equal, a state of affairs typically
traced to the land reform program.[63] Farmers prospered and landlords used the bonds to develop a strong urban economy, one that
became increasingly dominated by Taiwanese.[64] During the years of
Kuomintang rule on the mainland, the land reform program was
not implemented because landlords were KMT loyalists. But the

party owed Taiwan's landlords nothing.[65] The mainlanders retained control of the government and, most significantly, its growing, technologically sophisticated bureaucracy.

The trade-off probably saved the Kuomintang from another revolutionary defeat; it surely converted it from a debased, inefficient organization whose loss of the mainland revealed the depth of its corruption to a more popular and benign agent of political integration. Official party histories, and even some more critical, unofficial accounts, glorify the events of 1949.[66] The reason for the land reform program, however, was less Sun Yat-sen than it was common sense and pragmatic politics. Chiang's Kuomintang bureaucratic elite had no experience in managing an economy. The inflationary spiral on the mainland during the Nationalist years was testimony to the Nationalist bureaucracy's incompetence. It was also engaged in a power struggle with the military, humiliated by a presumably inferior Communist army, and lusting for blood. Many of them also believed that they had lost the civil war because they had deserved to, and were anxious not to repeat the same mistake twice (to "lose two revolutions in the same half-century").[67] A leading architect of land reform, Chen Cieng, writes that the rural villages were on the brink of revolution and that the Communists were ready to lend a hand. But land reform deprived them of an issue and the threat receded.[68] Besides, commerce has always been regarded as less worthy and less prestigious than government service; it is the "crooked road" in traditional Confucian thought.[69] Crooked road or not, the standard of living of Taiwanese in the private sector soon outstripped that of the mainlanders. Given the organization's reputation for corruption, Kuomintang bureaucrats had to live on their salaries in order to create a new tradition.[70]

STRUCTURE, MEMBERSHIP, AND INCENTIVES   The Kuomintang is a massive bureaucracy, but unlike the government civil service, it has no competitive exams. The elder Chiang did not take party organization very seriously, since he governed in the Confucian tradition of absolute loyalty and regarded the party as his own personal fiefdom. With the death of Chiang and his son Chiang Ching-kuo's assumption of power, intra-KMT disputes have become institutionally structured, and opposition political parties have won the right to organize.

To accommodate the organization to its primary role of integrating the Taiwanese, the Kuomintang created a bureaucracy that approximates that of the government: there are departments for economic affairs, finance, military intelligence, and so on. A party organization chart looks very much like a government organization manual. Party headquarters is located within the government complex and is guarded by Republic of China (ROC) soldiers. Government revenues fatten its treasury, as do several lucrative ties to illegal and marginally legal operations. But the party is less influential in economic policy making than are the Communist parties of The People's Republic of China or the Soviet Union.[71]

Of substantially greater importance is the establishment and maintenance of corporatist relationships with organized groups. Kuomintang technocrats work closely with farmers' organizations, labor unions, and business organizations. Kuomintang professionals operate hundreds of service centers, providing vocational training, job placement, free medical care, and technical help to farmers and business organizations. The party is responsible for the China Youth Corps, a boy and girl scout type of operation, which is one of the most popular summer programs for pre-collegiate youth. Kuomintang cells on college campuses spread the faith, and also keep an eye on those whose loyalty to the organization is suspect.[72] As Edwin Winkler explains:

It picks the candidates, runs the elections, and by many accounts recasts the vote when necessary. Much of this modus operandi, including the general theme of political artifice overriding natural society, follows directly from Sun Yat-sen's formulation of tutelary democracy for China. However, political machines work similarly in many parts of the world, including parts of the United States.[73]

The comparison of the KMT to an urban machine, perhaps Chicago's under Daley, is a good one. Party and interest groups are engaged in a mutually advantageous exchange. The comparison serves also to remind us of the great difference between the KMT and a genuinely totalitarian party. Membership in interest groups, while by no means compulsory, is certainly encouraged. As ex-

plained above, group leadership is not selected by the members of
the interest group, but is assigned by the government, generally
from the ranks of Kuomintang stalwarts who have reached manda-
tory retirement age, or have been given a golden parachute.

The Leninist decision-making structure of the organization has
changed little since its days on the mainland. There are three de-
liberative bodies: the Central Committee (75 members), which
elects the Central Standing Committee (19 members), and a Central Advisory Committee (144 members). Given the strongly interpersonal nature of Chinese organizational politics, the differences
between them are hard to fathom. Probably the Central Standing
Committee, which typically includes the major cabinet ministers,
is the most influential. But institutional position is not a sufficient
condition for political influence. In the Republic of China, party
members honor personal loyalty, reciprocal obligation, and interpersonal reciprocity more than official rank.

Since the role of the party is to provide cheerleading for bureaucratically initiated policy, its ownership and operation of the
Central News Agency, the *Central Daily News,* the Broadcasting
Corporation of China, the Central Motion Picture Corporation of
China, and the China Book Company gives it an information monopoly only slightly less pervasive than those of the People's Republic of China and the U.S.S.R. Nonparty news agencies
invariably have a Kuomintang representative in the editorial office.[74] The party, in cooperation with the Government Information
Office, enforces censorship.[75]

The rules of the game are rather open. Personal attacks on
Chiang Ching-kuo, favorable comments about the People's Republic of China, advocacy of an independent Taiwan, or any basic
challenge to the legitimacy of the Nationalist government are ta-
boo. As is true in many authoritarian societies, the media can
demand the resignation of ministers, accuse high-ranking officials
of corruption or stupidity, and even suggest that martial law (imposed in 1949 and repealed in 1987) is unnecessary (only because
of the absolute loyalty and devotion of the people to the Kuomintang, of course).[76]

The fate of martial law provides interesting evidence about how
ideas percolate in an authoritarian society. As we will see in the

next chapter, martial law was a symbol in the struggle between liberal and conservative Kuomintang factions. The absurdity of martial law was a frequent topic in casual cocktail party talk, and even occasionally was slipped into more formal gatherings (academic conferences, for example). The press generally avoided the topic. In 1986, however, plans to replace martial law were announced without more than a weak whine from the conservatives. Once martial law's departure was assured, the reasons why it could "never" be abolished were forgotten.

The opposition publishes under its own, quite unclear, rules. The government makes periodic sweeps, yanking publishing permission and closing offices. But opposition publications crop up again, are tolerated for a while, and are then shut down. The cycle continues unabated. You can find copies of opposition publications in newsstands, especially in the Taiwanese-dominated street markets, quite easily.[77] Bars and coffee houses are filled with gossip about the private lives of government officials, the stupidity and cupidity of the Chiang family, and even more seditious comments about *rapprochement* with the mainland. But Taiwan is a "partially free" society, and one is never certain when the rules will be tightened or relaxed.

Party and Government

The relationship between the Kuomintang and the government is not as tight as in Communist countries, as it does not initiate economic policy. Bureaucratic decisions are usually, not invariably, endorsed by the top-level party committees. Unlike Japan's Liberal Democratic Party, few party careerists have made their way into the top ranks of government. Unlike Communist parties, KMT membership is not reserved for the worthy: anyone over twenty can join. Upon being admitted, the new member agrees to abide by Kuomintang policy. No one has ever been expelled from the organization, however, nor do its new members pay much attention to the perfunctory pledge.[78] Once in, no renewal is required (other than paying dues), but to withdraw one is supposed to make a formal statement. Of course, few bother.[79] The party is organized to recruit on campuses and in the armed services, and it is here that most people join. Some prominent Taiwanese businesspeople have joined later as a consequence of their increasing economic influence, but they are the exception. The party currently enrolls about 2.5 million people, 80 percent of them Taiwanese.

In exploring the reasons for joining the KMT, most of our attention will be given to differences between mainlanders and Taiwanese, since a major item on the party's agenda is cooptation of the Taiwanese. It has succeeded in recruiting them, but has it been as successful in reducing differences between them and those who were party members before the defeat or their descendants?

There is a quite strong ideological component to the decision to join the Kuomintang, greater among the mainlanders than among the Taiwanese, but still apparent in both (Table 5-6). It is not uncommon to hear government bureaucrats refer to Sun Yat-sen's "Three Principles of the People" as the guiding rationale for their administrative careers.[80]

Among Taiwanese, it is still commonplace to hear the Kuomintang spoken of as the "mainlanders' party," even though the speakers are members. Writing in 1970, Douglas Mendel quotes a Taiwanese political activist as saying, "We Formosan candidates were treated more fairly by the prewar Japanese parties than the mainlander Chinese KMT leaders treat us now."[81] Such sentiments are scarce today since the Kuomintang has recruited young Taiwanese to stand for election, but they are not totally absent. The fact

TABLE 5-6
INDIVIDUAL REASONS FOR JOINING THE KUOMINTANG [78]

Reason	Taiwanese (n = 175) (%)	Mainlanders (n = 156) (%)
Peer pressure	22	24
To get ahead in business	51	13
To get ahead in government	5	31
Agreement with KMT ideology	22	32

Source: These data are from personal interviews with 175 Taiwanese businesspeople and 156 mainlander civil servants in 1983 and 1985. Thus, the sample is not a random selection of party members but is a good representation of business and government leaders.

that one-fifth of the Taiwanese Kuomintang members claim to have joined to foster the "Three Principles of the People" should be placed against the backdrop of lingering distrust of mainlanders. During the 1985 trial of the alleged killers of Henry Liu, the author of an anti-Chiang book, Taiwanese seemed less concerned about the international implications of the trial than about a concurrent scandal involving the misuse of credit union funds. They referred to the Liu case as a "fight among the mainlanders."[82]

Both groups respond about equally to peer pressure. One mainlander, speaking about his compulsory military service, explained to me: "The Kuomintang's political representative gave a speech, urging us to join. Nobody seemed terribly interested but most of us joined anyway. Nothing was gained but nothing was lost and what the hell." There is a powerful measure of propaganda in Taiwanese education, as happens in many authoritarian countries that believe their security to be subject to immediate threat: "Educational authorities seek to create a powerful loyalty to Chinese society and, specifically, to the state as exemplified by the government of the Republic of China (the Kuomintang government). Political training and the rudiments of group discipline begin in kindergarten with flag-raising ceremonies quite formally carried out."[83] Indoctrination begins early, comparable to the political indoctrination of children in the People's Republic of China or the Soviet Union, and surely more heavy-handed than the treatment by schools of the dominant political party in South Korea or Singapore.

Yet people join the Kuomintang for selective benefits more often than not. Mainlanders, with the economy effectively in Taiwanese hands, join because they believe that membership will further a government career and that promotion will come more rapidly. Taiwanese see the party as a way to enhance their business prospects. Chinese may be more anxious to find a legitimating ideology than are the Japanese, South Koreans, or Singaporeans, but they are just as anxious to get ahead and see the Kuomintang as an opportunity to do so. In Confucian corporatist societies (if Taiwan is typical), the individualist urge to get ahead is conspicuous. Even in a party that claims a revolutionary, ideologically driven past, people are induced to join for much the same reasons that they join organizations in open, pluralistic cultures. Some do so to further the cause, but more do so to advance their own financial well-being.

Recruitment and Integration

The recruitment of Taiwanese has occurred more in local politics than in national elections. Beginning in 1950, cities and counties elected mayors, councils, and magistrates. Unlike national elections, which still maintain the myth that Taiwan is a province of the mainland, the local ones occur every four years and have become keenly contested, serving as stepping stones for ambitious Taiwanese. Since the Kuomintang made its initial mark with land reform, it remains extraordinarily popular among farmers. Party candidates average about a 10 percent higher margin of victory in the rural areas.[84] The KMT has lost in Taipei and in other large cities, but has never been threatened in the villages. It polls around 70 percent, averaging only about 59 percent in Taipei but over 78 percent in the other sections of the island.[85] The organization seeks out and grooms educated, young Taiwanese businesspeople and provides them with generous financial support during the campaign. In this way the party hopes to elude the drift of the Taiwanese elite toward the opposition party.

But recruitment into the *inner circles* of the Kuomintang is another matter. The Central Committee and Central Standing Committee are 55 percent mainlander (compared with 20 percent of the rank and file). Of the members of these committees under fifty years of age, however, only 41 percent are mainlanders. Among the Taiwanese, all have had previous party experience in local elections. The mainlanders have not had such experience, being recruited to the party from the civil service. Taiwanese are more likely to have earned an advanced degree, usually in business or economics and from an American university. The mainlanders are more likely not to have gone beyond their initial college degree, earned in political science or history.[86]

But like all decision-making bodies, the KMT contains some who are more influential than others. Eleven people were singled out by me as taking an unusually active interest in economic policy.[87] All eleven had been employed at the higher reaches of either the Ministry of Economic Affairs or the Ministry of Finance and all are mainlanders. Reflecting the traditional division of the spoils, a Taiwanese business background shows their ease of access to "the crooked road." The most active members of the Central Committee, all mainlanders, nonetheless are likely to discuss proposed government policy with Taiwanese businesspeople. Typical of this mode of behavior is Tsiang Yien-si, former secretary-general of the Kuomintang.[88] Tsiang, another veteran of land reform, maintains a regular social and professional relationship with two prominent Taiwanese businessmen, the president of Tatung (the electronics manufacturer), a member of the Central Standing Committee, and the president of Taiwan Plastics, one of the largest manufacturers on the island, who is not a member of the Kuomintang.

The Kuomintang does seem to meet the criteria for the encompassing organization. Its major function is the integration of two disparate and potentially antagonistic factions: the mainlanders and the Taiwanese. While the integration is far from complete, the tension is less severe than it might have been. The Kuomintang is encompassing because it listens to (always), and incorporates (sometimes), the demands of Taiwanese-dominated business interest groups. Although the bureaucracy, mainlander-dominated, is likely to view rich Taiwanese businesspeople with suspicion and even hostility, the KMT reduces the degree of hostility. Business interest groups believe that their ability to influence the execution of policy if not the design of policy is due to their influence within the ruling party.[89]

Perhaps the expectation that organizations should encompass but not oppress is too great. Can a party be an agent of political modernization without losing control?[90] Taiwanese political scientists are much enamored of Western models of political development. They believe that economic progress is a forerunner of political growth (by which they mean competitive elections rather than conflict between intra-party factions). Some of them, such as Hu Fu, have long urged the Kuomintang to cease its harassment of opposition leaders, believing that political development is akin to an open electoral system with a stable opposition.[91] Hu was a major participant in the lobbying effort to persuade party leadership to meet with the mainland over a hijacked airliner, and to allow the opposition to organize. Hu's faction is not concerned about loss of control; it welcomes it.

Another group of scholars subscribes more to the conservative tradition in the study of political development, which requires only stability and an enlightened elite.[92] Since Taiwan has a good income distribution, a rising standard of living, and an elite that, by Asian standards, is enlightened, they argue that enough is enough. The issue is simple for Taiwanese scholars: your opinions on development depend on how much you admire Japan, since no one expects more political competition than exists there. Japanophiles believe that institutionalization of legitimate conflict is the crucial indicator of development.[93]

The proponents of Japanese-style government do not care whether the competition takes place within the KMT or between the Kuomintang and the emergent opposition parties; they want *competition*. Japan, so prominent in the tensions of the past, seems an ever-present force in Taiwanese politics today. Of less importance to the party theoreticians is the experience of their brethren on the mainland. In 1957, Mao wished for a "hundred flowers," got them, and promptly exiled the gardeners, moving to the "great leap forward" and finally the cultural revolution. In 1979, Deng Xiaoping invited critics to write their complaints on "Democracy Wall." They did, and he quickly silenced them.

The Kuomintang has no current inclination toward such ruthless deeds, except for the most extreme adherents of its most conservative faction; memories of its brutality in the past, however, should dampen uncritical optimism. With Chang Ching-kuo old and ill, only the second transfer of power in the Republic of China's four decades of rule on Taiwan is at hand. He has done everything possible to strengthen the position of the progressive party factions. But one should never underestimate the staying power of secular religious dogma; the old guard might once again see a chance to regain its declining influence. It is not without its supporters.[94]

The KMT's most liberal faction, however, believes that with economic development well underway, political development cannot be far behind. Since the members of this bloc subscribe to the theory of development that asserts that economic advancement leads inevitably to demands for political democracy, they believe that the only way to halt the course of political development is to retard economic growth. Since this course of action is impossible, they anticipate a political democracy at least as developed as Japan's.[95] If these events come to pass, the Kuomintang will be less encompassing.[96]

In 1987, with the President's health failing, martial law repealed, and the opposition becoming institutionalized, the KMT had become accustomed to moderate political conflict. After all, most of the opposition leaders sought only a Western-style democracy, although an independent Taiwan is always lurking beneath the public agenda. However, the sudden appearance of right-wing organizations, reminiscent of the old secret societies, suggests that the decline of the party as an encompassing organization might be speedier than it had anticipated. These organizations (believed to be financed partially by the conservative KMT factions) complained that the party had made too many concessions to the Democratic Progressive Party. At the same time, the opposition Democratic Progressive Party began complaining that the new civil law, which replaced martial law, did not go far enough.

In June, violence broke out during the debates on the repeal of martial law, when the DPP's protest was met with a counter-rally by the leading extreme right-wing groups, the Anti-Communist Patriotic Front and the China Patriotic Society. Unlike previous demonstrations, such as those in 1979, the government was not the target. This time the violence was caused by two opposing organizations whose hostility was a shock to the government. The government quickly assumed the role of peacemaker, above the warring factions, and turned the riots into a public relations coup. But, while the government has been able to pressure the right—for the moment—into backing off, the KMT for the first time is facing a genuinely conflictual society. There is every indication that the right-wing groups will form a political party.

The pressure for at least a modicum of pluralism in Taiwan, unlike the other authoritarian regimes in Asia, is rather explicitly part of the "official" legacy of Sun Yat-sen. Sun's belief in government of, by, and for the people (he admired and emulated the American rhetoric) has been a consistent source of pressure toward democratization. Additionally, the strong American presence (especially immediately after the Kuomintang defeat and during the Korean war) pushed Taiwan toward democratization. Many of the concessions made by the KMT were at the provincial or local level. The party has always run exceptionally well in these elections. However, a substantial array of interest groups (generally those initiated by the KMT) take these elections quite seriously, and conflict is more intense than among the Kuomintang's nationally oriented factions. More importantly, almost all of the winners in provincial and local elections are Taiwanese, not mainlanders. Thus, in addition to the pressure for political modernization generated by the "economic miracle," the political infrastructure has created equally potent expectations.[97]

SIX

FACTIONS IN ENCOMPASSING ORGANIZATIONS

Although there are opposition parties in the Asian governments, they are unlikely to become majorities. In South Korea the opposition is becoming organized, militant, and determined to introduce major changes in the nation's traditionally authoritarian mode of governance. In Singapore, on the other hand, only two opponents of the People's Action Party hold seats in the legislature. In Taiwan the opposition is developing institutional stability, with about 25 percent of the Legislative Yuan in opposition to the Kuomintang; however, only recently has it been able to engender a genuine opposition organization. When measures for the elimination of martial law began in 1986, the disparate opposition (which hitherto had been prohibited from creating a formal organization) began an attempt to increase the anti-Kuomintang vote.

The new party, the Democratic Progressive Party, cannot compete as openly as Japanese opposition parties, since the civil law drafted to replace martial law stipulates that all political parties must accept Sun Yat-sen's "Three Principles of the People" (no great risk, since there is little with which to disagree), support the Constitution (that is, the original document written by the Nationalists during their reign on the mainland), oppose Taiwanese independence (as a separate nation, with ties neither to the mainland nor to the Nationalist fiction about returning as "liberators"), and profess anti-Communism.[1] In a typical example of Taiwan's less aggressive authoritarianism, the DPP, a coalition of the various opposition factions traditionally active, announced its birth *before* the enabling legislation was ratified by the Legislative Yuan.[2]

Besides limiting the substance of party platforms, the election laws were biased in favor of the KMT. Democratic Progressive Party candidates were denied access to television, for example. Even so, the 1986 elections were an auspicious debut for the new party; it won twelve of the nineteen legislative races it entered and captured one-fourth of the popular vote, about the same as the unorganized opposition in the previous election.

FACTIONS AND INTRA-PARTY DISPUTES

Depending on your understanding of the severity of conflict, existence of stable factions *within* the dominant party can be considered an alternative to inter-party competition. Japan's Liberal Democratic Party (LDP) is often regarded as the example of the encompassing organization that nevertheless nurtures factions, each in competition for intra-party leadership. The LDP factions are quite stable, somewhat like the various caucuses that exist in the United States Senate and House of Representatives. The political process is one of alliances among LDP factions, but much of the substance of factional politics is nonideological. The competition between factions is less about policy and more about personnel. Of the LDP factions, each named for its leader, Bradley Richardson and Scott Flanagan write:

While factions stem from many different sources, such as graduation from common elite schools or espousal of a common ideology or interest, the primary basis for the organization of Liberal Democratic factions is a personalistic affiliation of rank-and-file members of parliament with one or another of the party's strongest politicians.[3]

Taiwan's Kuomintang too has factions, about as stable as those of the Liberal Democratic Party, but more tightly linked to policy preferences. Of course the more remote probability of Kuomintang electoral defeat may hinder the development of strong factional leaders.

The most enduring of the Kuomintang factions is the old

guard: those who came over with Chiang and were members of the remnants of Kuomintang organization in the 1940's. The old guard is in permanent alliance with the military-intelligence establishment. If for no other reason than because they are dying, this most conservative faction has been in decline for a decade or so. Many members can be seen hanging around the Legislative Yuan playing mah jong, looking for all the world like retirees in a nursing home. But although its future is bleak, the old guard can still pack an enormous punch, since it is the repository of purity. Old Nationalists still argue that the return to the mainland is possible and desirable, and they maintain passionately the fiction that the government in Taipei is the only legitimate government of all China.

Taiwan was under martial law from 1949 until 1987, an embarrassing and unnecessary reminder of the bad old days. Most of the old guard have personal memories of the defeat of the Nationalists and still regard the People's Republic of China as a bandit government bent on invading Taiwan, destroying the legitimate government, and imposing a brutally totalitarian one in its stead. Hence martial law became the old guard's most sacred cause.[4] About 40 percent of the citizens of the Republic of China were unaware of martial law and, of those who did know about it, only a handful noticed any loss of individual freedom. But its irrelevance did not discourage the old guard from opposing its abolition.[5] The motto of the old guard is the "three no's": no contact, no negotiation, no compromise. They recognize, however, that the Taiwanization of the Kuomintang dooms them and they speak of "adjusting" their hard-line stance (a process called the "two and a half no's" by the cynical media).

In the fall of 1986, the KMT announced its intention to remove martial law and to legitimate an opposition party. These acts were of major *symbolic* import.[6] Since martial law was *de facto* inoperative, the symbolism becomes all the more important; it means that the moderate and liberal/reformist factions of the party are on the ascent. The elimination of martial law was opposed strenuously by the conservatives to no avail.

The old guard is aided by a faction within the Kuomintang bureaucracy that seeks a return to influence by the party.[7] Distressed that the party is largely excluded from economic policy, this faction is as conservative as the old guard, but for different reasons. Whether or not they believe sincerely that the mainland is poised for invasion, they claim that this is so in the hope that fear of an attack from the mainland will restore the party to its original position as defender of the faith. Unlike the old guard's dreams of past glories, however, the young conservatives are most anxious to confront and defeat the opposition candidates, not by prohibiting their freedom of assembly through martial law, but with aggressive Kuomintang candidates who can win elections.[8] It was younger KMT legislators who lobbied successfully for the ROC's meeting with the mainland to negotiate a return of a highjacked commercial jet in 1986. They spoke in public about the "policy of the ostrich," and attracted the support of prominent opposition *dangwai* legislators, who suddenly found themselves on the front pages of major newspapers.

The Kuomintang reform wing is represented by younger party bureaucrats in league with mainlander civil servants in the Ministry of Economic Affairs, the Ministry of Finance, the Ministry of Foreign Affairs, and the Research and Evaluation Commission of the Executive Yuan. The liberal arts faculty of most universities also casts its lot with the progressives. The bureaucrats and academics have in common American graduate degrees and a belief in expanding political participation, relaxing the corporatist hold on interest groups, and strengthening the opposition's right to organize. The civil servants in these most prestigious government agencies are impatient with the old guard's single-minded obsession.[9]

The Kuomintang reform wing is not interested in reunification. It seeks to guide the ROC toward the development of a more open, pluralist system.[10] It repeatedly, almost defensively, attacks the People's Republic and, having done so, urges Taiwan not to emulate it. With this formula, the progressives have been able to argue for political development equal to economic development. Wei Yung, one of the most active in this group and director of the Research and Evaluation Commission, displays the style of the Kuomintang reformers:

By comparing the development strategies of the ROC and those of Communist China, we may draw a major conclusion, i.e., it is the enlightened teaching of Dr. Sun Yat-sen and the constitutional form of government in the ROC that have been the major moving force behind the modernization process on Taiwan. On the other hand, it is the closed and often erratic political system that has prevented the people of mainland China from achieving a high level of modernization. . . . In order to achieve modernization, a nation must have a flexible and open-ended ideology and political system.[11]

Finally, the technocrats within the Kuomintang are concerned largely with economic development and with continuing or perhaps reassessing the Taiwanese tradition of "growth with equity." Their values are well represented in the editorial policy of Taiwan's largest newspaper, the *United Daily News*. Like the left, the technocrats sport American degrees. If they have any political values, they are likely to resist the old guard's preference for heavy-handed statism because they are fascinated with the growth potential of market economies. The more conservative old guard is accustomed to the traditional statist economic policies of the early Nationalists, while the technocrats seek to reduce the role of government. Leading the attack on the state are a series of government-sponsored think tanks, located on university campuses with additional funding from business interest groups.[12] Coupled with their free market ideology, the Taiwanese members of this faction also suspect that the mainlanders are interested in developing a Philippine style of economic monopolies with party favorites being given a leg up.

The technocrats want to sell off the largest state-owned enterprises, Taiwan Power and China Steel. About one percent of Taiwan's business is government-owned, but this one percent employs 9 percent of the work force, produces 24 percent of value added, and holds 52 percent of Taiwan's assets in operation.[13] If more economic freedom leads to a demand for more political pluralism, they do not care—probably because they cannot, with good reason, imagine even a pallid imitation of Western pluralism taking root. Taiwanese businesspeople are conspicuous in this faction.

As committed as they are to a free market ideology, technocrats lobby hard against the old guard's traditional ally, the military.[14] The military consumes a larger share of GNP in Taiwan than in Japan, South Korea, or Singapore, but its share has been declining consistently. It is now about half what it was a decade ago.[15]

Ironically, this faction's quarrel with the old guard invokes the sacred name of Sun Yat-sen. Conservative mainlanders, steeped in the statist traditions of the Kuomintang, believe that the reduction of the role of the government in the economy might erase the gains in equity in exchange for more rapid growth. Hence the socialist portion of Sun's writings (rather than the sections dealing with democracy) are cited. The Taiwanese in this faction are clear about their priorities: equity is less important than growth.[16]

These factions compete on a more or less equal basis. The military–old guard faction was seriously damaged by Henry Liu's murder;[17] but the technocrats were equally injured by serious credit union scandals.[18] The reformers won a major (possibly decisive) victory in 1986, however, when the ROC government met with representatives of the People's Republic in Hong Kong to negotiate the return of an ROC airliner diverted to the mainland. Shortly, thereafter, the Tangwai Research Association, a leading opposition group, opened an office in Taipei to begin the task of building a serious opposition. The old guard regained some lost ground when demonstrations against martial law, undertaken to capitalize on the euphoric mood created by the opening with the mainland, failed to move the government toward a more accelerated pace of reform. However, the subsequent suspension of martial law made the right's victory hollow.

Not only is the balance of power precarious, with predictions of rises and falls more plentiful than in the Washington rumor mill, but the Kuomintang factions also represent serious policy alternatives, greater than those in the factions of Japan's Liberal Democratic Party.[19] The factions are stable, and not dependent on a single charismatic individual.[20]

Personal Cliques and Ideological Factions

As is true so often in Chinese political systems, the assumption of reciprocity of interpersonal relations is pervasive. Lien Sheng-yang writes, "The Chinese believe that reciprocity of actions should be as certain as a cause and effect and, therefore, when a Chinese acts he normally anticipates a response of return. Favors done for others are often considered what may be termed 'social investments' for which handsome returns are expected." John Weakland suggests a subtle modification: "The system of reciprocal aid . . . is centered around the concept of *jen-chi'ng* (human feelings) . . . as a gift and return favor are not conceived of as a bargain or as one being a condition for another. Chinese dislike such a matter of fact, businesslike view."[21] Anyone who has spent even a short time in Taiwan or the People's Republic does not need to be told about reciprocity.

When a faction's leader apparently loses influence, rumors of presidential disfavor abound. For every example of a demotion or resignation because of scandal or policy disagreement, there are three claiming the departed official was caught in bed with a cabinet minister's wife. But the factions do pursue their policies with the intention of altering, or preserving, the status quo.

The opposition also has its factions, ranging from the Taiwanese independence movement, through the reunification faction, to the moderates who hope to develop an electoral alternative to the Kuomintang. The opposition is less adamant than in South Korea or Japan but is more expressive than in Singapore. There have been no anti-government protests since 1979 of the magnitude of the anti-Narita protests in Japan or the persistent anti-government protests in South Korea. The brief flurry of disorder when the liberalization process was begun was not even remotely as intense as the South Korean fractures of the social fabric.[22] Taiwan's response to protests and demonstrations falls between the extremes of South Korea and Japan. South Korea adapts a more repressive line, and struggles with longer traditions of protest.

"Soft" Authoritarianism

These disputes are reasonably well covered in Taiwan's media and little effort is made to portray the Kuomintang as more monolithic than it is. Perhaps because it is less powerful than are the parties in other one-party systems, there is little effort to conceal its deliberations, especially those involving the role of government in the economy. Thus it was possible to assess the relative support that the various factions have achieved. In Table 6-1, we see that there are consistent differences between the Kuomintang's mainlander mem-

TABLE 6-1
RESPONSE TO FACTIONAL POLICY
PREFERENCES: PERCENTAGE AGREEING

Preference	Taiwanese (n = 175) (%)	Mainlanders (n = 156) (%)
The party should be strengthened *vis-á-vis* the Executive Yuan	63	45
The role of the government in the economy should be reduced	72	51
The goal of growth with equity is as important as ever	43	55

bers and its Taiwanese members, with each group acting to advance its own self-interest.

Strengthening the party would enhance the position of the Taiwanese, who comprise about 80 percent of its membership. Since the Kuomintang has never had the power of the Chinese Communist Party, those who seek to strengthen it are not necessarily reacting against a stubborn bureaucracy, as happens on the mainland. There, the often incompatible pressures of ideological purity and technological expertise have resulted in internal wars of major import, the cultural revolution being the most egregious example.

In Taiwan, the faction seeking to strengthen the party operates from a Western bias. Members of this faction are hardly "pluralists," but they are less addicted to unity and cohesion, less "Confucian." The Kuomintang has become the vehicle of the Taiwanese majority and they want it to speak for them with authority. Many of the academic Kuomintang members at the most prestigious universities are thoroughly familiar with the American "responsible party" debate, and believe that a stronger political party will lead to a more responsive government.[23]

Mainlanders (excluding the conservative factions) see the party slipping away and hence resist efforts to strengthen it (although academic supporters of the responsible party doctrine are usually mainlanders, since university faculties contain few Taiwanese). Of course the model to which the responsible party advocates claim closest allegiance is Japan's Liberal Democratic party, rather than either of the two American parties. The LDP's tightly knit system of recruitment, the old boy network that merges business and government, and the policy consensus are seen as avenues to power. Most of the rising Taiwanese stars are in the Taiwanese mold of pragmatic politics, rather than the more ideologically rigid mainlander tradition; hence Japan's supremely pragmatic LDP is a natural.

ETHNIC DISPUTES

Taiwanese preference for *laissez-faire* economics also stems from their perceived self-interest. The bureaucracies are still dominated by mainlanders. Although Taiwanese businesspeople get on well with the various bureaucracies, they are firm believers in the growth potential of free markets, with Japan once again providing the model. Their belief in free markets makes them afraid of the mainland, although their pragmatism compels them to seek a reconciliation. Ironically, the Taiwanese free marketeers suspect the mainlanders of harboring lingering statist preferences. The KMT was, lest we forget, under the tutelage of the U.S.S.R. during the early 1920's and Chiang Ching-kuo studied in Moscow. Party structure and organization, designed initially along Leninist lines, still retain some trappings of the Soviet party.

Mainlanders do entertain such notions. The corporatist decision-making structure of the Asian authoritarian systems is not ideally suited for free markets. Although the Asian political systems are predicated on market ideologies, only Hong Kong (a colony) can claim to be truly committed to a minimalist government. But the mode of intrusion is not similar to a socialist centrally planned economy. Government-business relations in Asian countries do not conform to either a free market or a centrally planned model of the economy; nor do they resemble the regulatory schemes prevalent in Western industrial pluralist systems.[24]

Taiwan's bureaucracy will be used as an example of the Asian style of government-interest group communication. Since most businesses are managed or owned by Taiwanese, and most bureaucracies are dominated by mainlanders, Taiwan is in need of more "encompassing" behavior than are the other Asian countries.

Mainlander bureaucrats brood about the anarchy of Taiwanese business; they too look to Japan, but for examples of an organized and cohesive business community. Taiwanese business people do not subscribe to the interventionist theories prevalent in Asia; they are more inclined toward purely free market ideas.[25] On the other hand, both the Taiwanese business community and the mainlander bureaucracy abhor the South Korean example of government reaching down into the decision-making process in individual firms.[26]

The Enduring Problem of Equity

Much the same sort of reasoning separates the two groups concerning the Kuomintang's traditional growth with equity programs. The truth of the matter is that the distribution of wealth has remained constant for the last decade, suggesting that the end of the "Taiwanese miracle" is at hand.[27] There may be nothing that can be done to restore what had come to be an expected reduction in the Gini index, but mainlander Kuomintang members fret about the Gini's stability more than Taiwanese do.[28]

Of course, there is a lot of mythology surrounding the growth with equity program, with government spokespersons claiming that Taiwan disproves both the theory that growth and equity are incompatible and the theory that dependency yields greater inequality. Other than the initial land reform efforts, there is some doubt about exactly what the government did to foster a decline in inequality. Richard Barrett and Martin Whyte write:

On balance the government clearly placed a much higher priority on economic growth than on income distribution. To some extent, though, the mainlander-dominated government stood above the newly emerging Taiwanese entrepreneurial elite and could not be made to serve their narrow class interests. In the end it seems that the decentralized, labor intensive pattern of growth itself, not government income policies, produced much of the redistribution that occurred.[29]

But even though there is more disconnection between incomes policy and income distribution than the ROC government cares to admit, the Kuomintang was there when it happened and can, like most governments, take credit when things go well.

Initially, the growth with equity program was sold to conservative Nationalists, including Chiang himself, as a means of reducing the threat of Communist infiltration, and had the land reform program not been constructed as it was, Taiwan's good record in income distribution would not have occurred. Since the United States supplied so much of the money, technology, and pressure for land reform, its egalitarian premise was perhaps due just a little less to Sun Yat-sen than the KMT currently believes. But in any case the labor-intensive period is ending. Agrarian origins to the contrary, much of the reduction in inequality has been a consequence of a declining rate of inequality *within* the industrial sector.[30] Initial economic planning models assumed that the development of labor-intensive industries would increase employment opportunities, that promoting mass education and raising the quality and quantity of education would produce people capable of taking advantage of these opportunities, and that a rational and progressive tax structure would merely augment these natural market forces.

Taiwan's Gini index declined from .51 in 1953 to .28 in 1985, an admirable and unusual record. But the high Gini in 1953 occurred *after* land reform.[31] In any case, the rates of growth in the agricultural sector are rapidly becoming a minor portion of Taiwan's total growth.[32] Also, the economy will become less labor-intensive, and this is the aspect of Taiwan's economic growth responsible for much of the decline in inequality.[33] This phase is just about over, since there is almost no unskilled labor left.

The leveling of Taiwan's income distribution (Taiwan publishes annual Ginis the way most countries publish GNP growth) has contributed to a trenchant debate. The old guard has suggested that the government design and enforce a progressive income tax more vigorously than has been the case in the past, signaling a move toward more state control and a "command" economy. The Taiwanese response is to propose even less intervention, letting the question of equity slide. In truth, all the government has "done" (after land reform) is *not* to soak the rich. It has developed an extraordinarily favorable investment climate, freeing designated industries from *any* taxes for at least five and usually ten years. Its tax revenues are low (18 percent of total income)[34] and its rate of savings has increased from 9 to 31 percent of GNP since 1952.[35]

This is not to say that the tax system has no effect on income distribution. The before and after tax Gini indexes show that the Gini has always been lower after taxes.[36] The rate of reduction is so low (about .002 percent), however, that its impact is minor. Herein lies the debate: to use the income tax more progressively to decrease the after-tax Gini or to leave things as they are.[37] The heavy investment in education, the avoidance of protectionism, and the refusal to require mergers seems to have achieved as much equality as possible.

The Stakes and the Struggle

For the party to "encompass," it must negotiate between two groups with differing goals, ideologies, and aspirations. The two groups are different culturally *and* economically. Unlike South Korea and Japan, which have a pure ethnic stock, Taiwan is heterogeneous. There is an almost experimental clarity in the division of ethnic identification. The Japanese disappeared and the Kuomintang established its rule within a period of only about five years. Mainland immigration ceased by 1953. During this brief period, the division of the spoils appeared as an acceptable alternative, but resulted in a sense of ethnic distance. The sense of separateness was probably stronger after the division of labor than before, since the original Taiwanese were from Fukien province in the south and the province closest to Taiwan, as were many of the mainlanders.

The politics of Taiwanese cultural identity lies close to the heart of the dispute between the People's Republic and the Republic of China about the future of Taiwan. Both governments assert that Taiwanese are ethnically and culturally identical to the Chinese on the mainland and that Taiwan is an integral part of China.[38] The Kuomintang and the mainland thus argue that to debate about two Chinas is comparable to claiming independent status for Texas or Hawaii, since Texas enjoyed a brief period of independence and Hawaii is separated from the mainland. The Taiwanese myth, the recapture of the mainland, and the Communist Party myth, that Taiwan is an integral part of the mainland and a purely "internal" matter, are both based on false assumptions about the majority on Taiwan.

Both sides agree that mainlanders have an advantage in that their cultural heritage is more directly derived from the Han homeland, which is bigger and more important than Taiwan, and that the Taiwanese language is less sophisticated than Mandarin. Some do not regard Taiwanese as a "real" language. With the occupation of Taiwan in 1949, Mandarin, not Taiwanese, became the language of commerce and education.[39] Taiwanese life style, cuisine, and art is not as elegant as the Mandarin culture. Commonly ascribed inferior status has on occasion fueled Taiwanese independence movements, prohibited as treason. It is possibly because of such feelings that Japan continues to exercise substantial influence, especially over upper-class Taiwanese.

Japan's language, culture, and style of life allow identification with a respected culture. Younger Taiwanese, especially the upwardly mobile offspring of their Japan-oriented elders, often seek social parity through the adoption of American life styles. With Taiwanese being pulled in at least two directions (and, with the possibility of a *rapprochement* with the mainland introducing the possibility of a third) the development of indigenous culture is hampered. Nevertheless, Taiwanese music and literature are just about as popular as either Chinese (Mandarin) or Western. There is, additionally, a developing interest in Taiwanese painting and lithography.

The decision to impose Mandarin was costly, but indicative of the attitude of mainlanders toward Taiwanese. Other than Mandarin, English is taught most often; still many Taiwanese working in hotels and restaurants speak Japanese more fluently than English, and speak Taiwanese better than Mandarin. With Taiwanese not taught at any level of education, and Taiwanese life styles not highly regarded, each year the distinction between Taiwanese and mainlanders becomes less apparent. For example, of the hundreds of restaurants in Taipei, no more than a handful serve Taiwanese cuisine, and only one in the districts frequented by tourists.

Aspiring Taiwanese are reminded, however gently, of their origins when they seek to become civil servants or teachers or to join the Kuomintang. Even with serious party efforts at integration, success is hard to come by since both sides regard the distinctions as legitimate. Conversations at social gatherings in Taipei quickly focus on varieties of speech, food preferences, and personality traits presumably associated with each ethnic group.[40] Taiwanese have begun seeking an identity and aggressively claiming ethnic identity much the same way blacks did in the United States in the 1960's, when they argued with school boards over teaching Swahili and wearing African clothes.

Of course the most apparent consequences of ethnic distinctions are the overrepresentation of Taiwanese in the private sector and the overrepresentation of mainlanders in the civil service. Even in provincial administration, at least one-third are mainlanders.[41] If political power follows economic power, then the days of the mainlanders are numbered; but the government in Confucian societies is a more revered symbol of authority than is a successful business. Although it is generally believed that Taiwanese enjoy a higher income than mainlanders, the symbolic effects of bureaucratic power endures and angers.[42]

The distribution of authority is made more complex by the transplanting of the Kuomintang elite from the mainland and the party's continuing claim to be the sole legitimate government. This assertion has legitimated the exclusion of Taiwanese from government. However, the present government has turned the argument around: it is now safe to recruit Taiwanese into the government since "the myth of sovereignty ensured that the Taiwanese who participated in politics would accept a social contract to treat mainlanders as equal nationals even though the logic of numbers gave increasing power to Taiwanese in electoral politics.[43]

Arguments about income distribution encourage Taiwanese participation. Since politics is an avocation of those with the time and money to indulge themselves, Taiwanese are a large pool of the eligibles. The irony of the presumably oppressed majority having as good or better a standard of living as the oppressors has not escaped either group, and in exchange for recruitment of Taiwanese into the government, the mainlanders anticipate a greater acceptance into the economic corridors of power and wealth.[44] Intermarriage speeds the integration of both groups: 60 percent of all mainlander marriages are to Taiwanese.

The Taiwanese-mainlander distinction is probably less abrasive than that among many of the world's ethnic groups occupying the same land as their opponents: India's Sikhs, Moslems, and Hindus are more murderous, to say nothing of the various tribes in the African nations. The Kuomintang has indeed been "encompassing," possibly out of necessity. Another reason for the KMT's success is the relative absence of congruent cleavages along class and ethnic lines, as is frequently the problem. There are not two classes, rich mainlanders and poor Taiwanese, but rather a subtle layering of classes, with ethnic intermixture: "Members of both . . . ethnic blocs . . . are present in all social classes, despite a common popular perception of Taiwan's peoples as made up of an upper Mainlander class and a lower Taiwanese class."[45]

Yet given the tradition of Confucian authority and the Chinese tradition of a heavy hand for the state in the economy, the KMT could have taken a different direction: it could have moved more in the direction of state capitalism, keeping a firmer hand on the economy as was done in South Korea, another former Japanese colony. Pye attributes the Kuomintang's benign transformation more to its humiliation by the People's Liberation Army, than to other possibilities (see page 136).[46] It is difficult to be arrogant in the face of a defeat by an allegedly inferior army. Mention has already been made of the determination of the party to avoid a second defeat on Taiwan. Fear of another humiliation is more a factor with the old fighters, however, than with their offspring.

As Taiwan's private sector developed, its major political institution lost much of its ideological zeal and became almost apolitical, if one can speak of a political party as being apolitical. Younger mainlanders openly mock their elders' incessant conversations about the past, the evils of Communism, the glories of the Nationalist armies, the defeat of Japan. If they go to American universities they absorb their pervasive insouciance. The last thing they care about is retaking the mainland, and even the traditional myth making on Taiwanese national holidays bores them. Whatever zeal existed in their families, as Table 6-2 shows, second-generation mainlanders are quite different from their elders, and more like the native Taiwanese.

The new generation of Kuomintang fast trackers are those who

TABLE 6-2
INTEREST IN POLITICS AND BUSINESS: PERCENTAGE
CLAIMING TO BE "VERY INTERESTED" OR "INTERESTED"

Interest	Mainlanders, by birthplace		Taiwanese (n = 175) (%)
	Mainland (n = 74) (%)	Taiwan (n = 82) (%)	
Politics	61	37	19
Business/finance	27	48	53

"all have specialized in management, economics, science, and technology, which is essential for a new era of high growth."[47] My information supports this finding. Among the younger (under fifty) members of the Kuomintang Central Committee, both mainlanders and Taiwanese were likely to have majored in economics or business; but in the over-fifty group the Taiwanese are more likely to have majored in economics or business while mainlanders majored in political science or history.[48] The political experience of the younger party members is likely to have been local while the older group has had experience in national politics. The policy component of local politics is unrelated to the mainland: zoning, pollution, and industrial development dominate Taiwanese politics just as in Europe and the United States.

Local politics is also an arena in which mainlanders and Taiwanese are more evenly balanced, and there is also a fair sprinkling of opposition members on city councils, which will surely increase as the new opposition party strengthens its organization. The struggle over orthodoxy is over and the agenda has shifted. The authorization by the party and government of legal opposition party organizations is merely the next step in the process of political development, the movement from state corporatism toward something akin to the social-state corporatism of Japan. As the passions of the past are replaced by the pragmatism of young Taiwanese and third- or fourth-generation mainlanders, technical skills, expertise, will become even more marketable.[49]

SEVEN

BUREAUCRATIC ENCOUNTERS

Mattei Dogan entitled his edited book about European bureaucracy *The Mandarins of Western Europe*.[1] This usage is appropriate since the first fully operative civil service was in imperial China, where mandarins—those who advanced by learning and conduct—could achieve influence with the emperor. The Confucian system of public administration conceded extraordinary prestige to the mandarin class. Confucian theorists also stressed the loyalty of the mandarins to the established distribution of wealth and power. The development of the independent influence of the mandarins was not seriously challenged in China until Mao's Cultural Revolution placed ideology ahead of education.

Institutionalized procedures for the recruitment, placement, and evaluation of civil servants began as early as the second century B.C. Public service was restricted to those deemed "worthy and talented."[2] European governments did not develop merit systems of civil service recruitment until the Industrial Revolution. The British civil service, which became the model throughout Europe, was not in place until the nineteenth century.[3]

But the Asian bureaucracy differs in important ways from the Western ones. Besides a lingering Confucian value system, there are institutional arrangements in Asia that distinguish its corporatism from the European corporatist governments.[4]

INSTITUTIONAL ARRANGEMENTS AND PRIORITIES

Both European and Asian corporatist states stress public-private sector cooperation. There is more governmental guidance in Asia, more fine-tuning of a capitalist economy largely run by the private sector. The intervention generally takes the form of market manipulation. There is more government tinkering with tax incentives for the development of new products, for example. Since Asian countries lagged behind European industrial democracies, there was more need for such incentives. Given the commitment to the use of the market, with implementation and compliance largely in private hands, Asian corporatist systems, much like their European counterparts, stress close coordination between public bureaucracy and private business. Chalmers Johnson writes:

This cooperation is achieved through innumerable, continuously operating forums for coordinating views and investment plans, sharing international commercial intelligence, making adjustments to conform to the business cycle or other changes in the economic environment, deciding on the new industries needed in order to maintain international competitive ability, and spreading both the wealth and the burdens equitably.[5]

Asian corporatist systems differ from European ones not so much in the commitment to collaboration between bureaucracies and interest groups as in the diversity and range of groups given legitimacy and in the relationship between bureaucracies and political parties. European corporatist systems are generally willing to grant legitimacy exclusively to business and labor, and then only to the peak associations given quasi-official status in their governments. In Asia, only business has acquired legitimacy and, given the priorities of the time, various kinds of businesses drop in and out of favor. There are, as Johnson suggests, innumerable opportunities for collaboration. But only in Japan is there the institutional legitimacy, the creation of formal mechanisms of exchange, that is typical of European corporatist governments.

There are just as many opportunities to *avoid* collusion in Taiwan, South Korea, or Singapore. In Japan the most respected business organization, the Keidanren, in tight coordination with the Ministry of International Trade and Industry (MITI), has shielded the MITI from the protestations of small business.[6] The MITI-

Keidanren collusion is so intimate that the line between public and private is indistinguishable.

But in other Asian systems peak associations are more beholden to the bureaucracy. The peak associations in Japan have been able to defy MITI, simply refusing to comply with its directives. The peak associations in Taiwan and South Korea have not been able—given the more authoritarian nature of the state—to become as independent; they are not, however, as subservient as critics suggest.[7] The balance of power is with the state, of course. But there are examples of segments of the private sector behaving like the Japanese—simply not complying.

Modes of Interest Accommodation

In all Asian systems, peak associations operate as auxiliary governments; in the authoritarian governments they are agents of implementation. They are not, in the bureaucratically preferred perfect world, the source of "pressure." In reality, successful economic policy depends on a compliant business community in much the same way that European corporate systems depend on a docile labor movement. The major distinction between the corporatism of Japan and that of South Korea, Taiwan, and Singapore is the relative mix of three means of structuring the relationship between the bureaucracy. Noting that "the fundamental problem of the state-guided growth system is that of the relationship between the state bureaucracy and privately owned business," Johnson proposes three components of business-bureaucracy encounters: self-control, state control, and public-private cooperation.[8]

Japan employs all three of these means, sometimes simultaneously. Self-control involves state designation of private organizations as enforcers of state-initiated policies. State control places management under government supervision while maintaining private ownership. Cooperation is a synthesis of the other two methods. It is the most difficult to achieve since it normally occurs after self-control and state control have been tried and each pattern of interaction has developed its own history and adherents. Japan has been successful in developing cooperation only after long and politically destructive disputes.

South Korea relies more heavily on state control than does Taiwan. Its bureaucracy prods and pushes the private sector into large conglomerates. Although less concentrated than is commonly assumed, its industry is huge by Taiwanese standards. The South Korean government has undertaken no efforts at income redistribution, but has pursued the creation of conglomerates single-mindedly.[9] The imprint of Japanese occupation was more vivid in South Korea than in Taiwan, and contemporary South Korean industry bears a close relationship to that of Japan. The Japanese *zaibatsu*, a centralized system of family control through holding companies, has its counterpart in the South Korean *chaebol*. The South Korean cartels are not as structurally advanced, however. *Chaebol* account for about 13 percent of GNP.

In stark contrast, the Taiwanese economy is small by Asian standards and minuscule in comparison with the active international corporations of the industrial democracies. Fewer than one-half of one percent of its manufacturing companies employ more than five hundred people. There are only three companies that could qualify even by the most generous standards as internationally competitive: Tatung (electronics), Formosa Plastics, and Nan-Ya. None are as large as the major South Korean *chaebol* such as Samsung, Hyundae, or Daewoo. In 1986, Tatung's sales were $900 million, Formosa Plastics' were $740 million, and Nan-Ya's were $1 billion. In contrast, Sansung's were $16 billion, Hyundae's were $2 billion, and Daewoo's were $11 billion.

Three-fourths of Taiwanese businesses employ fewer than six people, a condition that various bureaucracies regard as economically damaging to Taiwan's international stature. The South Korean government gives major credit advantages to its *chaebol*, preferring to put its money on those with a proven track record, whereas Taiwan has not used size of firm as a variable in the equation for determining the posture of the government. Because it emphasizes equality more than South Korea does (see Table 5-1), the government of Taiwan takes pride in the prevalence of small, family-owned businesses. The example most often given is that of a family noodle stand that becomes a family taxi company at night. Such a family would earn about $24,000 U.S. dollars.[10]

The accumulation of personal wealth, a policy very popular with mainlander bureaucrats not directly involved with economic planning and with Taiwanese politicians, is less popular with the technocratic cadres rising to influence in the last several years. Realistically, the opportunity for small businesses to accumulate capital is slim. As is true of most countries, bankruptcy is directly and inversely related to size. But some businesses do offer the possibility of upward mobility. The food stand operators (whose businesses employ the largest single component of the employed population) are most likely to move up into more stable enterprises of medium size (by Taiwan standards, employing ten or more people). The example invariably cited is the Sho Mei ice cream company, which moved from food stand to national distribution. Such examples are rare, but fuel the Taiwanese ambition much like the Horatio Alger stories once did in the United States. But although individual anecdotes of success and failure are abundant, the important point is that most businesses remain small when they replace failed ones. Money is easy to obtain, and market-biased interest rates have made it difficult for large firms to buy out small ones. An economy dominated by small businesses is likely to produce more income equality and less economic growth.[11]

But Taiwan's mainlander political leadership lusts after international respectability. With the number of embassies in Taipei shrinking, and those remaining generally being from the ranks of the other international untouchables, Taiwan wants to become another Korea. A nation of shopkeepers does not develop and export automobiles or computers. Taiwan's Tatung does export the odd television to the United States, and has facilities in several American cities for the distribution and maintenance of microcomputer monitors and other electronic components, but most of Taiwan's exports are from its small to medium business segment, which has no name recognition. The United States is enraged by Japan's unfavorable balance of trade. Taiwan's is equally unbalanced, but nobody even notices.

Two Contrasting Styles

Taiwan thus needs several large companies to get our attention. It needs to develop, cultivate, and maintain something comparable to South Korean *chaebol*. As long as its few companies with over five hundred employees are regarded as industrial giants, these things will not come to pass.[12]

The South Korean policy is straightforward and brutal.[13] Its Presidential Special Directive of 1974 dictates that the scale of enterprises should be enlarged to enable them to become internationally competitive and the managerial and financial capacities of families are limited, so privately held firms should go public. To achieve these goals, the directive induced corporations to comply by awarding "appropriate privileges" to well-managed public corporations, established a system of overseeing and controlling credit allocations and tax records, reduced the debt/equity ratio of large corporations by "managing the bank system appropriately," and reinforced tax surveillance and the outside audit system.

To comply with this directive, the Ministry of Finance produced a categorization of businesses based on the strength of their finances. Those firms with weak financial structure were directed to become strong. Until they did, they were prohibited from receiving new foreign loan guarantees, establishing or acquiring additional businesses, investing in stock, or acquiring nonoperating real estate. If compliance is a problem, the Financial Normalization Committee notifies banks not to extend low interest loans.

The Taiwanese counterpart is the Statute for the Encouragement of Investment, promulgated initially in 1960 and amended most recently in December, 1984. It provides for the Ministry of Economic Affairs to approve the merger of businesses. Upon approval, income tax payable as a result of the merger is waived and land values of the consolidated enterprise are entered as a credit against any remaining tax. If the merger involves a "productive enterprise" (all manufacturing, handicraft, mining, agriculture, forestry, fishing, animal husbandry, transportation, warehousing, public utilities, technical services, and hotels), the following additional benefits are available: a five-year "tax holiday" and accelerated depreciation on machinery and equipment to half of its service life.

The tone and intent of the two documents establishes South Korea as the more aggressive and Taiwan as the more conciliatory. Of course, in the execution of the statutes, the South Korean government meets resistance. Yet the growing international recognition of South Korea's economy is tribute to its stubborn determination, while the inability of Taiwan to become competitive is evidence of its less coordinated policy.

The ROC Ministry of Economic Affairs has tried to institute mergers, interpreting the law liberally. It does not merely "approve" them; rather it encourages them. But the result has been disappointing. Although most banks are government-owned, there is a small and medium industry credit fund with available credits maintained at $131 million, much like the American Small Business Administration, which the government created largely because of the pressure of the Taiwan Textile Federation.[14] The opportunities for punitive action, such as canceling incentives or revoking export licensing or registration, are reduced by such funds, and by the strength of the Taiwanese in the Kuomintang. The party, while not a policy-making organization, has on occasion been an effective advocate for Taiwanese businesspeople facing the possibility of sanctions. As a result, high-level civil servants constantly complain about the inability of the bureaucracy to restructure the economy as has been done in Korea, and about the anarchy of the economic structure, as compared with Japan's.[15]

Lawrence Lau lists the basic differences between the authoritarian governments of Taiwan and South Korea. First, in South Korea, income is concentrated at the high end, as "most development theorists would predict," while in Taiwan the distribution is more equal. Lau believes that the elite's adherence to Sun's "Three Principles of the People" (specifically the obligation to enhance the "people's livelihood") is partially responsible. As the Kuomintang is the official transmitter of Sun's ideas, its claim to being encompassing is reinforced.[16] Second, Taiwan's growth rate is more stable because of its conservative monetary policies. Third, South Korea maintains loose control over exchange rates, while Taiwan is very strict. Fourth, South Korea borrows heavily to finance its investment, while Taiwan relies on domestic savings. Fifth, South Korea is dominated by conglomerates, while Taiwan's economy consists of small business. Sixth, the South Korean government takes an active role in controlling market impulses, while Taiwan is more inclined to let the market run its course. In sum, "where South Korea has tended to enforce vigorously an elaborate roster of economic do's and don'ts, Taiwan's government has aimed instead to create an economic environment conducive to growth."[17]

The contrast extends to labor relations. Taiwan has adopted extensive labor laws and regulations, dealing with maximum hours, union negotiations, maternity leaves, child labor, retirement, compensation for industrial accidents, vacations, and the like. In typical state corporatist fashion, the bureaucracy has intervened to create a labor-management relationship as complex as those of the European societal corporatist governments. South Korea's economic miracle has tended to push labor-management relations to the side. South Koreans work longer hours, at lower wages, with fewer protections. Those who work for the huge conglomerates are better off. In typical Japanese fashion, they have begun to assume a paternalistic role. But this aside, South Korean workers are not as well off as are Taiwanese. Since Taiwan's per capita income is substantially higher than South Korea's, and since its income distribution is more equal, one can understand why South Korea continues to be shaken by massive protest and political instability while Taiwan does not. Virtually simultaneously with the South Korean government's capitulation and authorization of opposition parties and elections, Taiwan (unnoticed as usual) repealed martial law and held an election in which the opposition garnered about one-fourth of the vote.

As was demonstrated in the summer of 1987, anti-government forces are more intractable in South Korea than in Taiwan. If the behavior of protestors is any guide, many South Koreans do not regard the governing elite, or its political party, as legitimate. A reasonable explanation is the long history of the Kuomintang and the far less symbolically significant South Korean party history. Ironically, the consistent assertion by the Kuomintang that it is the legitimate government on the mainland, and the determination of the People's Republic to press for reunification, has created more of a sense of impermanence in Taiwan. North Korea could not possibly re-invade and reunify by force of arms. Nor, except in such equally rigid dictatorships like Albania, is it held in high regard. But, perhaps because of its attraction to the international community and its identification with a major Marxist revolution, the mainland's claim is recognized as valid.

The splash made by South Korea's entry into the American automobile market is a good example of the profound differences between the two countries. South Korea was justifiably proud, and Taiwan can only watch with envy: its export cars are a year or so away. But South Korea has limited car manufacturing to three firms, while Taiwan's industry is splintered among six manufacturers, each too small to benefit from mass production's cost-saving techniques. James Schiffman and Maria Shao encapsulate differences:

In South Korea, a few large business groups dominate, and the government is heavily involved in policy-making. Building markets is often more important . . . than profit. Taiwan is a land of mom and pop businesses, and government is less overt. Profit is king. . . . Despite common roots in Confucianism, they perceive that they have great differences. Koreans are seen as spenders, Chinese as savers. Koreans are characterized as aggressive, Chinese as cautious. . . . South Korea has only 7,000 trading companies. . . . Taiwan has 60,000 trading companies. Many of them consist of a boss, a telephone, a telex machine—and maybe the boss's wife as secretary.[18]

Bureaucratic Defeats in Authoritarian Societies

The running feud between the textile manufacturers and importers and the Ministry of Economic Affairs illustrates the frustration felt by mainlander bureaucrats. Until 1987, martial law allowed the government to impose mergers by simple decree. But martial law was never a realistic political option. Given the sensitivity of the bureaucracy to charges of exploitation, it is impossible for it to issue orders to the Taiwanese business community. This is not to suggest that, appearances to the contrary, the ROC bureaucracy is a captive of its regulated clientele, for this is demonstrably not the case. It has pushed hard to move from labor-intensive to capital-intensive industries by interpreting the strategic industries legislation very capriciously and has withstood a major assault from automobile manufacturers.

The last example illustrates well the give and take of an authoritarian bureaucracy. Dissatisfied with the quality of automobiles
produced by Yue Loong, a Taiwanese manufacturer, the Ministry of
Economic Affairs offered a manufacturing contract to Toyota. Previously, the importation of Japanese cars had been prohibited. The
early contract negotiations began in 1982, with strong opposition
from Taiwanese business leaders and from the Kuomintang. The
initial contract was withdrawn, and another was offered to Nissan,
as this company was willing to split the contract with Yue Loong.
In 1985, when the first automobile had yet to appear, the Ministry
of Economic Affairs, having yielded to domestic pressures to require
foreign investment in Yue Loong, liked the idea so much that it
began negotiations with Chrysler. Thus there will be four partners:
Yue Loong, Nissan, Chrysler, and the ROC government. Ultimately the plant will be in full swing, but years of protracted negotiations has been required.

The ROC government hopes that this venture will earn it a
measure of respect, as happened when South Korea exported automobiles in 1986. The desperation of the Ministry of Economic
Affairs, and the Executive Yuan, to begin the project is belied by
the length of the negotiations.[19] Still, the contract was negotiated.
The Ministry of Economic Affairs has also avoided strict construction of the strategic industries legislation, by giving high-tech companies a substantial advantage over heavy industry and minor
manufacturing.

RECRUITMENT AND COHESION

Japan is a homogeneous country with a consensual decision-
making culture. Its bureaucracy is, like those of Britain and France,
recruited from high achievers. Tokyo University's law faculty is the
equivalent of Oxford and Cambridge or L'Ecole Nationale d'administration. An astonishing 80 percent of Japanese upper-level
civil servants are graduates of Tokyo University.[20] There is a sense of
continuity or cohesion that common backgrounds and common
values creates.

There is also a hierarchy of prestige in the Japanese civil service, with the Ministry of International Trade and Industry being the most respected. The Taiwanese bureaucracy is neither so centrally recruited nor so cohesive in values. The Ministry of Economic Affairs is the most eagerly sought after plum, like the Ministry of Commerce and Industry or the Economic Planning Board in Korea, but recruitment to it is not through any specified path. About 200,000 people pass the civil service exam annually in Taiwan. The most frequently requested bureau is the Ministry of Economic Affairs, followed by the Ministry of Foreign Affairs, the Ministry of Finance, and the Ministry of Defense. Lagging well behind are the ministries of education, justice, and communication and a few minor commissions. The mechanism of selection allows a fair amount of negotiation: to those who pass, each ministry administers its own exam, and each candidate ranks his or her preferences.

Personalism and Corruption

Asian civil services, no less than their European counterparts, present an image of expertise. When governments undertake massive planning functions, stability is valuable. Interest groups and administrators cannot interact under conditions of uncertainty, and therefore both seek to regularize. Individual ministers come and go, but bureaucrats stay on. In the Asian authoritarian governments, executive turnover is not on the same level as in the European democracies; even Japan, which has a high rate of turnover compared with its neighbors, has not removed the Liberal Democrats from office in three decades, and the extent to which the various factions recruit and nurture political candidates from the bureaucracy provides even more stability.

Bureaucracies expand as regulations are promulgated and interest groups with a strong stake in decisions appear to contest them. Although the Asian governments are not big spenders in comparison with European governments, and hence there is more privatization, the blurred distinction between public and private fosters keen group interest. A major problem of the regulatory process is the relative dependence of each participant on the other, a debate

that led Schmitter to make his distinction between societal corporatism and state corporatism. The operative distinction is the degree of "penetration" of one by the other, and the degree of
"dependency" of one on the other.[21] When the blurring of the lines
is enhanced by recruitment from a common pool, as in Japan, it is
difficult to decide who is dependent on whom.[22] Irrespective of the
relative degrees of influence, bureaucracies rely on expertise—
technical skill—as a *political* resource. They are able to do so by
asserting their "neutral competence." Expertise is a potent weapon
in Asian politics, since it does not have to compete with responsiveness for legitimacy. The Weberian notion that the essence of
bureaucracy is recruitment and advancement according to merit is
buttressed by the Confucian ideal of affording great prestige to
learning. Hence the profession of government is a noble one.

But the spirits of Confucius and Weber conflict with another
equally well-established code of behavior: the exchange of personal
favors. Reciprocity competes well with neutral expertise, and the
politics of the area is replete with the giving and exchanging of
personal favors. Sometimes the exchange is between functional
equals who have different goods or services to offer, like the *blat* of
the Soviet Union. In other cases, the exchange is between patron
and protégé. Powerful patrons build strong cadres by the judicious
use of institutional power, and often personal loyalty or enmity is
more influential than ideology or even political advantage.

The most obvious examples are those of Japan, where in the
harsh assessment of Richardson and Flanagan:

the politician is more likely to tie his career to the rise of a particular
faction leader. . . . Japanese party factions, especially those in the LDP, are
not based on party issues or ideological differences and therefore serve no
representative function. . . . The most damaging impact of personalistic
norms . . . is found in their association with . . . political corruption. The
cultural norms of reciprocity, exchange of favors, and gift-giving seem
to legitimate influence peddling and bribery in the minds of many
Japanese."[23]

The instance most often cited is former Prime Minister Kakuei
Tanaka's conviction on the charge of accepting about $2 million in
bribes from Lockheed. In spite of the scandal, Tanaka continued to

hold his seat, actually increasing his margins of victory, presumably because people believed his defense (that he needed the money to help the needy). The comparable scandal in Taiwan—the illegal use of credit union funds—did result in the resignation of the ministers of finance and economic affairs, and possibly the resignation of the secretary-general of the Kuomintang, but very little else other than an escalation of charges of corruption by the nascent opposition party.[24]

The opportunities for interest groups in systems that accept interpersonal reciprocity are substantial. In Taiwan, Kuomintang leadership, especially Chiang Ching-kuo, have made much of the reduction of corruption, barring bureaucrats from bars, dance halls, and expensive restaurants. Soon after the death of the elder Chiang, forty-five members of the government, including ten members of the feared Garrison Command (military intelligence), were arrested for customs violations, and Chiang Kai-shek's personal secretary went to prison for bribery. A conspicuous jailing of twenty more bureaucrats on the same charge was designed to establish the incorruptible image of the civil service. Given the sleazy reputation of the party until the retreat from the mainland, the clean image was almost a necessity. As long as attention was focused on them, it meant that civil servants would be living largely on their salaries, a rarity in Chinese government. The issue is not corruption, but rather its extent and the use to which it is put. One of the most notorious scams on the island is the Kuomintang-managed Vocational Assistance Committee for Retired Soldiers, a large combine of smaller manufacturers. The misuse of funds by the party in this enterprise is notorious, but nobody cares very much, since it is unobtrusive.

Soon the novelty of no honest graft wore off and ROC bureaucrats began to drift easily into the rule of reciprocity. The exchange of favors became once again routine. Reciprocity's practitioners distinguish it from major scandals, although it often involves considerable amounts of money or other valuables. Misuse of money earned through reciprocity is a greater sin than the reciprocity itself.

The universal norm of reciprocity applies to *individual* behavior. Well-placed and skillful players of the game may have more influence than their location in the institutional scheme would warrant. Not only has Taiwan failed to merge its textile manufacturers; it has also failed to relegate textiles to a less favored category. Close Kuomintang ties and complex patterns of interpersonal reciprocity have kept the group leadership in a stronger position than its economic importance alone would merit.[25] Interest groups that are strategically located, such as those representing light manufacturing and high tech, may be influential because of their designation as the key to development, but skillful businesspeople in less favored industries can do just as well. Nonetheless, James Gregor's evaluation, that "the bureaucracy in the ROC is governed largely by impersonal . . . criteria" is in accord with my general impression.[26]

The Ministry of Economic Affairs

Taiwan's most prestigious bureaucracies illustrate Chalmers Johnson's discussion of "pilot agencies." He writes, "I am referring to such organs of state as Japan's Ministry of International Trade and Industry, the ROC's Ministry of Economic Affairs, Korea's Economic Planning Board, and Singapore's Economic Development Board and Jurong Town Corporation." (In Hong Kong the functions of the pilot agencies are performed solely by the banking community and by cartel-like organizations of private entrepreneurs.) These organizations perform "think tank" functions for their economies, chart the route for economic development, obtain a consensus for their plans from the private sector, act as "gatekeepers" for contacts with foreign markets and investors, and provide positive government support for private economic initiative.[27]

Taiwan's Ministry of Economic Affairs is just as Johnson describes it. In the bribery scandals of the late 1970's, only the Ministry of Finance was implicated, leaving Economic Affairs to blossom as the most glamorous of the cabinet ministries. The 1985 credit union scandals did touch the Ministry of Economic Affairs; however, accusations of bribery and fraud were confined to minor political appointees. Nevertheless, the resignation of the minister was demanded and received.

Given the obsession of Asian authoritarian governments with GNP growth, the prestige of the Ministry of Economic Affairs is understandable. (Its prestige among civil servants far exceeds that of the Ministry of Defense, an unobtrusive indicator of Taiwan's altered priorities.)[28] Besides planning for the private sector, the Ministry of Economic Affairs administers most of Taiwan's government-owned corporations.[29]

The ministry has been given the responsibility of shifting Taiwanese industry into high technology. It has gathered unto itself primary responsibility for economic planning, resource allocation, and even the approval or disapproval of specific contracts that do not conform to government plans. Intervening at such a minute level gives the ministry the chance for reciprocity.[30] It is here—with the granting or denial of explicit individual business proposals—that the tension between bureaucracy and business is greatest.

The Ministry of Economic Affairs is a good place to start describing the Taiwanese integration process; if Taiwanese are moving into the most honored ministry, real progress will have been made. Also we want to know more about the importance of party membership as opposed to neutral competence as a criterion for recruitment. Table 7-1, derived from personnel records, provides some answers.

As the table shows, there are *no* Taiwanese with the highest civil service rank employed in the Ministry of Economic Affairs. There are some at the second level, and the percentage of Taiwan-

TABLE 7-1
CHARACTERISTICS OF EXECUTIVES IN THE MINISTRY OF
ECONOMIC AFFAIRS, BY RANK AND BY BACKGROUND

Characteristic	Rank*				
	1	2	3	4	5
Age	61	58	50	46	39
% Taiwanese	—	25	40	60	65
% advanced degree	25	30	20	30	40
% economics/business training	30	26	30	42	50
% experience abroad	75	70	60	30	40
% government experience	88	75	80	40	10
% business experience	15	20	25	40	45
% Kuomintang	100	100	80	52	50

*1 = highest; 5 = lowest.

ese increases as one descends to the lowest ranks. The recruitment of Taiwanese into the lower ranks represents the inevitable: as the mainlanders die off and their offspring marry, Taiwanization will be complete.[31] Still, the blurring of initial distinctions continues.[32] There is no reason not to assume that some of the Taiwanese in lower ranks will advance, and that their places will be taken by other Taiwanese. Party membership decreases as rank declines, suggesting that either people join as they move up, or that the proportion of party members will decline when those now in lower ranks advance.

But advancement and even retention are not as structured as they would be in a fully rationalized bureaucracy. There is more room to move up or down for reasons unrelated to merit or performance. Some Taiwanese claim that the civil service exam is biased, since it is in Mandarin. (This claim is, of course, ludicrous since all Chinese dialects are written with the same characters in the same order: presumably those who claim so were either trying to snooker me or could not read.) Others claim that there is a "quota" of jobs for each province, thus ensuring the mainlanders' dominance since only they can trace their roots to one of the other (mainland) provinces.[33] Remember that, in Nationalist dogma, Taiwan is a province rather than a nation.

LOYALTY AND MERIT IN CONFLICT

The absence of a fully installed merit system reflects the difficulty Taiwan and the mainland have in separating merit from loyalty; in both countries there are ample supplies of party ideologues who equate loyalty with merit, and you can lose your job for disloyalty without access to administrative or judicial remedies.[34] Highly placed civil servants have sought to "leapfrog" especially talented Taiwanese over mainlanders by using the "special rating," a process that creates substantial opposition but is still done.[35] Various ministers make frequent recruiting forays into high schools and colleges, urging students to prepare themselves for a government career by studying business, economics, statistics, and international trade.

Judging from the career patterns in the Ministry of Economic Affairs, the choice of a technocratic education by college-bound youth is proceeding at full speed (Table 7-2).[36]

Different career paths build on deeper cultural differences to create problems in business-government relations not experienced by the other Asian authoritarian countries. Instead of the extraordinary homogeneity and virtually identical recruitment paths of business and government leaders in Japan, Taiwan suffers because of the traditional division. Ministers in Taiwan speak often of their admiration for Japan and especially for the one path to success, Tokyo University. Examination of the lowest ranks in the Ministry of Economic Affairs shows that only 32 of 83 came from National Taiwan University, the most prestigious university on the island.

The most widely cited work in the Taiwanese civil service (after Sun Yat-sen's "Three Principles of the People") is Ferrel Heady's *Comparative Public Administration*, which argues for meritocracy.[37] The younger civil servants, especially the Taiwanese, are very much in this mold. They are better educated than the mainlanders and less likely to belong to the Kuomintang. The reluctance of the younger Taiwanese civil servants to join the party is ironic, since the Kuomintang is the only organization explicitly pursuing political integration, seeking to insulate the bureaucracy from political squabbling, and arranging meetings of mutual accord between Taiwanese businesses and mainlander bureaucracies.

TABLE 7-2
CHARACTERISTICS OF THE TWO TOP RANKS OF THE
MINISTRY OF ECONOMIC AFFAIRS, BY ORIGIN OF RESPONDENT

Characteristic	Ranks 1 and 2	
	Taiwanese	Mainlander
% advanced degree	72	59
% economics/business training	42	38
% experience abroad	42	36
% government experience	33	45
% business/experience	61	38
% Kuomintang	41	58

Reverse Discrimination: The Private Sector

In response to the government's efforts toward integration, some companies have tried to find mainlanders, hoping to refute the widely held belief that mainlanders cannot earn a decent living. I examined the records of two Taiwanese-owned businesses, an insurance company, not central to the bureaucracy's high-technology drive, and a plastics manufacturing firm. The insurance company employs almost no mainlanders. The plastics manufacturing concern, heavily involved in the response to planning directives, has recruited a beginning cadre that is about 50 percent mainlander. The difference between the two is the extent to which the Ministry of Economic Affairs is aware of their hiring practices. Firms that are incorporated into the government's strategic industries planning have a higher profile. The Ministry can make life agony if it wishes to, and every mainlander hired is an investment in good business-government relations. But if a firm is unnoticed, the biases of the owners are apparent.

The centrality of the plastics company accounts for its compliance with integration. Even so, Taiwan is a giant step away from Japan, where there is more personnel interchange between private and public bureaucracies. In Taiwan, private businesses do not lure away bureaucrats; bureaucracies do attract some from the private sector, but these tend not to be mainlanders.

The Process of Interest Group Intermediation

Unquestionably there is more of the classic corporatist mode of interest group intermediation in Japan. There are peak associations and trade associations that have tight relationships with regulatory bureaucracies.[38] Taiwan does not pretend to approximate Japan's freedom to organize. The government sanctions or represses organizations and supplies them with officers. Estimates of membership range from one-third to one-half of the eligibles, and membership is not even remotely similar to the semi-compulsory organizations of European corporatism. Most of the trade associations are no more than paper organizations; a few enjoy substantial access because of individual reciprocity. Robert Silin notes that "managers of both large and small firms feel they operate at the will of the government, which is considered at best capricious," and that "people in industry feel strong antipathy toward government officials."[39] Yet my interviews with businessmen and their organizations reveal almost no idea of confrontation.

There are no peak associations, but there are two or three industrialists who enjoy a Japanese-style collaborative relationship with the bureaucracies. They meet regularly with top ministers in a variety of circumstances. Often their meetings are as structured as those in Japan. Joint sponsorship of various conferences on management, technology, investment, and so on are regularly arranged by government organizations, such as the China External Trade Development Council, think tanks, and business associations. Given the traditions of the country, there is invariably quite a bit of ceremony associated with each conference and many opportunities to talk privately.

The essence of the process is its reliance on reciprocity rather than institutional position. But interest groups rarely operate as a source of policy *initiation*, as occurs, occasionally, in Japan. The ROC government does not encourage challenges to its political monopoly and makes the rewards of compliance tempting. Acquiescence—reinforced by a Confucian tradition—is the norm. As one interviewee expressed it, "In terms of relative influence it appears that businesses are more inclined to adjust their performance in accordance with administrative expectations." But the exceptions are conspicuous because they are so rare: the fight over mergers and the delay of the automobile contract and currency reform are examples of a stubborn business community.

Another dispute about currency policy has all the earmarks of a pluralist fight. Importers have argued successfully for flexible exchange rates, defeating the exporters, who prefer to peg the new Taiwanese dollar (NT) to the U.S. dollar. Since the Ministry of Economic Affairs favors exports over imports, the outcome is even more remarkable. Importers carved out a close relationship with rival bureaucracies in order to battle with the Ministry of Economic Affairs. It responded with a ban on all Japanese imports.

Another issue is the role of state-owned enterprises in the economy. They are invariably in the red, and their position in the economy (as measured by the percentage of GNP generated by state-owned businesses) is declining annually. Once more than half the GNP, the state-owned firms now account for less than 20 percent.[40] If the government were intent on using its clout, it is unlikely that it would divest itself as rapidly as it has. (It still keeps a tight reign on financial transactions, however.)

The fact that the government of Taiwan is not a monolith and is vulnerable to interest group pressure should not obscure the essential aspect of its government—its moderate (or "soft") authoritarianism. The government monopolized policy initiation to a greater degree than is true in Japan, but to a lesser degree than occurs in Korea. It is free of traditional interest groups, much to the delight of Olson, who singles it out for special acclaim:

> There is one country so prototypical that it is worth special attention. . . . Taiwan has enjoyed fantastically high growth rates. The Japanese occupation . . . had repressed special-interest organizations in Taiwan, so the rapid growth is in accord with the theory offered in this book. . . . Countries with Taiwan's nearly complete absence of special-interest organization should be able to maintain something approximating full employment and full-capacity production even during an unexpected deflation or disinflation.[41]

The irony is that Taiwan is moving as fast as it can toward an autonomous economy. It will never become a pluralist system, but then neither will Japan. If it achieves its goal of becoming another Japan, the absence of groups that Olson applauds will become a remnant of times past.

No matter how the economy is organized, it is not the absence of interest groups that explains economic success. Rather the relative absence of narrow distributional coalitions is itself a result of a more collectivist value system. The chairman of the Chinese National Federation of Industries and the Chinese National Association of Industry and Commerce, a Taiwanese, explained:

> The economic interest groups in Taiwan are not so well organized and do not do as much lobbying as those in the United States and other Western countries. This is probably because the national policies of the Republic of China are guided by the three people's principles as upheld by Dr. Sun Yat-sen. On the economic side, the principle of people's livelihood con-

tains a well-designed model to balance the different interests of different economic groups while the economy is developed under the market system. There is, therefore, no need for a special interest group to lobby to urge the government to take action in its favor. For instance, ever since the beginning of the industrialization of Taiwan under the government of the Republic of China, policies have been adopted to develop industries without sacrificing the interest of the farmers. Another example is that the government has always taken measures in accordance with the principle of the people's livelihood to promote workers' welfare. This is why the trade unions of Taiwan are not as active as those in many other countries and Taiwan is well known as a country with the fewest labor problems. As a result of such guided policies and measures, there has been a continuous decrease in income inequity along with a tremendous expansion of the economy in the past thirty years.

It is not that these remarks are accurate; they express the normal, intensely personal commitment to the value system of Asian collectivism. Russian bureaucrats quote Lenin because they have to; members of Asian political elites are true believers. Whether the reason for this genuine commitment to conflict avoidance is because of "Confucianism" (and the cultural characteristics implied by the term) or because the Taiwanese have become accustomed to state corporatism and find it a reasonable way to organize political life, interest groups fit easily into the mode. The need, or even the will, to enforce compliance is conspicuously absent.

State corporatism without a secular theology might not be so successful at compartmentalization. Berger notes that South Korea and Taiwan, while repressing political opposition (more so in South Korea, less so in Taiwan), have "permitted the growth of participatory institutions centered around nonpolitical (primarily economic) concerns."[42] That economic concerns could be regarded as nonpolitical tells us much about the Confucian state corporatist system. Opposition can be compartmentalized.

Unquestionably there is no reason to equate corporatism, state or societal, with economic growth. The "economic miracle" of the Pacific Rim has generated quite a bit of curiosity, especially in Taiwan, where growth has been accompanied by a reduction of inequality. But state corporatism also exists in Mexico and Portugal, neither of which has been able to sustain consistent economic growth. Portugal has been described as "rural, Catholic, agricultural, paternalistic, and backward," a condition said to be appropriate for corporatism.[43] The serious decline of the Mexican economy, and the continued loss of support by the Partido Revolucionario Institutional (PRI), is another example of corporatism hindering development.[44] But did corporatism "cause" these conditions? Howard Wiarda answers that "in the broad political-cultural sense of implying the accumulated habits and behavior patterns of the Portuguese nation, corporatism was an independent variable, probably as important as class structure in determining political outcomes and maybe more so."[45]

A slightly different claim can be made for the uniquely Asian form of state corporatism, a form heavily flavored by the Confucian ethic. But Confucianism is not the accumulated habits and behavior patterns of Asian state corporatism. A conjunction of rapid industrialization and Confucian political traditions contribute, along with regional economic hegemony induced by Japanese imperialism, to Asian corporatism. This combination (and it would be pointless to try to unravel the causal chain) has produced a healthy economy and a political system that is "developing."

EIGHT

PLURALISM, CORPORATISM, AND CONFUCIANISM: A REPRISE

Why do people join organizations? Do they do so to enhance their individual well-being by gaining access to selective benefits? Or do they do so without any regard for their own circumstances but for the good of a cause, group, or country?

The answer is, as most of us might suspect, "it depends." It depends on the group or organization and it depends to a lesser extent on the culture. People in a very individualistic culture—the United States—are both selfish and altruistic; people join organizations because they believe passionately in their cause or to get cheap term insurance. They act both "rationally" and "irrationally." People join trade associations for different reasons than when they join single-issue organizations.

If there is altruism in a hyper-pluralist country, there is also individualism in an unquestionably collectivist one. Some people join the Kuomintang to get ahead in business. Since the Kuomintang's patron, Sun Yat-sen (like most Chinese intellectuals), did not hold commerce in high regard, he might be at least bemused to learn that so many of his disciples are in it for the money.

But a different result appears when we ask, not about the decision to join, but about the decision to renew. Given the high turnover rate in organizations, and the ephemeral nature of political passion, it is hardly surprising that most organizations find selective incentives or go out of business (or keep in business by a steady membership transfusion). How can such a predicament allow interest groups to serve as the connection between the rulers and the ruled? The answer is apparent. Interest groups are no better at representing than are legislatures—that is to say, not very good. The organizations that do the best job of representing their members are the single-issue groups, which political scientists and politicians have accused of heating up the political process beyond the point of reasonable compromise, of making a country ungovernable because of an uncontrollable proliferation of interest groups. The belief that interest groups are linking units, but that too many links is dangerous, is elegantly stated in a study of Spain's transition from authoritarian to democratic government: "The underorganization of Spanish democracy reduces the threat of the country's *becoming ungovernable through a proliferation of interest groups.*"[1]

So the risk of fragmentation is greatest when countries are beset by intractable interest groups, irrespective of the motives of individual choice. Since, as membership becomes more a matter of habit, selective benefits replace collective ones in all but the single-issue groups, it is presumably their difficulty in working within a system of compromise that makes them such a threat.

The societal corporatist countries are not troubled by an explosion of interest groups because they have developed a mode of interest group mediation that excludes all but a few peak associations not only from the influence process but also from the right to try to squeeze into it. Perhaps for this reason they are more "governable." They do not have consistently faster-growing economies as is often alleged, but they do have lower inflation, less unemployment, and as a consequence less political and civil unrest and more stability. Is corporatism, in either its societal or state variants, more just? Corporatism is neither a sham to exploit the working class nor a device to saddle corporations with endless regulations.

Societal corporatism does not lead to either more or less equality in income distribution. But state corporatism *might*. Taiwan reveals the possibilities; that other state corporatist systems are not more equitable does not mean that they can never be so.

The Taiwanese bureaucratic elite had an unusually low set of constraints upon its experiment in economic planning. Japan's colonial rulers used Taiwan primarily for agricultural exports. Although some elements of an industrial infrastructure existed, the island was virtually a pre-industrial enclave. The KMT's swift elimination of opposition left it able to do what it wished. It chose to build an economy in which it would be a guide, but with the Taiwanese receiving most of the economic rewards.[2] It is unlikely that these combinations of events and organizations could exist again.[3] Thomas Gold's excellent analysis of Taiwan's politics and economics concludes:

> What leaps out . . . is the way in which Taiwan's political elite, with a great deal of autonomy from particular social interests, effectively led sustained economic development through several crises and maintained stability in the bargain. . . . It . . . restructured society, channelled funds for investment, intervened directly in the economy, created a market system, devised indicative plans, determined the physical and psychological investment climate, and guided Taiwan's incorporation into the world capitalist system.[4]

Societal corporatism produces less profound results because, among other reasons, it has never had an empty canvas on which to paint its picture of an ideal world. State corporatism by itself is not necessarily the "cause" of prosperity and equity. One has only to observe Mexico's plummet into economic chaos to understand that state corporatism can lead just as easily to disaster.

The mode of conflict resolution is also a bad predictor of economic *growth*. To find examples of faster-growing corporatist systems we must turn to Asian state corporatism; the state corporatism in the Iberian tradition is both less stable and less prosperous. The Asian state corporatist countries, because they are so economically impressive, have attracted more attention than they would otherwise have done. There are many examples of state corporatism but only a few within the Confucian tradition. What "causes" their success? Is it the strong state, bureaucratically dominant over underorganized business and coopted labor? Presumably it is not for the reasons mentioned above; there are good examples of corporatism producing less than salutary results.

Is the Pacific Rim's success, then, because of Confucianism? This conclusion seems hard to accept, unless we keep in mind its secular, cultural, informal nature. A way of political life dominated by a meritocracy seems a reasonable way to govern, unless we are concerned with accountability (as Confucian scholars were not, except at the broadest level of a social contract). Gold argues that "ambition for self and family; high value on education and learning by copying exemplars; frugality; the family as an economic unit, and entrepreneurship" are Taiwanese cultural characteristics that contribute directly to a booming economy.[5]

The Asian political culture's stress on group loyalty rather than individualism sets it in obvious contrast to the United States. An open, competitive interest group system, at the heart of pluralist dicta, is quite foreign to Asian culture, and to a slightly lesser extent to European societal corporatism. Samuel Huntington expresses the difference well:

> In such a society, the critical need is to avoid competition and disharmony, and hence elaborate consultation within the group is required before a decision can be reached. Americans, on the other hand, are comfortable with open conflict, majority votes, and a more individualistic, "lone ranger" style of leadership.[6]

One need not call this cluster of cultural dictates "Confucianism," but these are attributes found more often in Asian than in Western society.

Of course we are concerned about accountability, a point often overlooked when American businesspeople admire Japanese coordination (forgetting that a healthy dose of bureaucratic intervention, or "meddling" in our way of thinking, is a long tradition in Asian government). It makes little difference whether they are as they are because of Confucianism, a strong bureaucracy, a tradition of stability as a legacy of colonial rule, or intense, seemingly unending external threats.

The efforts to install a competitive democracy in Japan did not succeed, nor will Taiwan become a two-party system (even as it removes most restrictions and sends its brightest bureaucrats scurrying all over the globe to study political parties) in the Western sense. Conversely, their mode of conflict resolution cannot be exported. As Berger writes, "Attempts by countries outside the region to emulate the East Asian example may well be futile. One may export the economic policies of, say, Taiwan, to an African country, but one can hardly expect Africans to adopt Confucian morality."[7]

Political culture and political socialization are too complex and intractable for a cross-national transfer. The point may appear obvious, but it is well to consider it in view of the current infatuation with things Asian and, to a lesser degree, things European. Corporatism's appeal, that it promotes cooperative rather than antagonistic government-business relations, requires a more collectivist culture than we would accept. Again, Huntington writes that "major differences have thus existed between American political values, with their stress on individualism, liberty, equality, and opposition to power and authority, and political values in other Western countries where values are more varied and more heavily weighted toward authority and hierarchy."[8]

These cultural differences are transmitted through family, school, media, friends, work groups, and so on, from generation to generation; they need to be explicitly implanted. But in Taiwan they are. Richard Wilson notes:

There are many positive reinforcers for the concept of group unity and for cooperation as the ideal group life. . . . Outside a fifth-grade classroom . . . is a sign which proclaims: "The struggle to obtain the victory of the group is the individual's victory." Group themes are a constant aspect of the literature which the children read.[9]

He found Taiwanese schoolchildren to be more intensely ideological, more committed to symbols of national unity, than their American counterparts.[10] Modes of conflict resolution are not the political equivalent of hair transplants.

If nothing much can be changed, we need to look once more at the styles of interest group intermediation. If policy adjustments are incremental unless one can duplicate conditions in the Pacific Rim, then can we conclude that at least the *process* of interest group intermediation is more responsive, or perhaps more representative, of the array of political groups extant in the society? Since corporatism constricts participation, does it provide more responsiveness to fewer groups?

The kinds of interaction structures found in state corporatist systems are different only in degree from the societal corporatist states. In the societal corporatist states, there is privileged access, a laying on of hands by the government, that effectively narrows the arena of interaction. Although not achieved by legislation or administrative fiat, the governments of Austria and Switzerland have identified and legitimated some participants and have excluded others.

The establishment of a cooperative relationship in state corporatist or in democratic states depends more on assessments of advantages and opportunities than on institutional arrangements. The wildly unregulated American political system, with the unsavory spectacle of candidates out-promising one another for the money of the political action committees is a result of ill-devised institutional reforms. But the PAC orgy is also a consequence of a political culture that is Darwinian in contrast to the societal corporatist or state corporatist regimes. Olson's prolonged disquisition on the costs and benefits of joining an organization is less appropriate to the countries he so much admires, where strongly internalized expectations devalue individualism. The influence peddling of a Michael Deaver is less valuable in political systems that have defined and constrained access.[11]

Defining access is what both corporatist and pluralist systems are all about. Influence peddling is pervasive in pluralist and authoritarian systems, but less so in corporatist ones (Austria and Japan are the exceptions). The uninterrupted reign of Japan's Liberal Democratic Party has created and maintained patterns of influence that are quite stable, possibly more so than in Taiwan, where factions have more of an ideological base and the rites of political passage are less clearly defined.

Charles Maier has argued that the modern corporatist state originated in the turmoil and social unrest following World War I. The wartime mobilization had integrated organized labor into the state-supervised decision-making system, and had blurred the distinction between public and private sectors. The transformation to corporatism was a conscious effort to exclude the less reliable and to ensure economic stability: "What permitted stability after 1924 was a shift in the focal point of decision making. Fragmented parliamentary majorities yielded to ministerial bureaucracies, or sometimes directly to party councils, where interest group representatives could more easily work out social burdens and rewards."[12]

Those excluded, principally the lower middle classes, suffered the ravages of inflation and flocked to the banners of radicals who condemned the "establishment." Although corporatism has been linked with the rise of Hitler's Germany and Mussolini's Italy, it is arguably more accurate to say that their initial support was from those excluded from the corporatist bargain.[13] The attraction of the French middle classes to Poujadism in the years after World War II has a similar ring, as has the "paranoid" streak in American politics. American populism generally attacks bigness—big business, big labor, big government—with equal ferocity; the likes of William Jennings Bryan, George Wallace, and the supporters of the various tax limitation schemes (such as Howard Jarvis in California) want to stop "them."[14] Corporatism does without doubt screen out participants, but does pluralism accomplish the same result without deliberation?

Both the societal corporatist and state corporatist regimes are "bifrontal." The first aspect of the bifrontal government is "statizing"—that is, gaining control of the political organizations and interests of a society.[15] Guillermo O'Donnell calls this process "conquest and subordination." In Latin America, the locus of O'Donnell's empirical work, conquest and subordination can take the form of a depoliticized working class, required for ambitious countries such as Brazil to join the international economic community. Depoliticization of the working class is an important aspect of the state corporatism of South Korea and Taiwan, and of Japan's state-societal corporatism (less now). A depoliticized, or at least coopted, labor movement also, as we have seen, was essential to the development of European societal corporatism. Whether it prospers and is incorporated, or is suppressed, an unassertive working class is a universal characteristic of corporatism. The other component is "privatization," the entry into the government of private organizations in their representative capacity.

Neither corporatist nor pluralist governments do very much of this, hence the desperate search for access in the United States and the political risk of drift toward unresponsiveness and instability in Asia. The pluralist version of the process of inclusion is "capture theory," the pejorative term suggesting that a bureaucracy is a creature of its regulated clientele. There is no pluralist equivalent of an economic segment being a creature of the bureaucracy that created and controls it. Yet the growth of government-initiated interest groups is apparent in the United States, especially during the periodic cycles of increased domestic expenditures such as the New Deal and the Great Society. But if the programs fade away, so do the attendant organizations. The various urban groups created during the 1960's, for example, are gone. Corporatism offers more stability in government-interest group relations. Unlike such arrangements in corporatist countries, however, pluralism's bureaucratically sponsored groups do not necessarily enjoy a political advantage.

In the United States, fragmentation of responsibility for policy gives interest groups the opportunity to continue competing after a major loss in one arena. The infamous "iron triangles" have withstood presidential assaults by creating a coalition between bureaucracies and interest groups that is surely comparable to the formal agreements of corporatism. These policy networks keep to a limited agenda, but the comparison to corporatism is still apt.

Societal and state corporatism and pluralist governments are not distinguished by the extent to which the state intrudes into economic life; they are differentiated by the structure of the interaction between interest groups and governments. Although there is always talk of change, the stability of the various systems is more impressive. Sweden may lose some of its cohesion, Taiwan may become less authoritarian, and the United States may become more collaborative. But it is inconceivable that any of these countries will change more than incrementally. Political systems survive if they fit well with political culture. Pluralism, corporatism, and Confucianism are examples of the fit.

The durability of political systems frustrates those who believe that pluralism has run its course. Reich, a leading popular critic of the failure of governments to ignore narrow distributional coalitions, writes:

Since the late 1960's, America's economy has been slowly unraveling. The economic decline has been marked by growing unemployment, mounting business failures, and falling productivity. Since about the same

time America's politics have been in chronic disarray. The political decline has been marked by the triumph of narrow interest groups, the
demise of broad-based political parties, a succession of one term presidents, and a series of tax revolts.[16]

The faddish nature of this sort of writing is apparent. Until the
Reagan years, Japan's corporatism was extolled and the inability of
pluralist systems to resist interest groups was a rarely challenged
assumption. Reagan is not a one-term president and, while one
would hardly argue against the notion that interest groups are often
able to thwart change, even a cautious reappraisal suggests that
fragmentation is not as extreme as Reich would have us believe.
With Reagan in his second term and tax protests receding, there is
no reason to assume that the United States must adopt corporatism
or become a Japanese colony.[17] On the other hand, a dose of corporatist fiscal acumen might have prevented the spending orgies of
Presidents Johnson and Reagan, and the deficits their policies
induced.

With the United States leading the international recovery of
the last half of the 1980's, the talk has shifted from corporatism to
privatization (not the penetration of government into private lives,
but rather the shifting of enterprises from public to private ownership). Britain has been selling off huge publicly owned assets.
Brazil, Mexico, and Chile are attempting to transfer more responsibility to the private sector. Japan has ended state monopolies in
communications and intends to sell its transportation system. But
these changes also will not restructure the established process of
interest group intermediation; privatization does not disenfranchise
groups anointed by corporatist governments.

If pluralism does not lead ultimately to disarray, societal corporatism does not threaten individual freedom and democratic processes as much as its critics believe.[18] Corporatism does sanction
and sponsor, bestowing the mantle of legitimacy. But pluralism accomplishes the identical result simply by allowing the natural attrition of the market to take its toll. Membership turnover and
organizational demise are more characteristic of pluralist than of
corporatist systems. Because of the ferocity of the market, those few
interest groups that can stay alive and establish access are only

slightly less anointed than the officially sanctioned organizations of corporatism. In both systems, only a few interest groups achieve access or power. The major differences among pluralism, societal corporatism, and state corporatism are in the distribution of influence between the public and private sectors rather than in the range of groups efficiently represented. State and societal corporatism arrange organizations in hierarchies, effectively granting selective benefits by government decree. Pluralistic governments face more of an assault in the public arenas of politics, especially in the United States. But in a decade or so, the Business Roundtable will still be quietly going about its tasks, while this year's most visible political action committees will be forgotten. It is after all in the legislative process that the groups in hyper-pluralistic systems find their niche. Because of the independence of policy networks, pluralism suffers from a more decentralized policy process than do state or societal corporatist governments.

Since legislatures are largely reactive institutions, responding to initiatives originated in the executive branches, much of the hoopla about interest groups buying legislators is distant from the policy *initiation* process. In policy initiation, the bureaucratic advantage over interest groups is substantial. By representing as technical and complex as many items as possible, bureaucracies define resources in a way that enhances their position. Only those groups with the money to acquire equally reliable technical information can expect to become part of the immediate, everyday clientele of an agency. The proportion of active interest groups that can achieve a parity of influence with their bureaucratic regulators is very small, irrespective of the mode of conflict resolution.

So also is the presumed pluralist virtue of accountability largely inaccurate. Modern government, whether organized according to the dictates of pluralism or of state or societal corporatism, is complex. Elected legislatures have no option but to delegate substantial portions of the policy-making function to bureaucracies. Bureaucracies, in turn, have to come to grips with their clientele, even if there is no "legal" reason for doing so.[19] Even though the cultures included in this book are quite different, are not their similarities more striking? State corporatism—if Taiwan is a good example—can contribute to the economic development that triggers demands for democratization. Less paternalism and more participation are coming to Taiwan within the next decade. Japan's mode of interest intermediation rather than the societal corporatism of Western Europe will be emulated.

The distance between the three modes of conflict resolution will narrow. Since they are ideal types, and since actual governments lean sometimes in one direction, sometimes in another, the erosion of unequivocal differences will be hastened even more. Some even believe that both corporatism and pluralism, since they both require or allow people to relinquish their participatory rights to organizations, will become increasingly inappropriate for postindustrial society.[20] This utopianism seems wide of the mark. All developing or industrial societies accommodate themselves to interest groups. Rather than wishing them away, pragmatic adjustment might be a better way of governing. There are excesses to be avoided among those governments that lean toward the extremes of the continuum; perhaps the United States is the most serious example of excess. Elections are awash in a sea of interest group money; political parties are slipping further into oblivion.

Too much should not be made of these public displays of disarray.[21] After all, there are only limited amounts of change available, and bureaucracies go about the day-by-day task of governing without fear of destruction. In the United States, mass media have made far too much of an alleged "Reagan revolution." Beneath the hoopla about "getting the government off our backs," little movement in this direction can be discerned. The proportion of GNP attributable to governments was 32 percent in 1979 and 37 percent in 1985.[22] Even Reagan's own egregious assertions about individualism contain strong threads of societal corporatism. His message is as much for moral or political obligation as for excessive individualism, for setting aside group interests (narrow distributional coalitions) in favor of the common interest, the "larger contours of public acceptability." The final verdict will probably see the Reagan "revolution" as nothing more than an evolution, a reaffirmation of the "basic structure of federal domestic functions," and an attempt to "conserve a predominately status quo, middle-class welfare state."[23] This position is not out of synchronization with the general tenets of public opinion, which has consistently shown acceptance of the established domestic welfare programs. Reagan's election had nothing to do with his ideology; there was no "mandate" for Tory radicalism, and very little actual institutional change.[24]

According to Harold Wilensky, the time is ripe for a corporatist challenge, since he believes corporatism flourishes when other representative institutions fail. But the evidence of failure is not persuasive.[25] What appeared in the 1970's to be massive revulsion toward government institutions turned out to be a less serious or stable collection of attitudes. A more probable outcome is an inclination in all industrial societies toward the center, a position that is eminently sensible and in keeping with public preferences.

NOTES

Preface

1. See Sterling Seagrave, *The Soong Dynasty* (New York: Harper and Row, 1985), for a lively description of Chiang as arch-fiend.

2. Fernando Henrique Cardoso, "On the Characterization of Authoritarian Regimes in Latin America," in David Collier, ed., *The New Authoritarianism in Latin America* (Princeton, N.J.: Princeton University Press, 1979), p. 39. The reference to income distribution is taken to imply a drift toward inequality. However, the data suggest that that assumption is inaccurate. See Gary S. Fields, *Poverty, Inequality, and Development* Cambridge, Eng.: Cambridge University Press, 1980), pp. 182–244. Costa Rica also has a hefty state presence in the economy. After the 1948 civil war, the government nationalized banking, power, and communications. In the 1970's the government formed public corporations (about 130) to guide economic development. Unfortunately, many of the decisions have resulted in price distortion and erratic economic growth.

3. Fields, *Poverty, Inequality, and Development*, pp. 228, 237–238; emphasis in original.

4. See Edward N. Muller and Mitchell A. Seligson, "Inequality and Insurgency," *American Political Science Review* 81 (June, 1987): 443.

5. Republic of China, Executive Yuan, Directorate-General of Budget, Accounting, and Statistics, *Report on the Survey of Personal Income Distribution in Taiwan Area, Republic of China, 1983* (Taipei, 1984), p. 30; Republic of China, Executive Yuan, Research, Development, and Evaluation Yuan, *Annual Review of Government Administration* (Taipei, 1985).

6. Confucius himself had less impact than, say, Jesus Christ. There are no doctrinal disputes about Confucius' teaching as there are in Christianity, nor have there been wars between adherents of Confucianism and various kinds of unbelievers. There is no analog to the Crusades, the Reformation, or the Inquisition. Chinese themselves often refer to *fu-chia* (the teachings of wise men) rather than to Confucianism. Even so, Confucianism is attacked from the left, by those who believe it encourages a veneration of the hierarchical past. For example, Confu-

ties, the Ming (founded in 1368), was to Confucianism as the United States is to James Madison. During the Ming years, Confucianism was a clear doctrine developed and proposed by a self-conscious group of intellectuals who wished to arrest social decay and to establish rule by enlightened elites, much as did Plato. To blame Confucianism for authoritarian government is comparable to blaming St. Paul for the Spanish Inquisition. See John W. Dardesss, *Confucianism and Autocracy* (Berkeley: University of California Press, 1983), pp. 13–14. See also Julia Ching, *Confucianism and Christianity* (Tokyo: Kodansha International, 1977), pp. 8–12.

7. Robert T. Holt and John E. Turner, *The Political Basis of Economic Development* (New York: Van Nostrand, 1966). More recently, Barrington Moore has compared the U.S.A., the U.S.S.R., and China, only to conclude that their political processes and policy outputs are more similar than most of us have previously thought.

8. Peter Hall, *Governing the Economy* (Oxford: Polity Press, 1986).

Chapter One

1. Thomas Hobbes, *Leviathan* (1651; New York: Collier, 1962), p. 100.

2. Gabriel A. Almond and Sidney Verba, *The Civic Culture: Political Attitudes and Democracy in Five Nations* (Boston: Little, Brown, 1965), p. 245.

3. David Truman, *The Governmental Process* (New York: Knopf, 1951), p. 33.

4. The best of these studies are: Donald R. Matthews, *United States Senators and Their World* (New York: Vintage, 1960); Lester Milbrath, *The Washington Lobbyists* (Chicago: Rand McNally, 1963); and Raymond A. Bauer, Ithiel de Sola Pool, and Lewis A. Dexter, *American Business and Public Policy* (New York: Atherton, 1963).

5. Truman, *Governmental Process*, p. 34.

6. Mancur Olson, *The Logic of Collective Action: Public Goods and the Theory of Groups* (Cambridge, Mass.: Harvard University Press, 1965).

7. Truman, *Governmental Process*, p. 23.

8. Olson, *Logic of Collective Action*, p. 61.

9. See, for example, James Q. Wilson, *Political Organizations* (New York: Basic Books, 1973), p. 21.

10. David Marsh, "On Joining Interest Groups," *British Journal of Political Science* 6 (July, 1976): 265.

11. As Presley was not referring to economic gratification, it seems appropriate to acknowledge that Olson uses the word "utility" theoretically, to suggest nonmonetary incentives. However, his examples invariably are economic.

12. Wilson, *Political Organizations* p. 29.

13. Terry Moe, *The Organization of Interests* (Chicago: University of Chicago Press, 1980), and John Hansen, "The Political Economy of Group Membership," *American Political Science Review*, 79 (March, 1985): 79–96.

14. Moe, *Organization of Interests*, p. 218.

15. Hansen, "Political Economy," p. 86.

16. Truman, *Governmental Process*, p. 106.

17. Keith Poole and Harmon Zeigler, *Women, Public Opinion, and Politics* (New York: Longman, 1985).

18. Hansen, "Political Economy," p. 90.

19. *Ibid.*, p. 93.

20. Truman, *Governmental Process*, p. 67.

21. *Ibid.*, p. 68. Olson says "market forces work against any organization that operates only in a part of the market" (Olson, *Logic of Collective Action*, p. 67.

22. See Anthony Oberschall, *Social Conflict and Social Movements* (Englewood Cliffs, N.J.: Prentice-Hall, 1973).

23. Schmitter argues that Nazi Germany began to lose its corporatist tendencies after 1936. See Philippe C. Schmitter, "Still the Century of Corporatism?, *Review of Politics* 85 (Jan., 1974): 85–131.

24. Donald Share, "Corporatism and Public Policy: The Literature and Its Application to Southern Europe," unpublished paper, 1981, p. 13.

25. See, for example, Karl Bracher, "Problems of Parliamentary Democracy in Europe," in Stephen Graubard, ed., *A New Europe?* (Boston: Houghton Mifflin, 1964).

26. Alfred Stepan, *The State and Society: Peru in Comparative Perspective* (Princeton, N.J.: Princeton University Press, 1978), p. 7.

27. Schmitter, "Still the Century of Corporatism?," p. 104.

28. See James M. Malloy, ed., *Authoritarianism and Corporatism in Latin America* (Pittsburgh: University of Pittsburgh Press, 1977).

29. See Ruth Berins Collier and David Collier, "Inducements versus Constraints: Disaggregating Corporatism," *American Political Science Review* 73 (Dec., 1979): 967–986.

30. Schmitter, "Still the Century of Corporatism?," pp. 102–103.

31. Amos Perlmutter, *Modern Authoritarianism* (New Haven, Conn.: Yale University Press, 1981), p. 122. The association of corporatism with a particular ideology is even more unadorned and inaccurate in Howard and Donnelly's essay. They present corporatism as a "principal form of contemporary right-wing regimes" and state that, "whatever the form, corporatism denies inherent personal dignity and equal concern and respect in the very bargain that defines the regime." See Rhoda E. Howard and Jack Donnelly, "Human Dignity, Human Rights, and Political Regimes," *American Political Science Review* 80 (Sept., 1986): 811–812.

32. J. T. Winkler, "Corporatism," *Archives of European Sociology* 17 (1976): 103. Charles Maier argues that corporatism can be understood as a response to militant unionism. See Charles S. Maier, "Preconditions for Corporatism," in John H. Goldthorpe, ed., *Order and Conflict in Contemporary Capitalism* (Oxford: Clarendon Press, 1984), pp. 39–59.

33. Alan Cawson, "Pluralism, Corporatism, and the Role of the State," *Government and Opposition* 13 (Spring, 1978): 187–198.

34. See Robert Salisbury, "Why No Corporatism in America?," in Philippe C. Schmitter and Gerhard Lehmbruch, eds., *Trends Toward Corporatist Intermediation* (Beverly Hills, Calif.: Sage, 1979), pp. 213–230, and Graham K. Wilson, "Why Is There No Corporatism in the United States?," in Gerhard Lehmbruch and Philippe C. Schmitter, eds., *Patterns of Corporatist Policy-Making* (Beverly Hills, Calif.: Sage, 1982), pp. 219–236. Both essays reach the same conclusion:

the United States has no peak associations, a declining labor movement, and little inclination to engage in sophisticated economic planning.

35. Peter J. Williamson, *Varieties of Corporatism* (Cambridge, Eng.: Cambridge University Press, 1986), p. 67.

36. Antonio Marongiu, *Medieval Parliaments: A Comparative Study* (London: Eyre and Spottiswoode, 1968), pp. 53–56.

37. See R. G. Davies and J. H. Denton, eds., *The English Parliament in the Middle Ages* (Philadelphia: University of Pennsylvania Press, 1981).

38. Share, "Corporatism and Public Policy," p. 4.

39. However, two strong corporatist countries, Switzerland and Japan, have no such religious homogeneity.

40. See Malloy, ed., *Authoritarianism and Corporatism.*

41. See John Chubb, *Interest Groups and the Bureaucracy* (Stanford, Calif.: Stanford University Press, 1983), pp. 8–10, for a discussion.

42. Theodore Lowi, *The End of Liberalism: Ideology, Policy, and the Crisis of Public Authority* (New York: Norton, 1969), p. 78, and "The Public Philosophy: Interest Group Liberalism," *American Political Science Review* 61 (March, 1967): 5–24. The most recent surfacing of Lowi's thesis is in David Stockman's condemnation of the Reagan budget process as being responsive solely to group pressure and incapable of carrying out a rational spending reduction program, believed by Stockman—with unintended borrowing from Rousseau—to represent the General Will. See Stockman, *The Triumph of Politics* (New York: Harper and Row, 1986).

43. Mancur Olson, *The Rise and Decline of Nations* (New Haven, Conn.: Yale University Press, 1982).

44. *Ibid.*, p. 47.

45. Stepan, *State and Society*, p. 30.

46. John C. Calhoun, *A Disquisition on Government*, in Benjamin F. Wright, ed., *Source Book of American Political Theory* (New York: MacMillan, 1929), p. 537; and Truman, *Governmental Process*, p. 51. See also Grant McConnell, *Private Power and American Democracy* (New York: Knopf, 1966), pp. 336–368.

47. Richard H. Solomon, *Mao's Revolution and the Chinese Political Culture* (Berkeley: University of California Press, 1971), p. 67.

48. As early as 196 B.C. the Chinese public service was reserved for those who were "worthy and talented." See Johanna M. Menzel, ed., *The Chinese Civil Service: Career Open to Talent?* (Boston: Little, Brown, 1963), pp. 66–81; see also Michael Lowe, *Everyday Life in Early Imperial China* (New York: Harper and Row, 1968), pp. 113–117.

49. John Fairbank, *The United States and China* (Cambridge, Mass.: Harvard University Press, 1959), pp. 28–42.

50. Joseph R. Levenson, *Confucian China and Its Modern Fate* (Berkeley: University of California Press, 1965), p. 16. In practice, civil servants learned about politics and acquired the necessary expertise to manage a polity while simultaneously proclaiming the value of traditional education. See John R. Watt, *The District Magistrate in Late Imperial China* (New York: Columbia University Press, 1972).

51. See W. T. de Bary, "Chinese Despotism and the Confucian Ideal: A Seventeenth-Century View," in John K. Fairbank, ed., *Chinese Thought and Institutions* (Chicago: University of Chicago Press, 1957), pp. 163–203.

52. Lucian W. Pye, *Asian Power and Politics* (Cambridge, Mass.: Belknap Press of Harvard University Press, 1985), p. 63.

53. Max Weber was among the first to observe that social class and bureaucratic success were linked irrespective of the impartiality of entrance examinations. See *The Religion of China* (Glencoe, N.Y.: Free Press, 1951), p. 135. See also Robert M. Marsh, *The Mandarins: The Circulation of Elites in China, 1600–1900* (New York: Free Press, 1961), p. 185.

54. Robert H. Silin, *Leadership and Values: The Organization of Large-Scale Taiwanese Enterprises* (Cambridge, Mass.: Harvard University Press, 1976), p. 25.

55. Pye, *Asian Power and Politics*, p. 70.

56. Kahn provides an account of an eighteenth-century monarch who resolved a potential conflict about the use of a canal. His mother's imperial barge was given preference over a grain tribute fleet with the approval of local officials who stood to suffer economically. See Harold L. Kahn, *Monarchy in the Emperor's Eyes: Image and Reality in the Ch'ien-Lung Reign* (Cambridge, Mass.: Harvard University Press, 1971), p. 94.

57. Arthur Wright, "Introduction," in Wright, ed., *Confucianism and Chinese Civilization* (Stanford, Calif.: Stanford University Press, 1975), p. xi. There is a fair amount of Confucianism in the approach to conflict taken by students of public management such as March and Simon, who regard conflict as evidence of a "breakdown in standard mechanisms of decision making." See James March and Herbert Simon, *Organizations* (New York: Wiley, 1957).

58. Pye, *Asian Power and Politics*, p. 27.

59. Robert Darnton, *The Great Cat Massacre and Other Episodes in French Cultural History* (New York: Vintage, 1985), pp. 3–4.

60. Tu Wei-ming, Confucian Thought: Selfhood as Creative Transformation (Albany: State University of New York Press, 1985), p. 138.

61. *Ibid.*, p. 139.

62. In Taipei, in 1986, the city government prepared to build yet another statue of Confucius, but was resisted successfully by apartment dwellers who objected to the invasion of their privacy by the crowds such an edifice was expected to bring.

63. There are, however, pro- and anti-Confucian cliques in both the People's Republic and Taiwan. Confucius' hometown, Qufu, has recently been refurbished. On Taiwan, a leading anti-Confucian disciple of John Dewey, Hu Shih, is highly regarded.

64. I am grateful to Richard Kraus for calling my attention to these similarities.

Chapter Two

1. Robert Salisbury, "An Exchange Theory of Interest Groups," *Midwest Journal of Political Science* 12 (Feb., 1969): 1–32.

2. Jack L. Walker, "The Origins and Maintenance of Interest Groups in America," *American Political Science Review* 77 (June, 1983): 396.

3. This description relies on Andrew McFarland, *Common Cause* (Chatham, N.J.: Chatham House, 1984).

4. *Ibid.*, p. 196.

5. *Ibid.*, p. 196.

6. This account relies upon Barbara Sinclair Deckard, *The Women's Movement* (3rd ed.; New York: Harper and Row, 1983), pp. 321–325.

7. *Ibid.*, p. 324.

8. Walker, "Origins and Maintenance," p. 403.

9. James Q. Wilson, *Political Organizations* (New York: Basic Books, 1973), p. 151.

10. This section is drawn from Harmon Zeigler, *The Politics of Small Business* (Washington, D.C.: Public Affairs Press, 1961), and from comments on this book by Terry Moe, *The Organization of Interests* (Chicago: University of Chicago Press, 1980), p. 194, and Wilson, *Political Organizations*, pp. 162–163. The Small Business Administration is now the source of numerous scams and the target of much corruption.

11. See McFarland, *Common Cause*, p. 46.

12. Peter B. Clark and James Q. Wilson, "Incentive Systems: A Theory of Organizations," *Administrative Science Quarterly*, 6 (Sept., 1961): 219–266.

13. *Ibid.*, pp. 134–135.

14. See G. L. Kristianson, *The Politics of Patriotism* (Canberra: Australian National University Press, 1966).

15. See McFarland, *Common Cause*, pp. 7–19, for an account of the small group network associated with the founding of Common Cause.

16. Sara Evans, *Personal Politics* (New York: Vintage, 1980), p. 44.

17. Salisbury, "Exchange Theory," p. 19.

18. Walker, Origins and Maintenance," p. 394.

19. Robert A. Dahl and Edward R. Tufte, *Size and Democracy* (Stanford, Calif.: Stanford University Press, 1973), p. 39.

20. Truman's critics are incorrect on this point. Surveys reveal that few people belong to multiple organizations; hence overlapping membership is said to be a fiction. However, Truman did not intend to use membership as a synonym for formal affiliation, but rather as an example of conflicting attitudes, each based on possibly incompatible group loyalties.

21. Mancur Olson, *The Logic of Collective Action: Public Goods and the Theory of Groups* (Cambridge, Mass.: Harvard University Press, 1965), p. 20.

22. Harmon Zeigler and G. Wayne Peak, *Interest Groups in American Society* (2nd ed.; Englewood Cliffs, N.J.: Prentice-Hall, 1972), p. 20. Much of the argument that follows comes from this source.

23. Murray Edelman, "Symbols and Political Quiescence," *American Political Science Review*, 54 (Sept., 1960): 701.

24. Walker, "Origins and Maintenance," p. 403.

25. David Truman, *The Governmental Process* (New York: Knopf, 1951), pp. 164–180.

26. William H. Riker, *The Theory of Political Coalitions* (New Haven, Conn.: Yale University Press, 1962).

27. Henry Kariel, *The Decline of American Pluralism* (Stanford, Calif.: Stanford University Press, 1961).

28. Roberto Michels, *Political Parties* (1911; New York: Free Press, 1962).

29. Andrew McFarland believes that a 20 percent negative response to a Common Cause survey is enough to kill a leadership proposed initiative. See McFarland, *Common Cause*, p. 98.

30. *Ibid.*, p. 106.

31. Harmon Zeigler, "Interest Groups in the States," in Virginia Gray, Herbert Jacob, and Kenneth Vines, eds., *Politics in the American States* (4th ed.; Boston: Little, Brown, 1983), pp. 125–126.

32. Moe, *Organization of Interests*, p. 216.

33. *Common Cause News*, April 7, 1987, p. 7.

34. See John R. Wright, "PACs, Contributions, and Roll Calls: An Organizational Perspective," *American Political Science Review* 79 (June, 1985): 400–414, for an excellent analysis of PAC organization.

35. Sar Levitin and Martha R. Cooper, *Business Lobbies: The Public Good and the Bottom Line* (Baltimore: Johns Hopkins University Press, 1984), p. 19.

36. Claus Offe, "Two Logics of Collective Action," in John Keane, ed., *Disorganized Capitalism* (Cambridge, Eng.: Cambridge University Press, 1985), p. 193.

37. Graham K. Wilson, *Business and Politics: A Comparative Introduction* (Chatham, N.J.: Chatham House, 1985), p. 33.

38. See Thomas Byrne Edsall, *The New Politics of Inequality* (New York: Norton, 1984), pp. 125–127.

39. Raymond A. Bauer, Ithiel de Sola Pool, and Lewis A. Dexter, *American Business and Public Policy* (New York: Atherton, 1963).

40. Salisbury, "Exchange Theory," pp. 1–32.

41. Walker, "Origins and Maintenance," p. 396.

42. Norman Luttbeg and Harmon Zeigler, "Attitude Consensus and Conflict in an Interest Group: An Assessment of Cohesion," *American Political Science Review* 60 (Sept., 1966): 655–666.

43. Harmon Zeigler and Keith Poole, "Political Woman: Gender Indifference," *Public Opinion*, Aug./Sept., 1985, pp. 48–62.

44. Moe, *Organization of Interests*, p. 208.

45. Jeffrey M. Berry, *The Interest Group Society* (Boston: Little, Brown, 1984), p. 124. See also Berry, *Lobbying for the People* (Princeton, N.J.: Princeton University Press, 1977).

Chapter Three

1. For a good account of the problems encountered, see Donald Share, "Corporatism and Public Policy: The Literature and Its Application to Southern Europe," unpublished paper, 1981.

2. Philippe C. Schmitter, "Still the Century of Corporatism?," *Review of Politics* 85 (Jan., 1974): 85–131.

3. See Gabriel Almond, "Corporatism, Pluralism, and Professional Memory," *World Politics* 35 (1983): 245–260, for a discussion of these problems.

4. *Ibid.*, p. 23.

5. *Ibid.*, p. 26.

6. *Ibid.*, p. 27.

7. Charles Lindblom, *Politics and Markets* (New York: Basic Books, 1977), pp. 185–189.

8. Andrew Shonfield, *Modern Capitalism: The Changing Balance of Public and Private Power* (London: Oxford University Press, 1965), p. 161.

9. Michael Watson, "Conclusion: A Comparative Evaluation of Planning Practice in the Liberal Democratic State," in Jack Hayward and Michael Watson, eds., *Planning, Politics, and Public Policy: The British, French, and Italian Experience* (Cambridge, Eng.: Cambridge University Press, 1975), p. 477.

10. Share, "Corporatism and Public Policy," p. 28.

11. Gerhard Lehmbruch, "Liberal Corporatism and Party Government," *Comparative Political Studies* 10 (April, 1977): 91–126.

12. See John Kenneth Galbraith, *The Anatomy of Power* (Boston: Houghton Mifflin, 1983), p. 87.

13. John Rawls, *A Theory of Justice* (Cambridge, Mass.: Harvard University Press, 1971).

14. Leo Panitch, "The Development of Corporatism in Liberal Democracies," *Comparative Political Studies*, 10 (April, 1977): 73.

15. The phrase, "social contract," is used by Share with appropriate irony. See Share, "Corporatism and Public Policy," p. 28.

16. Panitch, "Development of Corporatism," p. 86.

17. The following make the argument most completely: Robert Jackman, *Politics and Inequality* (New York: Wiley, 1975); Bruce Russett, "Inequality and Instability: The Relation of Land Tenure to Politics," *World Politics* 16 (1964): 442–454, and Jack Nagel, "Inequality and Discontent: A Nonlinear Hypothesis," *World Politics*, 26 (1974): 453–472.

18. David Collier and Ruth Berins Collier, "Who Does What, to Whom, and How," in James M. Malloy, ed., *Authoritarianism and Corporatism in Latin America* (Pittsburgh: University of Pittsburgh Press, 1977), p. 498.

19. See Graham K. Wilson, *Business and Politics: A Comparative Introduction* (Chatham, N.J.: Chatham House, 1985); Philippe C. Schmitter, "Reflections on Where the Theory of Neo-Corporatism Has Gone and Where the Praxis of Neo-Corporatism May Be Going," in Gerhard Lehmbruch and Philippe C. Schmitter, eds., *Patterns of Corporatist Policy-Making* (Beverly Hills, Calif.: Sage, 1982), p. 271; Lehmbruch, "Liberal Corporatism and Party Government," pp. 91–126.

20. Claus Offe, "The Attribution of Public Status to Interest Groups: Observations on the West German Case," in Suzanne Berger, ed., *Organized Interests in Western Europe: Pluralism, Corporatism, and the Transformation of Politics* (Cambridge, Eng.: Cambridge University Press, 1981), p. 143.

21. Schmitter, "Reflections,", pp. 271–273.

22. Brian Barry, "Does Democracy Cause Inflation?: Political Ideas of Some Economists," in Leon L. Lindberg and Charles S. Maier, eds., *The Politics of Inflation and Stagnation* (Washington, D.C.: Brookings Institution, 1985), pp. 280–317. See also Scott Lash, "The End of Neo-Corporatism?: The Breakdown of Centralized Bargaining in Sweden," *British Journal of Industrial Relations* 23 (July, 1985): 216–239.

23. Walter Korpi, *The Democratic Class Struggle* (London: Routledge and Kegan Paul, 1983), pp. 13–19.

24. Peter J. Williamson, *Varieties of Corporatism* (Cambridge, Eng.: Cambridge University Press, 1986), p. 34.

25. T. J. Pempel and Keiichi Tsunekawa, "Corporatism Without Labor?: The Japanese Anomaly," in Schmitter and Lehmbruch, eds., *Trends Toward Corporatist Intermediation*, pp. 231–269.

26. See David Halberstam, *The Reckoning* (New York: Morrow, 1986), pp. 153–188.

27. Robert Reich, *The Next American Frontier* (New York: Times Books, 1983); Ezra Vogel, *Japan as Number One* (Cambridge, Mass.: Harvard University Press, 1979).

28. Mancur Olson, *The Rise and Decline of Nations* (New Haven, Conn.: Yale University Press, 1982).

29. *Ibid.*, p. 47. Olson's data are drawn most often from the American states, while his generalizations are about nations, a curiosity that appears to have escaped notice.

30. See James Buchanan, *The Limits of Liberty* (Chicago: University of Chicago Press, 1975).

31. See Scott Lash, "The End of Neo-Corporatism?," pp. 216–239; see also Agne Gustafsson, "Rise and Decline of Nations: Sweden," *Scandinavian Political Studies* 9 (1986): 35–50.

32. See Mancur Olson, "A Theory of the Incentives Facing Political Organizations: Neo-Corporatism and the Hegemonic State," *International Political Science Review* 7 (1986): 165–189.

33. Olson, *Rise and Decline*, pp. 36–71.

34. Offe, "Attribution of Public Status to Interest Groups."

35. Manfred Schmidt, "Does Corporation Matter?," in Lehmbruch and Schmitter, eds., *Patterns of Corporatist Policy-Making*, pp. 252–256. This classification is similar to Schmitter's, at least with regard to the strong corporatist states. See Philippe C. Schmitter, "Interest Intermediation and Regime Governability in Contemporary Western Europe and North America," in Berger, ed., *Organizing Interests*, p. 294. But different criteria can produce different results. Colin Crouch places Japan in a weak corporatism category, on the basis of its uncoordinated labor-management relations. However, few would agree with this assessment. See Colin Crouch, "Conditions for Trade Union Wage Restraint," in Leon N. Lindberg and Charles S. Maier, eds., *The Politics of Inflation and Economic Stagnation* (Washington, D.C.: Brookings Institution, 1985), p. 116.

36. Heady had previously shown a strong relationship between a strong labor/socialist coalition and incomes policy. See Bruce W. Heady, "Trade Unions and National Wage Policies," *Journal of Politics*, 32 (May, 1970): 407–439.

37. Schmidt, "Does Corporatism Matter?," p. 257.

38. The use of strike volume as a measure of corporatism is especially troublesome, for it allows the definition to be part of the measurement. See Andrew Cox, "Corporatism as Reductionism: The Analytic Limits of the Corporatist Thesis," *Government and Opposition* 81 (Winter, 1982): 85–87. Even so, Schmidt is less "reductionist" than Schmitter, who has operationalized corporatism *exclusively* by the proportion of the work force in unions and the extent of centralism in union organization. See Almond, "Corporatism, Pluralism, and Professional Memory," p. 259, for an appraisal.

39. Kerry Schott, *Policy, Power, and Order* (New Haven, Conn.: Yale University Press, 1984), pp. 173–177.

40. The indicator of ideology, developed by Schmidt, consists of the proportion of cabinet seats held by social-democratic and left-wing parties, during the years from 1974 through 1978. The range of scores runs from 5 ("bourgeois hegemony") to 1 ("social-democratic hegemony"), with gradations between. See Schmidt, "Does Corporatism Matter?," p. 256. I extended the data to 1986, resulting in some changes in the original rankings. France dropped from "bourgeois hegemony" to "bourgeois dominance"; the Federal Republic of Germany changed from "social-democratic dominance" to a "balance."

41. Heidenheimer, Heclo, and Adams record the "left-wing vote" in the United States as 0, compared with an average of 33 percent in the other twenty countries. See Arnold J. Heidenheimer, Hugh Heclo, and Carolyn Teich Adams, *Comparative Public Policy* (2nd ed.; New York: St. Martin's, 1983), p. 156.

42. Thomas R. Dye, *Politics, Economics, and the Public* (Chicago: Rand Mc-Nally, 1966).

43. Gabriel Almond and Bingham Powell, *Comparative Politics: A Developmental Approach* (Boston: Little, Brown, 1966).

44. Susan B. Hansen, "Public Policy Analysis: Some Recent Developments and Current Problems," in Ada W. Finifter, ed., *Political Science: The State of the Discipline* (Washington, D.C.: American Political Science Association, 1983), p. 221.

45. Francis G. Castles, ed., *The Impact of Parties* (Beverly Hills, Calif.: Sage, 1982).

46. *Ibid.*, p. 15. He regards multivariate analysis as "too ambitious" given a "limited universe of discourse." Yet uncomplicated multivariate analysis for small samples is readily available, and significance tests for partial correlation (using n-2 for degrees of freedom) go down to 5.

47. In the tables and analyses that follow, corporatism will be used in combination with ideology, wealth, and labor in each multiple regression. Occasionally, these core variables will be supplemented with other appropriate ones.

48. Philippe C. Schmitter, "Still the Century of Corporatism?," *Review of Politics* 36 (Jan., 1974): 85–131.

49. I use an ethnic and homogeneity index devised by the Soviet Academy of Sciences and reproduced in George Thomas Kurian, *The New Book of World Rankings* (New York: Facts on File, 1984), pp. 48–49. It ranges from 7 (Tanzania), the least homogeneous, to 100 (North Korea), the most homogeneous.

50. I excluded the data on days lost to strikes, since it is a component of the corporatism index. The correlation with growth is trivial.

51. The use of longer-term data (1960–1982) did not appreciably change the general conclusion.

52. Because the n is small, although no smaller than is customary in studies of corporatism, I have used two measures of significance: the traditional one and Students T, less vulnerable to distortion with small samples.

53. Olson, *Rise and Decline*, p. 150.

54. The correlation between the ratio and proportion of GNP explained by government spending is .90.

55. Schmidt believes that Switzerland and Japan are unlike the other corporatist countries in that their corporatism is "private," yet is the functional equivalent of the more interventionist forms of corporatism. Schmidt, "Does Corporatism Matter?," p. 257.

56. Olson, "A Theory of Incentives," p. 187.

57. Olson, *Rise and Decline*, pp. 90, 91.

58. The ratio of total work force to strike days.

Chapter Four

1. Graham K. Wilson, *Business and Politics: A Comparative Introduction* (Chatham, N.J.: Chatham House, 1985), pp. 110, 113.

2. Philippe C. Schmitter, "Interest Intermediation and Regime Governability in Contemporary Western Europe and North America," in Berger, ed., *Organized Interests*, pp. 285–327.

3. Manfred Schmidt, "Does Corporatism Matter?," in Gerhard Lehmbruch and Philippe C. Schmitter, eds., *Patterns of Corporatist Policy-Making* (Beverly Hills, Calif.: Sage, 1982), pp. 244–256.

4. Francis G. Castles, ed., *The Impact of Parties* (Beverly Hills, Calif.: Sage, 1982).

5. Richard Rose, *Do Parties Make a Difference?* (2nd ed.; Chatham, N.J.: Chatham House, 1982), pp. 142–188.

6. Peter Hall, *Governing the Economy* (Oxford: Polity Press, 1986).

7. Rose, *Do Parties Make a Difference?*, p. 142.

8. Concerning the confusion on this issue, Schmidt concludes that "it is interesting to note, however, that the strength of the socialist milieu (measured by the left-wing vote) always varies inversely with the rate of unemployment" Schmidt, "Does Corporatism Matter?," p. 241).

9. *Ibid.*, p. 252.

10. David Cameron, "Social Democracy, Corporatism, Labour Quiescence, and the Representation of Economic Interests in Advanced Capitalist Society," in John H. Goldthorpe, ed., *Order and Conflict in Contemporary Capitalism* (Cambridge, Eng.: Cambridge University Press, 1985), pp. 144–178.

11. Hall, *Governing the Economy*, p. 80.

12. Robert Reich, *The Next American Frontier* (New York: Times Books, 1983), p. 15.

13. Both Olson and Reich agree that Britain is the best example of "institutional sclerosis." See Mancur Olson, *The Rise and Decline of Nations* (New Haven, Conn.: Yale University Press, 1982), p. 80.

14. Richard J. Estes and John Morgan, *The Social Progress of Nations* (New York: Praeger, 1984).

15. Michael Don Ward, *The Political Economy of Distribution* (New York: Elsevier, 1978), p. 181. The inequality index is a summary of: the Hibbs Z-score, which uses infant mortality, the number of doctors per 10,000 inhabitants, and the percentage of daily kilocalories per capita (HIBBZSCR); two inequality indexes based on the ratio of poverty to affluence (INEQ1, INEQ2); a measure of social mobility (SOCMOB); and the Gini index (GININDIV). The formula, with weights derived from factor loadings is: INEQUAL = .68 [INEQ2] + .75 [SOCMOB] + .98 [HIBBSZSCR] + .85 [INEQ1] + .60 [GININDIV] / D where D = number of missing cases for each variable, standardized.

16. Peter Katzenstein, *Small States in World Markets* (Ithaca, N.Y.: Cornell University Press, 1985), pp. 246–247.

17. Leo Panitch, "The Development of Corporatism in Liberal Democracies," *Comparative Political Studies* 10 (April 1977): pp. 67–68.

18. See the conclusions to Robert Jackman, "Socialist Parties and Income Inequality in Western Industrial Societies," *Journal of Politics*, 32 (May, 1970): pp. 135–149.

19. Ward, *Political Economy of Distribution*, pp. 44–45.

20. Corina M. Van Arnhem and Geurt J. Schotsman, "Do Parties Affect the Distribution of Incomes?: The Case of Advanced Capitalist Democracies," in Castles, ed., *The Impact of Parties*, pp. 332–352. This article argues that Gini indexes are lower in corporatist countries. But the article uses bivariate analysis with an n of 10, and defines corporatism on the single dimension of union centralization.

21. This account is taken from Gerhard Lehmbruch, "Liberal Corporatism and Party Government," *Comparative Political Studies* 10 (April, 1977): 91–126.

22. Katzenstein, *Small States*, p. 247.

23. See Thomas D. Lancaster and Gary Prevost, eds., *Politics and Change in Spain* (New York: Praeger, 1985), and Donald Share, "Spanish Economic Development: Delayed Development, Francoist Economic Policy, and Revolution from Above," Master's Thesis, Stanford University 1978, for discussions of economic problems related to authoritarian governments.

24. Lester C. Thurow, "A Surge in Inequality," *Scientific American*, May, 1987, p. 30. My italics.

25. Rose, *Do Parties Make a Difference?*, p. 133. See also W. D. Rubinstein, *Wealth and Inequality in Britain* (London: Faber and Faber, 1986), and David M. Smith, *Where the Grass Is Greener* (London: Penguin, 1979).

26. Schmitter, in "Interest Intermediation," puts forth the argument that corporatist governments avoid excessive "fiscal ineffectiveness."

27. Kerry Schott, *Policy, Power, and Order* (New Haven, Conn.: Yale University Press, 1984), p. 56.

28. Most still believe Sweden is free of strikes. See Walter Korpi, *The Working Class in Welfare Capitalism: Work, Unions, and Politics in Sweden* (London: Routledge and Kegan Paul, 1978), and Steven Kelman, *Regulating America, Regulating Sweden* (Cambridge, Mass.: MIT Press, 1981), for the old view, and Anders Leion, "Sweden," in B. C. Roberts, ed., *Industrial Relations in Europe: The Imperatives of Change* (London: Croom, Helm, 1985), pp. 204–221, for the revisionist view. See also Andrew Martin, "Wages, Profits, and Investment in Sweden," in Leon L. Lindberg and Charles S. Maier, eds., *The Politics of Inflation and Economic Stagnation* (Washington, D.C.: Brookings Institution, 1985), pp. 403–466.

29. Agne Gustafsson, "Rise and Decline of Nations: Sweden," *Scandinavian Political Studies* 9 (1986): 41.

30. Scott Lash, "The End of Neo-Corporatism?: The Breakdown of Centralized Bargaining in Sweden," *British Journal of Industrial Relations* 23 (July, 1985): 225–235.

31. Philippe C. Schmitter, "Still the Century of Corporatism?," *Review of Politics* 85 (Jan., 1974): 90.

32. *Ibid.*, p. 76.

33. Wilson, *Business and Politics*, p. 111.

34. Hugh Heclo and Henrik Madsen, *Policy and Politics in Sweden: Principled Pragmatism* (Philadelphia: Temple University Press, 1986), p. 316. This conclusion reminds us, again, of the imprecision of measures of corporatism. Possibly, Heclo and Madsen's argument could be made about each of the countries considered here. We are in dire need of a systematic, empirical assessment of corporatism. The arguments advanced in this chapter should be examined more exhaustively with a larger universe and more precise measurement. They are intended as suggestions, rather than conclusions.

35. Ulf Jacobsson, "Economic Growth in Sweden," in Arnold C. Harberger, ed., *World Economic Growth* (San Francisco: Institute for Contemporary Studies, 1984), pp. 59–94.

36. See Donald Share, "Spanish Economic Development."

37. Gary Prevost, "The Spanish Labor Movement," in Lancaster and Prevost, eds., *Politics and Change in Spain*, pp. 124–143.

38. Boetsch sums up the influence of the Spanish church: "Since the death of Franco in 1975 and throughout the transition toward a plural democracy, the Spanish church has played a critical and influential role. The degree of its influ-

ence stems from historical, political, and social factors, but its ability to act decisively and to command the respect of groups all along the political spectrum in
large part owes to its seasoning during the tumultuous decade [1965–1975]." See
Laurent Boetsch, "The Church in Spanish Politics," in Lancaster and Prevost,
eds., *Politics and Change in Spain*, p. 150.

39. See Howard R. Penniman and Eusebio M. Mujal-Leon, eds., *Spain at the
Polls, 1977, 1979, and 1982* (Durham, N.C.: Duke University Press, 1985). See
also Donald Share, *The Making of Spanish Democracy* (New York: Praeger, 1986).

40. Takeshi Ishida, "The Development of Interest Groups and the Pattern of
Political Modernization in Japan," in Robert E. Ward, ed., *Political Development in
Modern Japan* (Princeton, N.J.: Princeton University Press, 1968), p. 302.

41. Robert A. Scalapino, "Elections in Prewar Japan," in Ward, ed., *Political
Development in Modern Japan*, p. 283.

42. Lucian W. Pye, *China: An Introduction* (Boston: Little, Brown, 1972),
p. 30.

43. Michio Morishima, *Why Has Japan Succeeded?* (Cambridge, Eng.: Cambridge University Press, 1982), p. 60.

44. Schmitter, "Interest Intermediation," p. 293. However, Almond's critique
brings these conclusions into question. See Gabriel Almond, "Corporatism, Pluralism, and Professional Memory," *World Politics* 35 (1983): 245–260.

45. Schmitter, "Interest Intermediation," p. 93. Similar arguments are made
in Ted Gurr and Raymond Duval, "Civil Conflict in the 1960's: A Complete
Theoretical System with Parameter Estimates," *Comparative Political Studies* 6
(1973): 135–170, and Bruce Russett, "Inequality and Instability: The Relation of
Land Tenure to Politics," *World Politics* 16 (1964): 442–454.

46. Executive transfers, as defined in *The World Handbook of Political and
Social Indicators*, include both "regular" transfers, those that occur as a result of
elections, parliamentary votes of no confidence, or any other removal mechanism
common to a given political system. "Irregular" transfers are those resulting
from coups, insurrections, or revolutions. See Charles Lewis Taylor and David
A. Jodice, *World Handbook of Political and Social Indicators* (3rd ed.; New
Haven, Conn.: Yale University Press, 1983), vol. 2, pp. 79–105.

47. Ward, *Political Economy of Distribution*. Using the percentage of income
accruing to the top quintile, Muller and Seligson determine that income inequality is a reliable predictor of political violence. See Edward N. Muller and Mitchell
A. Seligson, "Inequality and Insurgency," *American Political Science Review* 81
(June, 1987): 426–429.

48. Douglas Hibbs, "Macroeconomic Policy and Political Parties," *American
Political Science Review* 73 (1979): 1467–1487; James Payne, "Inflation, Unemployment, and Left Wing Parties: A Reanalysis," *American Political Science Review*, 73
(1979): 181–185. Schmitter, in "Interest Intermediation," pp. 315–316, finds a
correlation between governability and the success of left-wing parties.

49. Schmitter, "Interest Intermediation," p. 321.

50. Colin Crouch, "Conditions for Trade Union Wage Restraint," in Leon
N. Lindberg and Charles S. Maier, eds., *The Politics of Inflation and Economic
Stagnation* (Washington, D.C.: Brookings Institution, 1985), p. 137.

51. Peter Katzenstein, "Small Nations in an Open International Economy:
The Converging Balance of State and Society in Switzerland and Austria, "in
Peter B. Evans, Dietrich Rueschemeyer, and Theda Skocpol, eds., *Bringing the
State Back In* (Cambridge, Eng.: Cambridge University Press, 1986), p. 227.

Austria—under Olson's scrutiny—is the poor relation of Europe, while here it is compared with Switzerland, the wealthiest country in Europe and, excluding an emirate or two, the world.

52. But surely some more precision or at least consistency would be helpful. In his introduction to *Patterns of Corporatist Policy-Making*, Lehmbruch regards Great Britain as an example of "medium" corporatism; in his essay in the same volume, Schmidt classifies the United Kingdom as "weak."

53. Hall, *Governing the Economy*, p. 269.

54. Possibly these countries might fit into Peter Williamson's "authoritarian-licensed" regimes. In this category, the state authorizes intermediary groups to cooperate in sustaining the social, political, and economic order but with a greater role for the state than is true in societal corporatism. See Peter J. Williamson, *Varieties of Corporatism* (Cambridge, Eng.: Cambridge University Press, 1986), p. 10.

55. Alan Cawson, "Introduction: Varieties of Corporatism: The Importance of the Meso-Level of Interest Intermediation," in Cawson, ed., *Organized Interests and the State* (Beverly Hills, Calif.: Sage, 1985), p. 9.

56. *Ibid.*, p. 11. The role of the state in establishing rules of exchange is discussed in Wolfgang Streek and Philippe C. Schmitter, "Community, Market, State—and Associations?: The Prospective Contribution of Interest Governance to Social Order," in Streek and Schmitter, eds., *Private Interest Government* (Beverly Hills, Calif.: Sage, 1986), pp. 1–29. See also Gerhard Lehmbruch, "Concertation and the Structure of Corporatist Networks," in Goldthorpe, ed., *Order and Conflict*, pp. 61–79.

57. This categorization resembles that of Katzenstein's. He distinguishes between "social corporatism" (centralized, cohesive labor organizations and weak and decentralized business associations) and "liberal corporatism" (strong, centralized business associations and decentralized labor organizations) (Katzenstein, *Small States*). See also Cameron, "Social Democracy," pp. 143–178.

58. Hall, *Governing the Economy*, p. 270.

59. Eric A. Nordlinger, *On the Autonomy of the Democratic State* (Cambridge, Mass.: Harvard University Press, 1981), pp. 168–170.

60. Harmon Zeigler, "Interest Groups and Public Policy: A Comparative, Revisionist Perspective," in Roger Scott, ed., *Interest Groups and Public Policy: Case Studies from the Australian States* (Melbourne: Macmillan of Australia, 1980), pp. 6–8.

61. Olson is especially hard on Australia, asking if any of his readers outside of Australia and its environs have ever purchased anything made there. He blames its protectionist tariff policy as much as its unions. But Japan, a hero country to Olson, has angered even its Asian neighbors by its protectionism. See Olson, p. 136. Treasurer Paul Keating, noting his country's continuing balance of payment problems, worried that Australia might become a "banana republic" if it continued to negotiate wages upward with the Australian Council of Trade Unions. See Hamish McDonald, "Down Under in a Hole," *Far Eastern Economic Review*, May 29, 1986, pp. 99–101.

62. See T. J. Pempel, "The Bureaucratization of Policymaking in Postwar Japan," *American Journal of Political Science* 18 (1974): 664.

63. See Wilson, *Business and Politics*, pp. 101–102.

64. Ruth Berins Collier and David Collier, "Inducements versus Constraints: Disaggregating 'Corporatism,' " *American Political Science Review* 73 (Dec., 1979): 967–986.

Chapter Five

1. T. J. Pempel and Keiichi Tsunekawa, "Corporatism Without Labor?: The Japanese Anomaly," in Philippe C. Schmitter and Gerhard Lehmbruch, eds., *Trends Toward Corporatist Intermediation* (Beverly Hills, Calif.: Sage, 1974), pp. 231–269.

2. For that matter, Mancur Olson's *The Rise and Decline of Nations* (New Haven, Conn.: Yale University Press, 1982) ignores corporatism, and the Europeans reciprocated until 1985. See Scott Lash, "The End of Neo-Corporatism?: The Breakdown of Centralized Bargaining in Sweden," *British Journal of Industrial Relations* 23 (July, 1985): pp. 215–239; see also Agne Gustafsson, "Rise and Decline of Nations: Sweden," *Scandinavian Political Studies*, 9 (1986): pp. 35–50.

3. James C. Hsiung, "East Asia," in Hsiung, ed., *Human Rights in East Asia: A Cultural Perspective* (New York: Paragon House, 1985), p. 7.

4. Barbara Crossette, "An Added Element in Asia: Confucianism," *New York Times*, June 5, 1987, p. 13.

5. H. G. Creel, *Confucius and the Chinese Way* (New York: Harper and Row, 1949), p. 256.

6. Leonard Shihlien Hsu, *The Political Philosophy of Confucianism* (London: Curzon, 1975), p. 176.

7. Pierre Do-dinh, *Confucius and Chinese Humanism* (New York: Funk and Wagnals, 1969).

8. Lucian W. Pye, *Asian Power and Politics* (Cambridge, Mass.: Harvard University Press, 1985), p. 55; Hsiung, "East Asia," p. 6.

9. Herman Kahn, *World Economic Development: 1979 and Beyond* (Boulder, Colo.: Westview, 1979), p. 118.

10. *Ibid.*, p. 121. Wu Teh-yao believes that the purest forms of Confucianism are found in Taiwan, Japan, and South Korea. See Crossette, "An Added Element."

11. Max Weber, *The Religion of China* (Glencoe, N.Y.: Free Press, 1951).

12. The Confucian abhorrence for commerce is similar to the presumed distaste of British old wealth for the industrial upper class. As we will see, on Taiwan public service is of greater prestige than private business, and hence government employment is controlled by the "mainlanders," while native Taiwanese control the economy.

13. Roderick MacFarquhar, "The Post-Confucian Challenge," *The Economist* (Feb. 9, 1980), pp. 67–72. The strongest case against Weber is Thomas Metzger, *Escape from Predicament: Neo Confucianism and China's Evolving Political Culture* (New York: Columbia University Press, 1977).

14. Peter L. Berger, *The Capitalist Revolution: Fifty Propositions About Prosperity, Equality, and Liberty* (New York: Basic Books, 1986), p. 158. Berger echoes with approval Robert Bellah's term, "Bourgeois Confucianism."

15. Richard H. Solomon, *Mao's Revolution and the Chinese Political Culture* (Berkeley: University of California Press, 1971), pp. 92–93.

16. Pye, *Asian Power and Politics*, p. 254.

17. *Ibid.*, p. 55.

18. *Ibid.*, p. 59; Hsiung, "East Asia," p. 8.

19. Hung Chao-tai, "Taiwan," in Hsiung, ed., *Human Rights in East Asia*, p. 90.

20. The analogy is in Michio Morishima, *Why Has Japan Succeeded?* (Cambridge, Eng.: Cambridge University Press, 1982), pp. 7–14.

21. Chalmers Johnson, "Political Institutions and Economic Performance: The Government-Business Relationship in Japan, South Korea, and Taiwan," in Robert Scalapino, S. Sato, and J. Wanadi, eds., *Asian Economic Development— Present and Future* (Berkeley: Institute of East Asian Studies, University of California, 1985), p. 70.

22. Pye, *Asian Power and Politics*, p. 216.

23. Ilpyong Kim, "South Korea," in Hsiung, ed., *Human Rights in East Asia*, p. 70. It is typical of Confucianism that it was judged relevant for the riots in South Korea in 1987. As the students were taking to the streets, a Confucian scholar reminded his readers of the possibility of losing the people's trust and hence the right to rule. An analog would have been for American intellectuals to urge a return to Edmund Burke, or Rousseau, during the riots of the 1960's and 1970's. See Crossette, "An Added Element." The strongest statement alleging Confucianism and authoritarianism are not necessarily the same is Metzger, *Escape from Predicament*, pp. 45–46.

24. Hung, "Taiwan," p. 100. Hu is also active in the reformist wing of the party.

25. Martial law was replaced by a civil code, with legislative approval taking place in June, 1987.

26. Pye, *Asian Power and Politics*, p. 232.

27. *Ibid.*

28. *Ibid.*, p. 254. See also Chan Heng Chee, "The Political System and Political Change," in Riaz Hassan, ed., *Singapore: Society in Transition* (London: Oxford University Press, 1976), pp. 30–51. Another interesting difference between Taiwan and Singapore concerns the family. Singapore's Prime Minister Lee accepts the controversial viewpoint popularized by William Shockley, that intelligence is inherited. People who do not graduate from a university are given inducements to be sterilized, while university graduates are given incentives to have large families. These two programs are undertaken to avoid "genetic deterioration." It is unlikely that Taiwan would give such programs much attention. The only interference in families is the law providing for equal distribution of estates when parents die. See *U.S. News and World Report*, April 13, 1987, p. 62.

29. *New York Times*, Feb. 11, 1985, p. A5. Earlier accounts, using Western standards, spoke, erroneously, of a "sweeping victory."

30. *New York Times*, Aug. 14, 1985, p. A13.

31. See Chapter One.

32. See John F. H. Purcell and Susan Kaufman Purcell, "Mexican Business and Public Policy," in James M. Malloy, ed., *Authoritarianism and Corporatism in Latin America* (Pittsburgh: University of Pittsburgh Press, 1977), pp. 191–226; Alice H. Amsden, "The State and Taiwan's Economic Development," in Peter B. Evans, Dietrich Rueschemeyer, and Theda Skocpol, eds., *Bringing the State Back In* (Cambridge, Eng.: Cambridge University Press, 1986), pp. 78–105; Stephen B. Wickman, "The Economy," in Frederica M. Bunge, ed., *South Korea: A Country*

Study (Washington, D.C.: U.S. Army, 1981), pp. 107–158; Edward S. Mason, Mahn Je Kim, Dwight H. Perkins, Kwang Suk Jim, and David C. Cole, *The Economic and Social Modernization of Korea* (Cambridge, Mass.: Harvard University Press, 1980), pp. 244–294, and T. J. S. George, *Lee Kuan Yew's Singapore* (London: Deutsch, 1973), chs. 6, 7.

33. Lindblom has alerted us to the existence of the market as an instrument of central bureaucratic planning. See Charles Lindblom, *Politics and Markets* (New York: Basic Books, 1977), p. 93.

34. Olson, *Rise and Decline*, pp. 48, 50.

35. *Ibid.*, p. 48.

36. Similar objections are made by Gustafsson, "Rise and Decline," p. 37.

37. Pye, *Asian Power and Politics*, pp. 56–89.

38. George, *Lee Kuan Yew's Singapore*, pp. 110–131.

39. By the middle 1980's, South Korea's rate of inflation had declined to the average for the region.

40. See Willard D. Sharpe, "Success Achieved by Taiwan and Korea Obscures Different Roads to Development," *Asian Wall Street Journal*, May 6, 1985, p. 23.

41. See Mason, Kim, Perkins, Jim, and Cole, *Economic and Social Modernization*, p. 265.

42. Ruth Berins Collier and David Collier, "Inducements versus Constraints: Disaggregating 'Corporatism' " *American Political Science Review* 73 (Dec., 1979): 979.

43. The original legislation regarding labor unions was written in 1929, when the KMT ruled the mainland. This legislation, amended in 1975, specifies that strikes may be called when a majority of the union votes in secret ballot after arbitration has been "proved a failure." A strike may not disturb the peace or inflict personal injury; nor may the union wage demand exceed the "standard wage." Some of this language is silly; no one has ever defined a "standard wage," and no Taiwanese worker would work for the minimum wage, as the going rate is many times more. Nor would any government allow a disturbance of the peace. The requirement for arbitration and majority vote is comparable to that of the American National Labor Relations Board and to the labor legislation fashioned by the Thatcher government in Britain.

The portions of the martial law document relating to strikes are somewhat redundant. As originally promulgated in 1934 and amended in 1948 and 1949, martial law did not prohibit strikes. It did, however, give the President discretionary power to do so. The document states that, "within an area under martial law, the commander-in-chief . . . may prohibit traders' strikes, workers' strikes, students' strikes or other strikes of the people and force the strikers to restore the original status." See U.S. House of Representatives, Subcommittee on Pacific and Asian Affairs, *Martial Law on Taiwan and United States Foreign Policy Interests* (Washington, D.C.: Government Printing Office, 1982), p. 178.

The labor union legislation establishes the procedure for arbitration (a Labor Dispute Arbitration Board) and specifies that strikes cannot be called until the dispute has "been brought to the Labor Dispute Arbitration Board for judgment." See Republic of China, Industrial Development and Investment Center, *Labor Laws and Regulation of the Republic of China* (Taipei, Oct., 1984), pp. 33, 50. There are occasional work stoppages, but the unions are careful to call them "sit-ins" or "sit-downs," thus—they believe—escaping the need to comply with the legislation.

The legislation was never rigorously enforced; no administrative order suppressing a strike was ever issued. The Taiwanese work force strikes at about the same rate as does the Japanese (See Table 5-1).

The number of disputes seems to rise and fall. The period of greatest labor unrest was 1981–1982, with 1,060 and 1,303 disputes recorded. In 1983, there were only 42. The most important reasons for disputes, irrespective of their incidence, are (1) dismissal or wrongful severance, (2) management said to be in arrears on wages, and (3) injury compensation. The settlement agreements are very rarely simply a return to the status quo. Rather, there are "dismissals by agreement," "dismissals with severance pay," "payment of wages in arrears," or "injury compensation." Wage increases as a consequence of strikes is a rarity. Few examples of disputes over working hours exist; the work month is about 200 hours. Taiwan's record in industrial accidents is comparatively good. The ratio of accidents to economically active population is .0003. This compares favorably with Singapore (.005), South Korea (.007), and, the worst, Hong Kong (.03). The United States' ratio is .06. See Republic of China, Executive Yuan, Directorate-General of Budget, Accounting, and Statistics, *Yearbook of Labor Statistics, 1985)* (Taipei, 1986), pp. 26, 875, and George Thomas Kurian, *The New Book of World Rankings* (New York: Facts on File, 1984). Since South Korea has less GNP per capita, a poor record in income distribution, and a dismal history of industrial accidents, the confrontations of 1987 were almost a foregone conclusion. The wave of strikes that followed a relaxation of restrictions illustrates the pent-up frustrations of South Korea workers.

The status of unions in the new civil law is not yet known, as implementation of the civil code has just begun. Since neither martial law nor labor union legislation specifically prohibited strikes, lifting martial law has had no legal effect on unions. The newly enacted National Security Law makes no mention of strikes, nor is labor legislation included in the list of sixteen laws declared inoperative because of an end to martial law. See Maria Chang, "How Will the Lifting of Martial Law Affect Labor Strikes in Taiwan," unpublished memorandum to the author, July 20, 1987.

44. Theodore Cohen, *Remaking Japan* (New York: Free Press, 1987).

45. See Republic of China, Industrial Development and Investment Center, *Labor Laws and Regulations of the Republic of China*, (Taipei, 1984).

46. Fox Butterfield, "Why Asians Are Going to the Head of the Class," *New York Times Education Life*, Aug. 3, 1986, pp. 18–22. Concerning the "thought reform" efforts in the People's Republic of China, Lifton attributes the Chinese variant of the technique to Confucianism. See Robert Jay Lifton, *Thought Reform and the Psychology of Totalism* (New York: Norton, 1963).

47. See Pye, *Asian Power and Politics*, p. 54.

48. Berger, *Capitalist Revolution*, p. 158.

49. *Ibid.*, p. 166.

50. *Ibid.*, p. 163.

51. Bruce Cumings, "The Origins and Development of the Northeast Asian Political Economy: Industrial Sectors, Product Cycles, and Political Consequences," *International Organization* 38 (Winter, 1984): 1–40. Concerning the exploitation of women, Diamond writes "One is reminded of the immigrant girls working in the sweatshops of New York at the turn of the century, while their brothers studied to be doctors and lawyers at City College" (Nora Diamond, "Women and Industry in Taiwan," *Modern China* 5 [July, 1979]: 327). In 1984,

Taiwan created, within the framework of an elaborate Labor Standards Law, provisions for the special problems of female workers. Female workers were given an eight-week maternity leave, with full wages (a month if there was a miscarriage). Since maternity leave is one of the hottest topics on the agenda of feminists in the United States, they might look to Taiwan as a model, along with most other industrially developed countries. Data on implementation are not yet available. See Republic of China, Industrial Development and Investment Center, *Labor Standards Law*, Aug., 1984.

52. Berger, *Capitalist Revolution*, p. 163.

53. Robert E. Ward, "Reflections on the Allied Occupation and Planned Political Change in Japan," in Ward, ed., *Political Development in Modern Japan* (Princeton, N.J.: Princeton University Press, 1968), pp. 478, 519. See also Richard L. Engstrom and Chu Chi-hung, "The Impact of the 1980 Supplementary Election on Nationalist China's Legislative Yuan," *Asian Survey* 24 (April, 1984): 447–458.

54. See Charles H. C. Kao and Ben Chie-liu, "Socioeconomic Development in Taiwan: An Analysis of Its Quality and Life Advancement," in Kwoh Ting-li and Tzong Shian-yu, eds., *Experiences and Lessons of Economic Development in Taiwan* (Taipei: Academia Seneca, 1982), p. 456.

55. Pye, *Asian Power and Politics*, p. 231.

56. See T. J. Pempel, *Policy and Politics in Japan: Creative Conservatism* (Philadelphia: Temple University Press, 1982), pp. 309–310, and Hung Chao-tai, "The Kuomintang and Modernization in Taiwan," in Samuel P. Huntington and Clement H. Moore, eds., *Authoritarian Politics in Modern Society: The Dynamics of Established One-Party Systems* (New York: Basic Books, 1970), p. 420.

57. Henry Kao, an opposition candidate, was elected mayor of Taipei shortly after the mainlanders showed up. Thereafter, the office was appointive. Kao lives comfortably in Taipei, where I interviewed him, as a token opposition leader quite loyal to the Kuomintang. When Amnesty International contacts him about political prisoners, he forwards the letter to the government.

58. The closest approximation is Switzerland. See Peter J. Katzenstein, *Corporatism and Change: Austria, Switzerland, and the Politics of Industry* (Ithaca, N.Y.: Cornell University Press, 1984). However, interest groups are more independently powerful than political parties in Switzerland.

59. See Douglas Mendel, *The Politics of Formosan Nationalism* (Berkeley: University of California Press, 1970), pp. 26–41, for an accounting of the events of 1947.

60. Television programs, invariably in Mandarin, are captioned for Taiwanese who cannot understand the language.

61. Some of their relatives now serve in the Legislative Yuan.

62. Land reform has been losing some of its luster in the last several years because of artificially low commodity prices, encouraging the shift from agrarian to urban labor.

63. Kuo Tai-chyn, "An Analysis of the Taiwan Experience: Policies and Social Factors," *Issues and Studies* 21 (Jan., 1985): 104.

64. The "land to the tiller" phrase is authentic Kuomintang history. It was initially used by Sun Yat-Sen.

65. See Amsden, "The State and Taiwan's Economic Development," p. 79. Barrington Moore concludes Kuomintang became a reactionary organization similar to European fascist parties. Barrington Moore, Jr., *Social Origins of Dictatorship*

and Democracy (Boston: Beacon Press, 1966), pp. 187–201.

66. See especially Chin Hsiao-Yi, "Chiang Kai-shek's Understanding of and Implementation of Sun Yat-sen's Revolutionary Ideology Program," unpublished paper, Taipei, 1981.

67. Interviews with Kuomintang bureaucrats who arrived in Taiwan in 1949 and participated in the land reform scheme.

68. See Chen Cieng, *Land Reform in Taiwan* (Taipei: China Publishing Co., 1968), pp. 47–48.

69. Robert H. Silin, *Leadership and Values: The Organization of Large-Scale Taiwanese Enterprises* (Cambridge, Mass.: Harvard University Press, 1976), p. 75.

70. It is generally agreed that corruption in the Republic of China is low by Asian standards, surely far lower than was the case when the KMT ruled the mainland. The party's image was tarnished badly, however, in 1985, with the appearance of evidence of substantial corruption in the Department of Economic Affairs and other agencies responsible for fiscal policy. Private credit unions—apparently with the knowledge of some high-level bureaucrats—channeled funds to one of Taiwan's largest businesses by using forged credit statements. Yet the magnitude of the scandal was surely not as great as that of former Japanese Prime Minister Tanaka's Lockheed bribe. "Honest graft" in Taiwan is less of a problem than in Mexico, which has a one-party government similar to Taiwan's. See Ralph Clough, *Island China* (Cambridge, Mass.: Harvard University Press, 1978), pp. 52–54.

71. Interview with Yien Si-chiang, Secretary-General, Central Committee, Kuomintang, Feb. 10, 1985.

72. This unsavory aspect of Kuomintang behavior should not be ignored; Taiwanese students in the United States are reluctant to talk to other Taiwanese because of their fear.

73. Edwin A. Winkler, "Roles Linking State and Society," in Emily Martin Ahern and Hill Gates, eds., *The Anthropology of Taiwanese Society* (Stanford, Calif.: Stanford University Press, 1981), p. 57.

74. Interview with Betty Yu, reporter, *Central Daily News*, Feb. 23, 1985.

75. The Orwellian irony of calling a censorship bureau an information office has escaped the Taiwanese.

76. Interview with Chao Yao-tung, Minister, Ministry of Economic Affairs, March 10, 1985.

77. During the trial of the Bamboo Gang for the murder of Henry Liu, presumably because he authored an unflattering portrait of Chiang Ching-kuo, I purchased the book openly at just such a stand. In addition to the tacit tolerance for Liu's book, there are a number of critical studies available in most bookshops. Some of these are from the "loyal opposition," and resemble the pathetic show dissent of the U.S.S.R. But others, such as Hsieh Cheng-i's *Inside and Outside the Kuomintang* (Taipei: Min-ch'uan t'ung-hsun-she, 1980), are highly critical but remain in circulation. See A. James Gregor and Maria Hsia Chang, *The Republic of China and U.S. Policy* (Washington, D.C.: Ethics and Public Policy Center, 1983).

78. Interview with Fred C. H. Lee, Office of International Affairs, Central Committee, Kuomintang, March 9, 1985.

79. Interview with Simon Wang, IBM Taiwan Corporation, Feb. 12, 1983.

80. Pye believes that the close proximity of ideology to everyday life is a consequence of the fact that "the Chinese are not comfortable with power unless it is cloaked in a moralistic ideology." (*Asian Power and Politics*, p. 231).

81. Mendel, *Politics of Formosan Nationalism*, p. 24.

82. Their cynicism was hardly abated by the trial. The defendants claimed to be operating on government orders, and one persistent rumor involved the president's son. But at no time did any defense attorney pursue this line of questioning by asking, "What did Chiang know and when did he know it?"

83. Richard W. Wilson, *Learning to Be Chinese: The Political Socialization of Children in Taiwan* (Cambridge, Mass.: MIT Press, 1970), p. 46. The Chinese political culture has generally regarded education as an opportunity to indoctrinate as well as to teach. (See Solomon, *Mao's Revolution*, pp. 506–508.

84. Data from all elections through 1980, made available by the Kuomintang to the author.

85. From KMT data. Vote fraud is always a likely occurrence in authoritarian countries. My impression is that it is less of a problem in Taiwan than in Mexico.

86. From KMT personnel files.

87. Each of the 104 (out of a possible 133) members were asked to list those whom they regarded as most active and interested in economic policy.

88. He was removed in 1985.

89. In the Legislative Yuan the Taiwanese Kuomintang legislators elected in 1980 were twice as likely as those serving in perpetuity, from the mainland, to introduce "interpellation" regarding a decision by the Ministry of Economic Affairs to award a manufacturing contract to a Japanese firm. The interpellation began in 1983 and, as of 1986, the contract had not been finally negotiated.

90. Raymond D. Gastil and James D. Seymour believe that Taiwan is more likely to change appreciably than is the People's Republic. See "Supporting Democracy in the People's Republic of China and The Republic of China (Taiwan)," in Gastil, ed., *Freedom in the World: Political Rights and Civil Liberties* (New York: Freedom House, 1984), p. 135.

91. Interview with Hu Fu, Professor, Department of Political Science, National Taiwan University, March 9, 1985.

92. See Robert E. Ward, "Introduction," ed., *Political Development in Modern Japan*, in Ward, pp. 6–7.

93. See Suzanne Berger and Michael J. Piore, *Dualism and Discontinuity in Industrial Societies* (Cambridge, Eng.: Cambridge University Press, 1980), for an exposition on the subject of institutionalization.

94. Chiang Kai-shek's widow, the venerable and infamous propagandist for the old "China Lobby," loathes her stepson, ROC President Chiang (the elder Chiang's heir by an earlier marriage) and he reciprocates. She is a powerful symbol of old guard hardliners, and was in Taiwan in 1986 seeking to undermine Chiang's carefully planned moves toward a more open society.

95. Like most systems in the throes of change, Taiwan is maintaining its symbolic posture of defiance against the mainland and a pledge to "liberate" it. It seeks to avoid alienating the conservatives. In the same fashion, Gorbachev is resurrecting Lenin to bless his reforms, and Deng condemns Western ideas (Maria Chang, "Transition Through Accretion: Institutionalizing a Competitive Party System in Taiwan," paper delivered to the Symposium on Political Reform of the Republic of China on Taiwan, Associated Chinese Social Scientists of North America, Baltimore, May 8–10, 1987).

96. Chang believes that the inability of any faction to gain the upper hand is a deliberate policy anticipating Chiang's death. He cannot groom his own successor because of the gradual but steady democratization of the country. To do so

would raise doubts about the sincerity of his commitment to two-party competition. Thus each faction is balanced against the other with carefully parceled out victories in order to enhance the probability of a collective leadership. See Maria Hsia Chang, "The Crisis of Succession on Taiwan," *Global Affairs*, Spring, 1986, pp. 141–156. See also "The Succession Question," *Asia Week*, May 25, 1986, pp. 34–36.

97. Gregor and Chang, *Republic of China and U.S. Policy*, pp. 60–79.

Chapter Six

1. Lest we faint with horror, recall that parties in the Federal Republic of Germany that are believed to "harm or abolish the basic libertarian democratic order or to endanger the existence of the Federal Republic" are prohibited. The Verfassungschutz enforced a "decree against radicals" and arrests have been made for "calling in question the courts or the electoral system." See Raymond D. Gastil, ed., *Freedom in the World, 1986–1987* (New York: Greenwood, 1987), p. 279. In 1987, its first full year of existence, the Democratic Progressive Party, although struggling to unite disparate factions, was reformist rather than revolutionary, courting working-class voters rather than appealing to the lost cause of Taiwanese independence. Nevertheless, its legislative members launched a spirited attack on the National Security Bill (the legislation replacing martial law) as too vague. As an example of the precision they seek, DPP legislators wish for those convicted under the terms of martial law to be able to appeal under the new legislation. See Carl Goldstein, "A Tiger Seeking Claws," *Far Eastern Economic Review*, May 14, 1987, pp. 24–26.

2. "A New Security Blanket," *Far Eastern Economic Review*, Jan., 1987, p. 14; "A Two Pronged Test," *Far Eastern Economic Review*, Dec., 1986, pp. 36–37; Harvey J. Feldman, "Taiwan Moves Toward a Two-Party System," *New York Times*, Dec. 27, 1986, p. 15.

3. Bradley M. Richardson and Scott C. Flanagan, *Politics in Japan* (Boston: Little, Brown, 1984), p. 100.

4. Interview with Yen Chia-kan, former President of the ROC, March 16, 1983.

5. Chinese Human Rights Association, *Report on the Survey of Human Rights in the Republic of China on Taiwan* (Taipei: The Association, 1984), pp. 12–19.

6. The most important impact of removing martial law will be to exempt civilians from the jurisdiction of military courts; other aspects of martial law (labor regulation, censorship) will remain unaffected, as separate legislation duplicates the original martial law.

7. The full-time party bureaucracy is heavily involved in factional politics, and forms alliances with KMT members who are active or influential in the government bureaucracy, the universities, the legislature, interest groups, and the media.

8. Interview with Chen Li-an, Deputy Secretary-General and Director of International Affairs, Central Committee, Feb. 21, 1984.

9. Interview with Chen Chien-jen, Director, Department of North American Affairs, Ministry of Foreign Affairs, Jan. 22, 1984.

10. Interview with Hu Fu, April 11, 1985.

11. In Republic of China, Executive Yuan, Research, Development, and Evaluation Yuan, *Annual Review of Government Administration* (Taipei, 1985), p. 51.

12. One of the most active is the Institute of Economics at National Chung-Hsing University.

13. Research, Development, and Evaluation Yuan, *Annual Review of Government Administration* (1985).

14. The Garrison Command, the most important intelligence unit, has been responsible for implementation of martial law, which, however, had fallen into disuse well before its suspension. Without martial law, the Garrison Command's responsibilities are in question.

15. As an example of Taiwan's somewhat slipshod authoritarianism, the military budget is supposed to be a secret. But since many bureaucrats like to play games, all one has to do is ask them to nod when you quote the right figure. Seven percent of GNP is about right. (This is the figure used by the *Asian Wall Street Journal*, which is sold in newsstands all over Taipei.)

16. I am grateful to Tsai Cheng-wen, Department of Political Science, National Taiwan University, for introducing me to the tension between mainlanders and Taiwanese about equity.

17. Liu died in San Francisco in 1985. High-ranking military officials were indicted, tried, and convicted, but the issue remains in doubt as appeals, renunciations of old confessions, and new evidence cloud the process. His most apparent offense was his authorship of an unflattering biography of ROC President Chiang Ching-kuo; during the trial, however, Liu's activities as a double agent (for the ROC and the People's Republic) came to light.

18. In 1985, a large credit union used individual investors' funds for investment in various enterprises, enriching its directors until the investments went sour; the government (which until then had no guaranteed bank deposits) paid those who lost their investments. It also quickly established a deposit guarantee law. The Ministry of Economic Affairs, the Ministry of Finance, and several lesser bureaucracies were implicated and their ministers' resignations were accepted.

19. Mab Huang, "Democratization on Taiwan," in Gastil, ed., *Freedom in the World*, p. 285.

20. "The Succession Question," *Asia Week*, May 25, 1986, pp. 34–36.

21. Lien Sheng Yang, "The Concept of *Pao* as a Basis for Social Relations in China," in John K. Fairbank, ed., *Chinese Thought and Institutions* (Chicago: University of Chicago Press, 1973), p. 291; John Weakland, "The Organization of Chinese Culture," *Psychiatry* 13 (April, 1950): 364. Ross Terrill makes a convincing case that a substantial portion of the factional infighting in the People's Republic of China originated in personal jealousies and hatreds. See Ross Terrill, *The White-Boned Demon* (New York: Morrow, 1984).

22. See David E. Apter and Nagayo Sawa, *Against the State: Politics and Social Protest in Japan* (Cambridge, Mass.: Harvard University Press, 1984), and Harold C. Hinton, *Korea Under New Leadership: The Fifth Republic* (New York: Praeger, 1983).

23. Among the more conspicuous proponents of this view are Hu Fu and Tsai Cheng-wen, Department of Political Science, National Taiwan University, and Thomas Lee, of Tamkang University.

24. Berger believes, however, that an informal business-government elite manages the Hong Kong economy in a way similar to that of the other Asian political-economic systems. See Peter L. Berger, *The Capitalist Revolution: Fifty Propositions About Prosperity, Equality, and Liberty* (New York: Basic Books, 1986), p. 158.

25. Interview with Chao Yao-tung, Minister, Ministry of Economic Affairs, May 18, 1983.

26. See Leroy P. Jones and Il Sakong, *Government, Business, and Entrepreneurship in Economic Development: The Korean Case* (Cambridge, Mass.: Harvard University Press, 1980).

27. Republic of China, Executive Yuan, Directorate General of Budget, Accounting, and Statistics, *Report on the Survey of Personal Income Distribution in Taiwan Area, Republic of China, 1983* (Taipei, 1984), p. 9.

28. On the other hand, bureaucratic publications have ceased discussing income distribution. Compare the 1980 Ministry of Economic Affairs report, *Economic Development in the Republic of China* (Taipei, 1980) with the 1984 Council for Economic Planning and Development's 1984 report, *Economic Development, Taiwan: Republic of China,* (Taipei, 1984).

29. Richard E. Barrett and Martin King Whyte, "Dependency Theory and Taiwan: Analysis of a Deviant Case," *American Journal of Sociology* 87 (March, 1982): 1982. See also Shirley W. Y. Kuo, Gustav Ranis, and John C. H. Fei, *The Taiwan Success Story: Rapid Growth with Improved Distribution in the Republic of China, 1952–1979* (Boulder, Colo.: Westview, 1981).

30. Paul K. J. Liu, "Economic Aspects of Rapid Urbanization in Taipei," *Academia Economic Papers,* March, 1979, p. 19.

31. Barrett and Whyte, "Dependency Theory and Taiwan," p. 1082. The 1953 data are unreliable.

32. Republic of China, Council for Economic Planning and Development, *Taiwan Statistical Data Book, 1985* (Taipei, 1985), p. 58.

33. Taiwan Institute of Economic Research, *Postwar Development of the Economy of Taiwan* (Taipei: The Institute, Oct., 1983), p. 7.

34. Republic of China, Ministry of Finance, *Government Finance of the Republic of China* (Taipei, Jan., 1985).

35. Republic of China, Industrial Development and Investment Center, *Categories and Criteria for Special Encouragement of Important Productive Enterprises, March, 1985, and Income Tax Law, March, 1985* (Taipei, 1985).

36. Kuo, Ranis, and Fei, *Taiwan Success Story,* p. 140.

37. John C. H. Fei, "Ideology of Economic Development in Taiwan," paper delivered at the Conference on Experiences and Lessons of Economic Development in Taiwan, Taipei, Dec. 18–20, 1981; see also Walter Galenson, ed., *Economic Growth and Structural Change in Taiwan* (Ithaca, N.Y.: Cornell University Press, 1979).

38. Douglas Mendel, *The Politics of Formosan Nationalism* (Berkeley: University of California Press, 1970), p. 1.

39. There is no difference between written Taiwanese and written Mandarin, but spoken Taiwanese is not merely a dialect; it is unintelligible to Mandarin speakers.

40. Of course, much the same sorts of conversations occur any time there are foreigners present. The stereotypical descriptions of crude Bavarians as compared with sophisticated Berliners come to mind.

41. Tung Ming-lee, *A Study of the Social Increase of the Population in Taiwan* (Taichung: Population Study Center, 1978), p. 12.

42. It is difficult to verify the truth about who makes the most money. Detailed statistics are kept about yearly wages, but not about money earned by family units running a variety of enterprises besides a regular job (noodle stands, taxis, etc.). Bureaucratic salaries are being raised at about 8 percent a year, higher for vice ministers and ministers. See Research, Development, and Evaluation Yuan, *Annual Review* (1985), p. 51, and Republic of China, Executive Yuan, Directorate General of Budget, Accounting, and Statistics, *Yearbook of Labor Statistics, 1984* (Taipei, 1985).

43. Lucian W. Pye, *Asian Power and Politics* (Cambridge, Mass.: Harvard University Press, 1985), pp. 232–233.

44. A visible symbol of resistance is Y. C. Yang, Chairman of the Formosa Plastics Group, who does not speak a word of Mandarin.

45. Hill Gates, "Dependency and the Part-Time Proletariat in Taiwan," *Modern China* 5 (July, 1979): 388.

46. Pye, *Asian Power and Politics*, pp. 233–234.

47. Chen Li-an, quoted in *Asia Week*, May 25, 1986, p. 39.

48. From KMT personnel files.

49. Even in the unlikely event that Chiang's careful balancing of factions is undone, and the old guard is returned to a share of the power, the transition process will not stop, since it reflects economic and demographic development as much as factional politics.

Chapter Seven

1. Mattei Dogan, ed., *The Mandarins of Western Europe* (New York: Wiley, 1975).

2. Johanna M. Menzel, ed., *The Chinese Civil Service: Career Open to Talent* (Boston: Little, Brown, 1963), pp. 66–81. See also David Apter, *The Politics of Modernization* (Taipei: Rainbow Press, 1967), p. 266.

3. Fritz Morstein Marx, *The Administrative State* (Chicago: University of Chicago Press, 1957).

4. Chalmers Johnson, "Introduction: The Taiwan Model," in James C. Hsiung, ed., *Contemporary Republic of China: The Taiwan Experience* (New York: American Association for Chinese Studies, 1981), pp. 9–18.

5. *Ibid.*, p. 13.

6. Graham K. Wilson, *Business and Politics: A Comparative Introduction* (Chatham, N.J.: Chatham House, 1985), p. 95.

7. Alice H. Amsden, "The State and Taiwan's Economic Development," in Peter B. Evans, Dietrich Rueschemeyer, and Theda Skocpol, eds., *Bringing the State Back In* (Cambridge, Eng.: Cambridge University Press, 1986), pp. 97–98.

8. Chalmers Johnson, *MITI and the Japanese Miracle: The Growth of Industrial Policy, 1925-1975* (Stanford, Calif.: Stanford University Press, 1982), pp. 309–312.

9. Leroy P. Jones and Il Sakong, *Government, Business, and Entrepreneurship in Economic Development: The Korean Case* (Cambridge, Mass.: Harvard University Press, 1980), p. 279. The similarities to De Gaulle's France are arresting. Hall's

detailed examination of French planning reveals that banks in France were *directed* to make capital available in a way that "favored the development of large enterprises. . . . At the heart of the program was a set of policies encouraging industrial concentration" (Peter Hall, *Governing the Economy* [Oxford: Polity Press, 1986], p. 167).

10. Chao Yao-tung, former Minister of Economic Affairs, enjoys explaining that mergers are unpopular because all Chinese want to be the boss.

11. Tibor Scitovsky, "Economic Development in Taiwan and South Korea, 1965–1981," in Lawrence J. Lau, ed., *Models of Development: A Comparative Study of Economic Growth in South Korea and Taiwan* (San Francisco: Institute for Contemporary Studies, 1986), pp. 175–176. Another, more hostile, interpretation is that businesses are kept small to avoid the creation of sources of power capable of competing on even terms with the bureaucracy. The evidence does not support this assertion. See Edwin A. Winkler, "Statism and Familism on Taiwan," in George C. Loege and Ezra F. Vogel, eds., *Ideology and Competitiveness* (Boston: Harvard Business School, 1987), pp. 182–183.

12. On the perception of Taiwanese of business size and power see Kwoh Ting-li and Wan An-yeh, "Economic Planning in the Republic of China," paper presented at the Conference on Experience and Lessons of Economic Development in Taiwan, Taipei, Dec. 18–20, 1981, p. 9.

13. The following account is taken from Jones and Sakong, *Government, Business, and Entrepreneurship*, pp. 99, 281–284.

14. Interviews with Chen Sun, Vice Chairman, Council for Economic Planning and Development, April 3, 1985; with Mon Hsiu-chang, Taiwan Textile Federation, May 2, 1985, and Wang Jen-huong, advisor, Ministry of Economic Affairs, May 3, 1986.

15. Chao Yao-tung, formerly the Minister of Economic Affairs and later Chairman of the Council for Economic Planning and Development, is an especially ardent critic of such circumstances.

16. See Lawrence J. Lau, "Introduction," in Lau, ed., *Models of Development,* p. 8.

17. *Ibid.,* p. 10.

18. James R. Schifman and Maria Shao, "South Korea and Taiwan: Two Strategies," *Wall Street Journal,* May 1, 1986, p. 1.

19. A similar arrangement between Vivitar, Zeiss, and the ROC domestic optical industry to manufacture a reflex lens has not come to fruition because the government wants to market the product under a Taiwanese, not Japanese, name. As a junior-level bureaucrat put it, "No more Radio Shacks." Disliked as they are, the Taiwanese surrogates for American manufacturers have converted the country from a third world backwater to the world's eleventh largest trading nation. For example, of the 7 million imported bicycles bought in the United States in 1986, 83 percent are Taiwanese, using the Schwinn label rather than that of the Giant Manufacturing Company, the Taiwanese manufacturer. Personal computers labeled Texas Instruments are stacked next to Multitechs—one for sale in the United States and the other for the local market. Although national pride compels the bureaucracy to encourage Taiwanese to use their own brands, established market shares based upon American product names are not willingly surrendered. See Douglas R. Sease, "Trade Tangle," *Wall Street Journal,* May 27, 1987, pp. 1, 22.

20. Akira Kubota, *Higher Civil Servants in Japan: Their Social Origins, Educational Backgrounds, and Career Patterns* (Princeton, N.J.: Princeton University Press, 1969), p. 72.

21. Philippe C. Schmitter, "Still the Century of Corporatism?," *Review of Politics* 86 (Jan., 1974): 85–131.

22. See Richard Samuels, *The Politics of Regional Policy in Japan* (Princeton, N.J.: Princeton University Press, 1979), for an argument that Japan, in its regional and local politics, is less corporatist than is commonly supposed.

23. Bradley M. Richardson and Scott C. Flanagan, *Politics in Japan* (Boston: Little, Brown, 1984), p. 182.

24. No one in Taipei can decide whether implication in the credit union scandal or public appearance with a mistress is the more important reason for the dismissal.

25. Taiwan wishes to earn contracts from manufacturers of designer clothes, as Hong Kong has done, rather than from discount houses; hence, it seeks larger companies that can negotiate favorably against the tough Hong Kong competition. A good example is Inter-Classico, which formerly made inexpensive synthetic shoes but now is leaving the cheap shoe market to South Korea and the People's Republic and concentrating upon the designer shoe market; its director began studying shoe-designing in Florence and plowed profits back into automated equipment. See Sease, "Trade Tangle," pp. 1, 22.

26. James Gregor, "Comparative Political Stability: The Philippines and the ROC on Taiwan," *Issues and Studies* 23 (Jan., 1987): 20.

27. Chalmers Johnson, "Introduction," p. 14.

28. Others have noted the waning influence of the military. See Amsden, "The State and Taiwan's Economic Development," p. 100.

29. The Ministry embarked on an ambitious privatization scheme that it hopes will convert the public corporations, especially those that are lagging, into privately owned cartels.

30. James Gregor believes that the involvement of highly placed officials with such minutial is characteristic of most Asian governments (personal communication with the author).

31. I do not mean to belittle the differences. Mainlander scholars themselves are frank. Wei Yung, a fast-track mainlander who directs research and evaluation, writes of the "incompetent rule of the first Chinese Governor-General in Taiwan that eventually led to a widespread rebellion by the Taiwanese [that in turn] left a deep scar on the relationships between the Mainlanders and Taiwanese on the Island" (Wei Yung, "Taiwan: A Modernizing Chinese Society," in Paul K. T. Sihm, ed., *Taiwan in Modern Times* [New York: St. Johns University Press, 1973], p. 444).

32. Edwin A. Winkler, "National, Regional, and Local Politics," in Emily Martin Ahern and Hill Gates, eds., *The Anthropology of Taiwanese Society* (Stanford, Calif.: Stanford University Press, 1981), p. 33.

33. Taiwan's literacy rate is 90 percent. Since education is compulsory through grade 9, most illiteracy is concentrated in the older segments of the population. The alleged quota system would mean that the offspring of mainlanders would list their province of origin as one on the mainland—for example, Sichuan—while Taiwanese would list Taiwan as their "province." I can find no evidence that a quota system exists. As is true of most countries, rumors about discrimination are common.

34. The actual language is far less foreboding. Besides routine annual ratings, there is a "special rating" that is issued "whenever a major contribution or serious misconduct has been made" (Republic of China, Executive Yuan, *Briefing on the Functions of the Ministry of Personnel* [Taiwan: Nov., 1984]). In practice, very few have suffered and most have benefitted from such reviews.

35. Interview with Chao Yao-tung, Minister, Ministry of Foreign Affairs, Feb. 1, 1983.

36. Dogan distinguishes the "traditional" mandarins, who were likely to have majored in liberal arts, from the "modern" mandarins who select economics, finance, or business administration. The traditional ones are on the decline. Taiwan, as does Europe, supports his contention. See Mattei Dogan, "The Political Power of the Western Mandarins," in Dogan, ed., *Mandarins of Western Europe*, pp. 16–17.

37. Heady writes of the need for a technocratic redefinition of the role of universities, concentrating on the training of a professional stratum technocratically oriented by the criteria of specialization and efficiency. See Ferrel Heady, *Comparative Public Administration* (New York: Longman, 1979), p. 324.

38. The business-government relation in Japan is well assessed in Wilson, *Business and Politics*, pp. 88–102.

39. Robert H. Silin, *Leadership and Values: The Organization of Large-Scale Taiwanese Enterprises* (Cambridge, Mass.: Harvard University Press, 1976), p. 16.

40. Republic of China, Executive Yuan, Research, Development, and Evaluation Yuan, *Annual Review of Government Administration* (Taipei, 1985). See also Alice H. Amsden, "Taiwan's Economic History: A Case of Etatisme and a Challenge to Dependency Theory," *Modern China* 5 (July, 1979): 341–380. George T. Crane argues that state-generated capital, rather than dependency, is the crucial factor in Taiwan's "miracle." See "The Taiwanese Ascent: System, State, and Movement in World Economy," in Edward Friedman, ed., *Ascent and Decline in the World System* (Beverly Hills, Calif.: Sage, 1982), pp. 93–114.

41. Mancur Olson, *The Rise and Decline of Nations* (New Haven, Conn.: Yale University Press, 1982), p. 218.

42. Peter L. Berger, *The Capitalist Revolution: Fifty Propositions About Prosperity, Equality, and Liberty* (New York: Basic Books, 1986), p. 160.

43. Howard J. Wiarda, *Corporatism and Development: The Portuguese Experience* (Amherst: University of Massachusetts Press, 1977), p. 328.

44. See John F. H. Purcell and Susan Kaufman Purcell, "Mexican Business and Public Policy," in James M. Malloy, ed., *Authoritarianism and Corporatism in Latin America* (Pittsburgh: University of Pittsburgh Press, 1977), pp. 191–226.

45. Wiarda, *Corporatism and Development*, p. 332.

Chapter Eight

1. Peter McDonough, Samuel H. Barnes, and Antonio Lopez, "The Growth of Democratic Legitimacy in Spain," *American Political Science Review* 80 (Sept., 1986): 755. My italics.

2. The Kuomintang's defeat on the mainland was a good indication of the depths to which it had sunk. Along with a genuine fear of losing again, the massive American aid was accompanied by hard lobbying to prevent the KMT from reverting to its statist ideology. There is a lively debate about the events leading to Taiwan's eventual explosive growth. One theory emphasizes the freedom of the KMT; the other suggests that, while the party had little domestic opposition, it was in effect a U.S. puppet. A strong statement to this effect is from Gates, who accuses those who believe in the enlightened dictatorship of the KMT of relying too heavily "on the capability of a befuddled and illegitimate client gov-

ernment to protect a population for which it has historically shown little sympathy" (Hill Gates, "Dependency and the Part-Time Proletariat in Taiwan," *Modern China* 5 [July, 1979]: 383). I cast my lot between the extremes of Platonic guardians and corrupt buffoons.

3. The case for uniqueness is made in Alice H. Amsden, "Taiwan's Economic History: A Case of Etatisme and a Challenge to Dependency Theory," *Modern China* 5 (July, 1979): 341–380. "Dependency theory," which normally claims that client states are bled dry to fuel a colonial power, is of dubious value in discussing Taiwan. It has had at least two periods of dependency, the Japanese and the United States (which surely had run its course by 1979, when we withdrew diplomatic recognition). Its continued prosperity may have been given an initial thrust by either of the "colonial" powers, but sooner or later a client nation has to sink or swim. Rather than dependency being economically unhealthy for a dependent country, Taiwan suggests the opposite result. It was more of a traditional colony when the Japanese ran it, however. No matter how you describe dependency theory, being in an actual colonial relationship is not the same as being a client. On the various kinds of dependency, a defense of client relationships, and a refutation of dependency theory as appropriate to Taiwan see Richard E. Barrett, "Dependency Theory and Taiwan: Analysis of a Deviant Case," *American Journal of Sociology* 87 (March, 1982): 1064–1089.

4. Thomas B. Gold, *State and Society in the Taiwan Miracle* (Armonk, N.Y.: Sharpe, 1986), p. 122. However, the real take-off began when the bureaucracy began to disengage from the economy. See Samuel P. S. Ho, *Economic Development of Taiwan, 1860–1970* (New Haven, Conn.: Yale University Press, 1978).

5. Gold, *State and Society*, p. 126.

6. Samuel P. Huntington, *American Politics: The Promise of Disharmony* (Cambridge, Mass.: Harvard University Press, 1981), p. 56. See Chie Nakane, *Japanese Society* (Berkeley: University of California Press, 1970), for a good account of such tendencies. Robert Bellah, Richard Madsen, William M. Sullivan, Ann Swidler, and Steven M. Tipton, *Habits of the Heart* (Berkeley: University of California Press, 1985), longs for a less individualistic America. But others have found little difference in political socialization between the two cultures. See Akira Kubota and Robert E. Ward, "Family Influence and Political Socialization in Japan: Some Preliminary Findings in a Comparative Perspective," *Comparative Political Studies* 3 (July, 1970): 140–175. Additionally, Europeans are more likely than Americans to believe that "the individual owes his first duty to the state and only secondarily to his personal welfare," but neither group of respondents can compare with the 92 percent of *Mexicans* who agreed with this statement. Plainly, attribution of group loyalty to Confucianism alone is in error. My interviews with KMT members used this question, and not a single respondent disagreed with it, but such would have been true also of members of the PRI in Mexico. See Donald J. Devine, *The Political Culture of the United States* (Boston: Little, Brown, 1972), p. 193.

7. Peter L. Berger, *The Capitalist Revolution: Fifty Propositions About Prosperity, Equality, and Liberty* (New York: Basic Books, 1986), p. 155.

8. Huntington, *American Politics*, p. 51.

9. Richard W. Wilson, *Learning to Be Chinese: The Political Socialization of Children in Taiwan* (Cambridge, Mass.: MIT Press, 1970), p. 34.

10. Comparing his findings to those of the extensive examinations of political socialization in the United States, Wilson notes that, whereas for American

children, symbols associated with voting and political participation become more salient, for Taiwanese children, it is ideology, the Three Principles of the People (Sun Yat-sen's principal work), that increases in importance.

11. This point is made well by Wilson's work on France. See Frank K. Wilson, "French Interest Group Politics: Pluralist or Neocorporatist?," *American Political Science Review* 77 (Dec., 1983): 895–910.

12. Charles S. Maier, *Recasting Bourgeois Europe* (Princeton, N.J.: Princeton University Press, 1975), p. 353.

13. The belief that a dispossessed lower middle class was the foundation for either the German or Italian fascist successes is generally accurate but not without substantial exceptions. The distinction between Italian and German fascism is major; Italian fascism incorporated much of the old elite structure corroded by World War I while Germany's fascism displaced established elites. Maier therefore calls Nazism "the revolt against the corporatist state" (*ibid.*, p. 593). Lipset argued that the rise of Nazism corresponded with the demise of the centrist parties; hence, he believes a "realignment" occurred. See Seymour Martin Lipset, *Political Man* (Garden City, N.Y.: Doubleday, 1960), p. 133. However, Hamilton asserts that the lower-middle-class support for Nazism has been exaggerated. See Richard F. Hamilton, *Who Voted for Hitler?* (Princeton, N.J.: Princeton University Press, 1982).

14. See Richard Hofstadter, *The Paranoid Style in American Politics* (New York: Vintage, 1968).

15. See Guillermo A. O'Donnell, "Corporatism and the Question of the State," in James M. Malloy, ed., *Authoritarianism and Corporatism in Latin America* (Pittsburgh: University of Pittsburgh Press, 1977), p. 44.

16. Robert Reich, *The Next American Frontier* (New York: Times Books, 1983), p. 3.

17. Tax reform may emerge as the lone triumph in an otherwise dismal second term; this issue was more heavily lobbied than any other, including aid to the Contras. Yet the law was passed.

18. See, for example, Lindsay Wright, "The Future of Democracy: Corporatist or Pluralist?," in Raymond D. Gastil, ed., *Freedom in the World: Political Rights and Civil Liberties* (New York: Freedom House, 1985), pp. 73–95.

19. These thoughts are the message of "public choice," as enunciated by James Buchanan, *The Limits of Liberty* (Chicago: University of Chicago Press, 1975).

20. Roger Benjamin, *The Limits of Politics: Collective Goods and Political Change in Postindustrial Societies* (Chicago: University of Chicago Press, 1980).

21. The same caution applies to "Iragua," the most serious evidence of malfeasance during the Reagan years, but of no major or permanent impact upon the actual institutions of government.

22. This measure is not necessarily a good indicator of a heavy government presence. Japan's respective proportions are 32 and 33 percent; yet no one would suggest that the United States approaches Japan's corporatism. Additionally, some of the spending increase is explained by increased state spending on social programs in response to the national government's efforts to increase defense spending while scaling back domestic expenditures. See Richard P. Nathan, "Institutional Change Under Reagan," in John L. Palmer, ed., *Perspectives on the Reagan Years* (Washington, D.C.: Urban Institute Press, 1986), pp. 121–146.

23. Hugh Heclo, "Reaganism and the Search for a Public Philosophy," in Palmer, ed., *Perspectives on the Reagan Years*, pp. 57, 58, 60.

24. There was less of a conservative mandate in 1984 than in 1980. Warren Miller concludes: "Ronald Reagan may have been reelected in part because he had moved the government to the ideological right; he was *not* reelected with a mandate to move further towards the goals of his conservative supporters. The 1980 election clearly turned in fair part on a desire for a shift to the right in the government's ideological center of gravity. . . . Four years later, however, popular sentiment for ideologically oriented policy change had moved as decisively in favor of wanting *more liberal* governmental policies as it had been in support of a conservative turn four years earlier." See Warren E. Miller, "The Election of 1984 and the Future of American Politics," in Kay Lehman Schlozman, ed., *Elections in America* (Boston: Allen and Unwin, 1987), p. 300.

25. Harold L. Wilensky, *The New Corporatism: Centralization and the Welfare State* (Beverly Hills, Calif.: Sage, 1976).

BIBLIOGRAPHY

Almond, Gabriel. "Corporatism, Pluralism, and Professional Memory." *World Politics* 35 (1983): 245–260.

Almond, Gabriel, and Bingham Powell. *Comparative Politics: A Developmental Approach.* Boston: Little, Brown, 1966.

Almond, Gabriel A., and Sidney Verba. *The Civic Culture: Political Attitudes and Democracy in Five Nations.* Boston: Little, Brown, 1965.

Amsden, Alice H. "The State and Taiwan's Economic Development." In Peter B. Evans, Dietrich Rueschemeyer, and Theda Skocpol, eds., *Bringing the State Back In,* pp. 79–95. Cambridge, Eng.: Cambridge University Press, 1986.

———. "Taiwan's Economic History: A Case of Etatisme and a Challenge to Dependency Theory." *Modern China* 5 (July, 1979): 341–380.

Apter, David. *The Politics of Modernization.* Taipei: Rainbow Press, 1967.

Apter, David E., and Nagayo Sawa. *Against the State: Politics and Social Protest in Japan.* Cambridge, Mass.: Harvard University Press, 1984.

Asia Week. "The Succession Question," May 25, 1986, pp. 34–36.

Barrett, Richard E. "Dependency Theory and Taiwan: Analysis of a Deviant Case." *American Journal of Sociology* 87 (March, 1982): 1064–1089.

Barrett, Richard E., and Martin King Whyte. "Dependency Theory and Taiwan: Analysis of a Deviant Case." *American Journal of Sociology* 87 (March, 1982):

Barry, Brian. "Does Democracy Cause Inflation?: Political Ideas of Some Economists." In Leon L. Lindberg and Charles S. Maier, eds., *The Politics of Inflation and Stagnation,* pp. 280–317. Washington, D.C.: Brookings Institution, 1985.

Bauer, Raymond A., Ithiel de Sola Pool, and Lewis A. Dexter. *American Business and Public Policy.* New York: Atherton, 1963.

Bellah, Robert N., Richard Madsen, William M. Sullivan, Ann Swidler, and Steven M. Tipton, *Habits of the Heart.* Berkeley: University of California Press, 1985.

Benjamin, Roger. *The Limits of Politics: Collective Goods and Political Change in Postindustrial Societies.* Chicago: University of Chicago Press, 1980.

Bentley, Arthur. *The Process of Government.* San Antonio, Tex.: Principia Press of Trinity University, 1949. Orig. pub. 1908.

Berger, Peter L. *The Capitalist Revolution: Fifty Propositions About Prosperity, Equality, and Liberty.* New York: Basic Books, 1986.

Berger, Suzanne, and Michael J. Piore. *Dualism and Discontinuity in Industrial Societies.* Cambridge, Eng.: Cambridge University Press, 1980.

Berry, Jeffrey M. *The Interest Group Society.* Boston: Little, Brown, 1984.

———. *Lobbying for the People.* Princeton, N.J.: Princeton University Press, 1977.

Boetsch, Lawrent. "The Church in Spanish Politics." In Thomas D. Lancaster and Gary Prevost, eds., *Politics and Change in Spain,* pp. 144–167. New York: Praeger, 1985.

Bracher, Karl. "Problems of Parliamentary Democracy in Europe." In Stephen Graubard, ed., *A New Europe?* pp. 245–264. Boston: Houghton Mifflin, 1964.

Buchanan, James. *The Limits of Liberty.* Chicago: University of Chicago Press, 1975.

Buchanan, William. "A Governable Country." Paper presented at the Suntory Foundation Symposium, "Japan Speaks," Osaka, Jan. 1981.

Butterfield, Fox. "Why Asians Are Going to the Head of the Class." *New York Times Education Life,* Aug. 3, 1986, pp. 18–22.

Calhoun, John C. *A Disquisition on Government.* In Benjamin F. Wright, ed., *Source Book of American Political Theory.* New York: Macmillan, 1929.

Cameron, David. "Social Democracy, Corporatism, Labour Quiescence, and the Representation of Economic Interests in Advanced Capitalist Societies." In John H. Goldthorpe, ed., *Order and Conflict in Contemporary Capitalism,* pp. 144–178. Cambridge, Eng.: Cambridge University Press, 1985.

Cardoso, Fernando Henrique. "On the characterization of Authoritarian Regimes in Latin America." In David Collier, ed., *The New Authoritarianism in Latin America,* pp. 33–57. Princeton, N.J.: Princeton University Press, 1979.

Castles, Francis G., ed. *The Impact of Parties.* Beverly Hills, Calif.: Sage, 1982.

Cawson, Alan. "Introduction: Varieties of Corporatism: The Importance of the Meso-Level of Interest Intermediation." in Alan Cawson, ed., *Organized Interests and the State.* pp. 1–21. Beverly Hills, Calif.: Sage, 1985.

———. "Pluralism, Corporatism, and the Role of the State." *Government and Opposition* 13 (Spring, 1978): 187–198.

Chan Heng Chee. "The Political System and Political Change." In Riaz Hassan, ed., *Singapore: Society in Transition,* pp. 30–51. London: Oxford University Press, 1976.

Chang, Maria Hsia. "The Crisis of Succession on Taiwan." *Global Affairs,* Spring, 1986, pp. 141–156.

———. "Transition Through Accretion: Institutionalizing a Competitive Party System in Taiwan." Paper delivered to the Symposium on Political Reform of the Republic of China on Taiwan, Associated Chinese Social Scientists of North America, Baltimore, May 8–10, 1987.

Chen, Cieng. *Land Reform in Taiwan.* Taipei: China Publishing Co., 1968.

Chin, Hsiao-yi. "Chiang Kai-shek's Understanding of and Implementation of Sun Yat-sen's Revolutionary Ideology Program." Unpublished paper, Taipei, 1981.

Chinese Human Rights Association. *Report on the Survey of Human Rights in the Republic of China on Taiwan.* Taipei: The Association, 1984.

Ching, Julia. *Confucianism and Christianity.* Tokyo: Kodansha International, 1977.

Chubb, John. *Interest Groups and the Bureaucracy.* Stanford, Calif.: Stanford University Press, 1983.

Clark, Peter B., and James Q. Wilson. "Incentive Systems: A Theory of Organizations." *Administrative Science Quarterly* 6 (Sept. 1961): 219–266.

Clough, Ralph. *Island China*. Cambridge, Mass.: Harvard University Press, 1978.

Collier, David, and Ruth Berins Collier. "Who Does What, to Whom, and How." In James M. Malloy, ed., *Authoritarianism and Corporatism in Latin America*, pp. 479–512. Pittsburgh: University of Pittsburgh Press, 1977.

Collier, Ruth Berins, and David Collier. "Inducements versus Constraints: Disaggregating 'Corporatism.' " *American Political Science Review* 73 (Dec., 1979): 967–986.

Common Cause News. April 7, 1987, p. 7.

Cox, Andrew. "Corporatism as Reductionism: The Analytic Limits of the Corporatist Thesis." *Government and Opposition* 81 (Winter, 1982): 79–95.

Crane, George T. "The Taiwanese Ascent: System, State, and Movement in World Economy." In Edward Friedman, ed., *Ascent and Decline in the World System*, pp. 93–114. Beverly Hills, Calif.: Sage, 1982.

Creel, H. G. *Confucius and the Chinese Way*. New York: Harper and Row, 1949.

Crossette, Barbara. "An Added Element in Asia: Confucianism." *New York Times*, June 5, 1987, p. 13.

Crouch, Colin. "Conditions for Trade Union Wage Restraint." In Leon N. Lindberg and Charles S. Maier, eds., *The Politics of Inflation and Economic Stagnation*, pp. 105–139. Washington, D.C.: Brookings Institution, 1985).

Cumings, Bruce. "The Origins and Development of the Northeast Asian Political Economy: Industrial Sectors, Product Cycles, and Political Consequences." *International Organization* 38 (Winter, 1984): 1–40.

Dahl, Robert A., and Edward R. Tufte. *Size and Democracy*. Stanford, Calif.: Stanford University Press, 1973.

Dardess, John W. *Confucianism and Autocracy*. Berkeley: University of California Press, 1983.

Darnton, Robert. *The Great Cat Massacre and Other Episodes in French Cultural History*. New York: Vintage, 1985.

Davies, R. G., and J. H. Denton, eds. *The English Parliament in the Middle Ages*. Philadelphia: University of Pennsylvania Press, 1981.

de Bary, W. T. "Chinese Despotism and the Confucian Ideal: A Seventeenth-Century View." In John K. Fairbank, ed., *Chinese Thought and Institutions*, pp. 163–203. Chicago: University of Chicago Press, 1957.

Deckard, Barbara Sinclair. *The Women's Movement*. 3rd ed. New York: Harper and Row, 1983.

Devine, Donald J. *The Political Culture of the United States*. Boston: Little, Brown, 1972.

Diamond, Nora. "Women and Industry in Taiwan." *Modern China* 5 (July, 1979): 317–340.

Do-dinh, Pierre. *Confucius and Chinese Humanism*. New York: Funk and Wagnals, 1969.

Dogan, Mattei, ed. *The Mandarins of Western Europe*. New York: Wiley, 1975.

———. "The Political Power of the Western Mandarins." In Mattei Dogan, ed., *The Mandarins of Western Europe*. New York: Wiley, 1975.

Dye, Thomas R. *Politics, Economics, and the Public*. Chicago: Rand McNally, 1966.

Edelman, Murray. "Symbols and Political Quiescence." *American Political Science Review* 54 (Sept., 1960): 695–704.

Edsall, Thomas Byrne. *The New Politics of Inequality*. New York: Norton, 1984.

Engstrom, Richard L., and Chu Chi-hung. "The Impact of the 1980 Supplementary Election on Nationalist China's Legislative Yuan." *Asian Survey* 24 (April, 1984): 447–458.

Estes, Richard J., and John Morgan. *The Social Progress of Nations.* New York: Praeger, 1984.

Evans, Sara. *Personal Politics.* New York: Vintage, 1980.

Fairbank, John. *The United States and China.* Cambridge, Mass.: Harvard University Press, 1959.

Far Eastern Economic Review. "A New Security Blanket," Jan. 22, 1987, pp. 12–13.
———. "A Two Pronged Test," Dec., 1986, pp. 36–37.

Fei, John C. H. "Ideology of Economic Development in Taiwan." Paper delivered at the Conference on Experiences and Lessons of Economic Development in Taiwan, Taipei, Dec. 18–20, 1981.

Feldman, Harvey J. "Taiwan Moves Toward a Two-Party System." *New York Times,* Dec. 27, 1986, p. 15.

Fields, Gary S. *Poverty, Inequality, and Development.* Cambridge, Eng.: Cambridge University Press, 1980.

Galbraith, John Kenneth. *The Anatomy of Power.* Boston: Houghton Mifflin, 1983.

Galenson, Walter, ed. *Economic Growth and Structural Change in Taiwan.* Ithaca, N.Y.: Cornell University Press, 1979.

Gastil, Raymond D., ed. *Freedom in the World, 1986–1987.* New York: Greenwood, 1987.

Gastil, Raymond D., and James D. Seymour. "Supporting Democracy in the People's Republic of China and the Republic of China (Taiwan)." In Raymond D. Gastil, ed., *Freedom in the World: Political Rights and Civil Liberties,* pp. 119–320. New York: Freedom House, 1984.

Gates, Hill. "Dependency and the Part-Time Proletariat in Taiwan." *Modern China* 5 (July, 1979): 381–407.

George, T. J. S. *Lee Kuan Yew's Singapore.* London: Deutsch, 1973.

Gold, Thomas B. *State and Society in the Taiwan Miracle.* Armonk, N.Y.: Sharpe, 1986.

Goldstein, Carl. "A Tiger Seeking Claws." *Far Eastern Economic Review,* May 14, 1987, pp. 24–26.

Gregor, A. James. "Comparative Political Stability: The Philippines and the ROC on Taiwan." *Issues and Studies* 23 (Jan., 1987): 11–22.

Gregor, A. James, and Maria Hsia Chang. *The Republic of China and U.S. Policy.* Washington, D.C.: Ethics and Public Policy Center, 1983.

Gurr, Ted, and Raymond Duval. "Civil Conflict in the 1960's: A Complete Theoretical System with Parameter Estimates." *Comparative Political Studies* 6 (1973): 135–170.

Gustafsson, Agne. "Rise and Decline of Nations: Sweden." *Scandinavian Political Studies* 9 (1986): 35–50.

Halberstam, David. *The Reckoning.* New York: Morrow, 1986.

Hall, Peter. *Governing the Economy.* Oxford: Polity Press, 1986.

Hamilton, Richard F. *Who Voted for Hitler?* Princeton, N.J.: Princeton University Press, 1982.

Hansen, John. "The Political Economy of Group Membership." *American Political Science Review* 79 (March 1985): 79–96.

Hansen, Susan B. "Public Policy Analysis: Some Recent Developments and Current Problems." In Ada W. Finifter, ed., *Political Science: The State of the Discipline*, pp. 217–246. Washington, D.C.: American Political Science Association, 1983.

Heady, Bruce W. "Trade Unions and National Wage Policy." *Journal of Politics* 32 (May, 1970): 407–439.

Heady, Ferrel. *Comparative Public Administration*. New York: Longman, 1979.

Heclo, Hugh. "Reaganism and the Search for a Public Philosophy," in John L. Palmer, ed., *Perspectives on the Reagan Years*, pp. 31–64. Washington, D.C.: Urban Institute Press, 1986.

Heclo, Hugh, and Henrik Madsen. *Policy and Politics in Sweden: Principled Pragmatism*. Philadelphia: Temple University Press, 1986.

Heidenheimer, Arnold J., Hugh Heclo, and Carolyn Teich Adams. *Comparative Public Policy*. 2nd ed. New York: St. Martin's, 1983.

Hibbs, Douglas. "Macroeconomic Policy and Political Parties." *American Political Science Review* 73 (1979): 1467–1487.

Hinton, Harold C. *Korea Under New Leadership: The Fifth Republic*. New York: Praeger, 1983.

Ho, Samuel P. S. *Economic Development of Taiwan, 1860–1970*. New Haven, Conn.: Yale University Press, 1978.

Hobbes, Thomas. *Leviathan*. New York: Collier, 1962. Orig. pub. 1651.

Hofstadter, Richard. *The Paranoid Style in American Politics*. New York: Vintage, 1968.

Holt, Robert T., and John E. Turner. *The Political Basis of Economic Development*. New York: Van Nostrand, 1966.

Howard, Rhoda E., and Jack Donnelly. "Human Dignity, Human Rights, and Political Regimes." *American Political Science Review* 80 (Sept., 1986): 801–817.

Hsiung, James C. "East Asia." in James C. Hsiung, ed., *Human Rights in East Asia: A Cultural Perspective*. New York: Paragon House, 1985.

Hsiung, James C., ed. *Human Rights in East Asia: A Cultural Perspective*. New York: Paragon House, 1985.

Hsu, Leonard Shih lien. *The Political Philosophy of Confucianism*. London: Curzon, 1975.

Huang, Mab. "Democratization on Taiwan." In Raymond Gastil, ed., *Freedom in the World: Political Rights and Civil Liberties*. New York: Freedom House, 1984.

Hung Chao-tai. "Taiwan." In James C. Hsiung, ed., *Human Rights in East Asia: A Cultural Perspective*. New York: Paragon House, 1985.

Huntington, Samuel. *American Politics: The Promise of Disharmony*. Cambridge, Mass.: Harvard University Press, 1981.

Ishida, Takeshi. "The Development of Interest Groups and the Patterns of Political Modernization in Japan." In Robert E. Ward, ed., *Political Development in Modern Japan*, pp. 293–336. Princeton, N.J.: Princeton University Press, 1968.

Jackman, Robert. *Politics and Inequality*. New York: Wiley, 1975.

———. "Socialist Parties and Income Inequality in Western Industrial Societies." *Journal of Politics* 32 (May, 1970): 135–149.

Jacobsson, Ulf. "Economic Growth in Sweden." In Arnold C. Harberger, ed., *World Economic Growth*, pp. 59–94. San Francisco: Institute for Contemporary Studies, 1984.

Johnson, Chalmers. "Introduction: The Taiwan Model." In James C. Hsiung, ed.,

Contemporary Republic of China: The Taiwan Experience. New York: American Association for Chinese Studies, 1981.

————. *MITI and the Japanese Miracle: The Growth of Industrial Policy, 1925–1975.* Stanford, Calif.: Stanford University Press, 1982.

————. "Political Institutions and Economic Performance: A Comparative Analysis of Japan, South Korea, and Taiwan." Project on Development, Stability, and Security in the Pacific-Asian Region, Institute of East Asian Studies, University of California, Berkeley, 1983.

————. "Political Institutions and Economic Performance: The Government-Business Relationship in Japan, South Korea, and Taiwan." In Robert Scalapino, S. Sato, and J. Wanadi, eds., *Asian Economic Development—Present and Future.* Berkeley: Institute of East Asian Studies, University of California, 1985.

Jones, Leroy P., and Il Sakong. *Government, Business, and Entrepreneurship in Economic Development: The Korean Case.* Cambridge, Mass.: Harvard University Press, 1980.

Kahn, Harold L. *Monarchy in the Emperor's Eyes: Image and Reality in the Ch'ien-Lung Reign.* Cambridge, Mass.: Harvard University Press, 1971.

Kahn, Herman. *World Economic Development: 1979 and Beyond.* Boulder, Colo.: Westview, 1979.

Kao, Charles H. C., and Ben-chie Liu. "Socioeconomic Development in Taiwan: An Analysis of Its Quality and Life Advancement." In Kwoh-ting Li and Tzong-shian Yu, eds., *Experiences and Lessons of Economic Development in Taiwan,* pp. 445–476. Taipei: Academia Seneca, 1982.

Kariel, Henry. *The Decline of American Pluralism,* Stanford, Calif.: Stanford University Press, 1961.

Katzenstein, Peter J. *Corporatism and Change: Austria, Switzerland, and the Politics of Industry.* Ithaca, N.Y.: Cornell University Press, 1984.

————. "Small Nations in an Open International Economy: The Converging Balance of State and Society in Switzerland and Austria." In Peter B. Evans, Dietrich Rueschemeyer, and Theda Skocpol, eds., *Bringing the State Back In,* pp. 227–251. Cambridge, Eng.: Cambridge University Press, 1986.

————. *Small States in World Markets.* Ithaca, N.Y.: Cornell University Press, 1985.

Kelman, Steven. *Regulating America, Regulating Sweden.* Cambridge, Mass.: MIT Press, 1981.

Korpi, Walter. *The Democratic Class Struggle.* London: Routledge and Kegan Paul, 1983.

————. *The Working Class in Welfare Capitalism: Work, Unions, and Politics in Sweden.* London: Routledge and Kegan Paul, 1978.

Kristianson, G. L. *The Politics of Patriotism.* Canberra: Australian National University Press, 1966.

Kubota, Akira. *Higher Civil Servants in Japan: Their Social Origins, Educational Backgrounds, and Career Patterns.* Princeton, N.J.: Princeton University Press, 1969.

Kubota, Akira, and Robert E. Ward. "Family Influence and Political Socialization in Japan: Some Preliminary Findings in a Comparative Perspective." *Comparative Political Studies* 2 (July, 1970): 140–175.

Kuo, Shirley W. Y., Gustav Ranis, and John C. H. Fei. *The Taiwan Success Story: Rapid Growth with Improved Distribution in the Republic of China, 1952–1979.* Boulder, Colo.: Westview, 1981.

Kuo Tai-chyn. "An Analysis of the Taiwan Experience: Policies and Social Factors." *Issues and Studies* 21 (Jan., 1985): 42–56.

Kurian, George Thomas. *The New Book of World Rankings.* New York: Facts on File, 1984.

Lancaster, Thomas D., and Gary Prevost, eds. *Politics and Change in Spain.* New York: Praeger, 1985.

Lash, Scott. "The End of Neo-Corporatism?: The Breakdown of Centralized Bargaining in Sweden." *British Journal of Industrial Relations* 23 (July, 1985): 215–239.

Lau, Lawrence J. "Introduction." In Lawrence J. Lau, ed., *Models of Development: A Comparative Study of Economic Growth in South Korea and Taiwan,* pp. 1–12. San Francisco: Institute for Contemporary Studies, 1986.

Lehmbruch, Gerhard. "Concertation and the Structure of Capitalism." In John H. Goldthorpe, ed., *Order and Conflict in Contemporary Capitalism,* pp. 61–80. Oxford: Clarendon Press, 1984.

———. "Liberal Corporatism and Party Government." *Comparative Political Studies* 10 (April, 1977): pp. 91–126.

Leion, Anders. "Sweden." In B. C. Roberts, ed., *Industrial Relations in Europe: The Imperatives of Change,* pp. 204–221. London: Croom, Helm, 1985.

Levenson, Joseph R. *Confucian China and Its Modern Fate.* Berkeley: University of California Press, 1965.

Levitin, Sar, and Martha R. Cooper. *Business Lobbies: The Public Good and the Bottom Line.* Baltimore: Johns Hopkins University Press, 1984.

Lien, Sheng Yan. "The Concept of *Pao* as a Basis for Social Relations in China." In John K. Fairbank, ed., *Chinese Thought and Institutions,* pp. 291–309. Chicago: University of Chicago Press, 1973.

Lifton, Robert Jay. *Thought Reform and the Psychology of Totalism.* New York, Norton, 1963.

Lindblom, Charles. *Politics and Markets,* New York: Basic Books, 1977.

Lipset, Seymour Martin. *Political Man.* Garden City, N.Y.: Doubleday, 1960.

Liu, Paul K. J. "Economic Aspects of Rapid Urbanization in Taipei." *Academia Economic Papers,* March, 1979.

Lowe, Michael. *Everyday Life in Early Imperial China.* New York: Harper and Row, 1968.

Lowi, Theodore. *The End of Liberalism: Ideology, Policy, and the Crisis of Public Authority.* New York: Norton, 1969.

———. "The Public Philosophy: Interest Group Liberalism." *American Political Science Review* 61 (March, 1967): 5–24.

Luttbeg, Norman, and Harmon Zeigler. "Attitude Consensus and Conflict in an Interest Group: An Assessment of Cohesion." *American Political Science Review* 60 (Sept., 1966): pp. 655–666.

MacFarquhar, Roderick. "The Post-Confucian Challenge." *The Economist,* Feb. 9, 1980, pp. 67–72.

Maier, Charles S. "Preconditions for Corporatism." In John H. Goldthorpe, ed., *Order and Conflict in Contemporary Capitalism,* pp. 39–59. Oxford: Clarendon Press, 1984.

———. *Recasting Bourgeois Europe.* Princeton, N.J.: Princeton University Press, 1975.

Malloy, James M., ed. *Authoritarianism and Corporatism in Latin America.* Pittsburgh, University of Pittsburgh Press, 1977.

March, James, and Herbert Simon. *Organizations.* New York: Wiley, 1957.

Marongiu, Antonio. *Medieval Parliaments: A Comparative Study*. London: Eyre and Spottiswoode, 1968.

Marsh, David. "On Joining Interest Groups." *British Journal of Political Science* 6 (July, 1976): pp. 257–271.

Marsh, Robert M. *The Mandarins: The Circulation of Elites in China, 1600–1900*. New York: Free Press, 1961.

Martin, Andrew. "Wages, Profits, and Investment in Sweden." In Leon L. Lindberg and Charles S. Maier, eds., *The Politics of Inflation and Economic Stagnation*, pp. 403–466. Washington, D.C.: Brookings Institution, 1985.

Marx, Fritz Morstein. *The Administrative State*. Chicago: University of Chicago Press, 1957.

Mason, Edward S., Mahn Je Kim, Dwight H. Perkins, Kwang Suk Jim, and David C. Cole. *The Economic and Social Modernization of Korea*. Cambridge, Mass.: Harvard University Press, 1980.

Matthews, Donald R. *United States Senators and Their World*. New York: Vintage, 1960.

McConnell, Grant. *Private Power and American Democracy*. New York: Knopf, 1966.

McDonald, Hamish. "Down Under in a Hole." *Far Eastern Economic Review*, May 29, 1986, pp. 99–101.

McDonough, Peter, Samuel H. Barnes, and Antonio Lopez. "The Growth of Democratic Legitimacy in Spain." *American Political Science Review* 80 (Sept., 1986): 735–760.

McFarland, Andrew. *Common Cause*. Chatham, N.J.: Chatham House, 1984.

Mendel, Douglas. *The Politics of Formosan Nationalism*. Berkeley: University of California Press, 1970.

Menzel, Johanna M., ed. *The Chinese Civil Service: Career Open to Talent?* Boston: Little, Brown, 1963.

Metzger, Thomas A. *Escape from Predicament: Neo Confucianism and China's Evolving Political Culture*. New York: Columbia University Press, 1977.

Michels, Roberto. *Political Parties*. New York: Free Press, 1962. Orig. pub. 1911.

Milbrath, Lester. *The Washington Lobbyists*. Chicago: Rand McNally, 1963.

Miller, Warren E. "The Election of 1984 and the Future of American Politics." In Kay Lehman Schlozman, ed., *Elections in America*, pp. 293–320. Boston: Allen and Unwin, 1987.

Moe, Terry. *The Organization of Interests*. Chicago: University of Chicago Press, 1980.

Moore, Barrington, Jr. *Authority and Inequality Under Capitalism and Socialism*. Oxford, Eng.: Clarendon Press, 1987.

Morishima, Michio. *Why Has Japan Succeeded?* Cambridge, Eng.: Cambridge University Press, 1982.

Muller, Edward N., and Mitchell A. Seligson. "Inequality and Insurgency." *American Political Science Review* 81 (June, 1987): 425–451.

Nagel, Jack. "Inequality and Discontent: A Nonlinear Hypothesis." *World Politics* 36 (1974): 453–472.

Nakane, Chie. *Japanese Society*. Berkeley: University of California Press, 1970.

Nathan, Richard P. "Institutional Change Under Reagan." In John L. Palmer, ed., *Perspectives on the Reagan Years*, pp. 121–146. Washington, D.C.: Urban Institute Press, 1986.

Nordlinger, Eric A. *On the Autonomy of the Democratic State*. Cambridge, Mass.: Harvard University Press, 1981.

Oberschall, Anthony. *Social Conflict and Social Movements*. Englewood Cliffs, N.J.: Prentice-Hall, 1973.

O'Donnell, Guillermo A. "Corporatism and the Question of the State." In James M. Malloy, ed., *Authoritarianism and Corporatism in Latin America*, pp. 47–88. Pittsburgh: University of Pittsburgh Press, 1977.

Offe, Claus. "The Attribution of Public Status to Interest Groups: Observations on the West German Case." In Suzanne Berger, ed., *Organizing Interests in Western Europe: Pluralism, Corporatism, and the Transformation of Politics*. Cambridge, Eng.: Cambridge University Press, 1981.

———. "Two Logics of Collective Action." In John Keane, ed., *Disorganized Capitalism*, pp. 170–219. Cambridge, Eng.: Cambridge University Press, 1985.

Olson, Mancur. *The Logic of Collective Action: Public Goods and the Theory of Groups*. Cambridge, Mass.: Harvard University Press, 1965.

———. *The Rise and Decline of Nations*. New Haven, Conn.: Yale University Press, 1982.

———. "A Theory of the Incentives Facing Political Organizations: Neo-Corporatism and the Hegemonic State." *International Political Science Review* 7 (1986): 165–189.

Panitch, Leo. "The Development of Corporatism in Liberal Democracies." *Comparative Political Studies* 10 (April, 1977): 61–90.

Payne, James. "Inflation, Unemployment, and Left Wing Parties: A Reanalysis." *American Political Science Review* 73 (1979): 181–185.

Pempel, T. J. "The Bureaucratization of Policymaking in Postwar Japan." *American Journal of Political Science* 18 (1974): 647–664.

———. *Policy and Politics in Japan: Creative Conservatism*. Philadelphia: Temple University Press, 1982.

Pempel, T. J., and Keiichi Tsunekawa. "Corporatism Without Labor?: The Japanese Anomaly." in Philippe C. Schmitter and Gerhard Lehmbruch, eds., *Trends Toward Corporatist Intermediation*, pp. 231–270. Beverly Hills, Calif.: Sage, 1979.

Penniman, Howard D., and Eusebio M. Mujal-Leon, eds. *Spain at the Polls, 1977, 1979, and 1982*. Durham, N.C.: Duke University Press, 1985.

Perlmutter, Amos. *Modern Authoritarianism*. New Haven, Conn.: Yale University Press, 1981.

Poole, Keith, and Harmon Zeigler. *Women, Public Opinion, and Politics*. New York: Longman, 1985.

Prevost, Gary. "The Spanish Labor Movement." In Thomas D. Lancaster and Gary Prevost, eds., *Politics and Change in Spain*, pp. 125–143. New York: Praeger, 1985.

Purcell, John F. H., and Susan Kaufman Purcell. "Mexican Business and Public Policy." In James M. Malloy, ed., *Authoritarianism and Corporatism in Latin America*, pp. 191–226. Pittsburgh: University of Pittsburgh Press, 1977.

Pye, Lucian W. *Asian Power and Politics*. Cambridge, Mass.: Harvard University Press, 1985.

———. *China: An Introduction*. Boston: Little, Brown, 1972.

Ranis, Gustav. "Prospects of Taiwan's Economic Development." In Kwoh Ting-li and Tzong Shian-yu, eds., *Experiences and Lessons of Economic Development in Taiwan*, pp. 511–525. Taipei: Academia Sinica, 1982.

Rawls, John. *A Theory of Justice*. Cambridge, Mass.: Harvard University Press, 1971.

Reich, Robert. *The Next American Frontier*. New York: Times Books, 1983.

Republic of China, Council for Economic Planning and Development. *Economic Development, Taiwan: Republic of China.* Taipei, 1984.
———. *Taiwan Statistical Data Book, 1985.* Taipei, 1985.
Republic of China, Executive Yuan. *Briefing on the Functions of the Ministry of Personnel.* Taipei, Nov., 1984.
Republic of China, Executive Yuan, Directorate General of Budget, Accounting, and Statistics. *Report on the Survey of Personal Income Distribution in Taiwan Area, Republic of China, 1983,* Taipei, 1984.
———. *Yearbook of Labor Statistics, 1984.* Taipei, 1985.
Republic of China, Executive Yuan, Research, Development, and Evaluation Yuan. *Annual Review of Government Administration.* Taipei, 1985.
———. *Income Tax Law, March, 1985.* Taipei, 1985.
Republic of China, Industrial Development and Investment Center. *Categories and Criteria for Special Encouragement of Important Productive Enterprises, March, 1985.* Taipei, 1985.
———. *Labor Laws and Regulations of the Republic of China.* Taipei, 1981.
———. *Labor Laws and Regulations of the Republic of China.* Taipei, Oct., 1984.
———. *Labor Standards Law.* Taipei, Aug., 1984.
Republic of China, Ministry of Economic Affairs. *Economic Development in the Republic of China, 1980.* Taipei, 1980.
Republic of China, Ministry of Finance. *Government Finance of the Republic of China.* Taipei, Jan., 1985.
Richardson, Bradley M., and Scott C. Flanagan. *Politics in Japan.* Boston: Little, Brown, 1984.
Riker, William H. *The Theory of Political Coalitions.* New Haven, Conn.: Yale University Press, 1962.
Rose, Richard. *Do Parties Make a Difference?* 2nd ed. Chatham, N.J.: Chatham House, 1982.
Rubinstein, W. D. *Wealth and Inequality in Britain.* London: Faber and Faber, 1986.
Russett, Bruce. "Inequality and Instability: The Relation of Land Tenure to Politics." *World Politics* 16 (1964): 442–454.
Salisbury, Robert, "An Exchange Theory of Interest Groups." *Midwest Journal of Political Science* 12 (Feb., 1969): pp. 1–32.
———. "Why No Corporatism in America?" In Philippe C. Schmitter and Gerhard Lehmbruch, eds., *Trends Toward Corporatist Intermediation,* pp. 213–230. Beverly Hills, Calif.: Sage, 1979.
Samuels, Richard. *The Politics of Regional Policy in Japan.* Princeton, N.J.: Princeton University Press, 1979.
Scalapino, Robert A. "Elections in Prewar Japan." In Robert E. Ward, ed., *Political Development in Modern Japan,* pp. 249–291. Princeton, N.J.: Princeton University Press, 1968.
Schiffman, James R., and Maria Schao. "South Korea and Japan: Two Strategies." *Wall Street Journal,* May 1, 1986, p. 36.
Schmidt, Manfred. "Does Corporatism Matter?" In Gerhard Lehmbruch and Philippe C. Schmitter, eds., *Patterns of Corporatist Policy-Making,* pp. 237–258. Beverly Hills, Calif.: Sage, 1982.
Schmitter, Philippe C. "Interest Intermediation and Regime Governability in Contemporary Western Europe and North America." in Suzanne Berger, ed., *Organized Interests in Western Europe: Pluralism, Corporatism, and the Transfor-*

mation of Interests, pp. 285–327. Cambridge, Eng.: Cambridge University Press, 1981.

———. "Reflections on Where the Theory of Neo-Corporatism Has Gone and Where the Praxis of Neo-Corporatism May Be Going." In Gerhard Lehmbruch and Philippe C. Schmitter, eds., *Patterns of Corporatist Policy-Making*, pp. 259–397. Beverly Hills, Calif.: Sage, 1982.

———. "Still the Century of Corporatism?" *Review of Politics* 85 (Jan., 1974): 85–131.

Schott, Kerry. *Policy, Power, and Order*. New Haven, Conn.: Yale University Press, 1984.

Scitovsky, Tibor. "Economic Development in Taiwan and South Korea, 1965–1981." In Lawrence J. Lau, ed., *Models of Development: A Comparative Study of Economic Growth in South Korea and Taiwan*, pp. 135–146. San Francisco, Institute for Contemporary Studies, 1986.

Seagrave, Richard H. *Mao's Revolution and the Chinese Political Culture*. Berkeley: University of California Press, 1971.

Sease, Douglas R. "Trade Tangle." *Wall Street Journal*, May 27, 1987, pp. 1, 22.

Share, Donald. "Corporatism and Public Policy: The Literature and Its Application to Southern Europe." Unpublished paper, 1981.

———. *The Making of Spanish Democracy*, New York: Praeger, 1986.

———. "Spanish Economic Development: Delayed Development, Francoist Economic Policy, and Revolution from Above." Master's thesis, Stanford University, 1978.

Sharpe, Willard D. "Success Achieved by Taiwan and Korea Obscures Different Roads to Development." *Asian Wall Street Journal*, May 6, 1985, p. 35.

Shonfield, Andrew. *Modern Capitalism: The Changing Balance of Public and Private Power*. London: Oxford University Press, 1965.

Silin, Robert H. *Leadership and Values: The Organization of Large-Scale Taiwanese Enterprises*. Cambridge, Mass.: Harvard University Press, 1976.

Smith, David M. *Where the Grass Is Greener*. London: Penguin, 1979.

Solomon, Richard H. *Mao's Revolution and the Chinese Political Culture*. Berkeley: University of California Press, 1971.

Stepan, Alfred. *The State and Society: Peru in Comparative Perspective*. Princeton, N.J.: Princeton University Press, 1978.

Streek, Wolfgang, and Philippe C. Schmitter. "Community, Market, State—and Associations?: "The Prospective Contribution of Interest Governance to Social Order," In Wolfgang Streek and Philippe C. Schmitter, eds., *Private Interest Government*, pp. 1–29. Beverly Hills, Calif.: Sage, 1986.

Tai, Hung-chao. "The Kuomintang and Modernization in Taiwan." In Samuel P. Huntington and Clement H. Moore, eds., *Authoritarian Politics in Modern Society: The Dynamics of Established One-Party Systems*, pp. 97–159. New York: Basic Books, 1970.

Taiwan Institute of Economic Research. *Postwar Development of the Economy of Taiwan*. Taipei: The Institute, Oct., 1983.

Taylor, Charles Lewis, and David A. Jodice. *World Handbook of Political and Social Indicators*, vol. 2. 3rd ed. New Haven, Conn.: Yale University Press, 1983.

Terrill, Ross. *The White-Boned Demon*. New York: Morrow, 1984.

Thurow, Lester C., "A Surge in Inequality." *Scientific American*, May, 1987, pp. 30–37.

Truman, David. *The Governmental Process*. New York: Knopf, 1951.

Tu Wei-ming. *Confucian Thought: Selfhood as Creative Transformation*. Albany: State University of New York Press, 1985.

Tung, Ming-lee. *A Study of the Social Increase of the Population in Taiwan*. Taichung: Population Study Center, 1978.

U.S. House of Representatives, Subcommittee on Pacific and Asian Affairs. *Martial Law on Taiwan and United States Foreign Policy Interest*. Washington, D.C.: Government Printing Office, 1982.

Van Arnhem, Corina M., and Geurt J. Schotsman. "Do Parties Affect the Distribution of Incomes?: The Case of Advanced Capitalist Democracies." In Francis G. Castles, ed., *The Impact of Parties*, pp. 352–362. Beverly Hills, Calif.: Sage, 1982.

Vogel, Ezra. *Japan as Number One*. Cambridge, Mass.: Harvard University Press, 1979.

Walker, Jack L. "The Origins and Maintenance of Interest Groups in America." *American Political Science Review* 77 (June, 1983): 390–403.

Ward, Michael Don. *The Political Economy of Distribution*. New York: Elsevier, 1978.

Ward, Robert E. "Reflections on the Allied Occupation and Planned Political Change in Japan." In Robert E. Ward, ed., *Political Development in Modern Japan*, pp. 477–535. Princeton, N.J.: Princeton University Press, 1968.

Watson, Michael. "Conclusion: A Comparative Evaluation of Planning Practice in the Liberal Democratic State." In Jack Hayward and Michael Watson, eds., *Planning, Politics, and Public Policy: The British, French, and Italian Experience*, pp. 236–349. Cambridge, Eng.: Cambridge University Press, 1975.

Watt, John R. *The District Magistrate in Late Imperial China*. New York: Columbia University Press, 1972.

Weakland, John. "The Organization of Chinese Culture." *Psychiatry* 13 (April, 1950): 361–370.

Weber, Max. *The Religion of China*. Glencoe, N.Y.: Free Press, 1951.

Wei, Yung. *Modernization in the Republic of China: Planning for a Future of Growth, Equity, and Security*. Taipei: Center for Public and Business Administration, National Chenchi University, 1984.

———. "Taiwan: A Modernizing Chinese Society." In Paul K. T. Sihm, ed., *Taiwan in Modern Times*. New York: St. Johns University Press, 1973.

Wiarda, Howard J. *Corporatism and Development: The Portugese Experience*. Amherst: University of Massachusetts Press, 1977.

Wickman, Stephen B. "The Economy." In Frederica M. Bunge, ed., *South Korea: A Country Study*, pp. 107–158. Washington, D.C.: U.S. Army, 1981.

Wilensky, Harold L. *The New Corporatism: Centralization and the Welfare State*. Beverly Hills, Calif.: Sage, 1976.

Williamson, Peter J. *Varieties of Corporatism*. Cambridge, Eng.: Cambridge University Press, 1986.

Wilson, Frank K. "French Interest Group Politics: Pluralist or Neocorporatist?" *American Political Science Review* 77 (Dec., 1983): 895–910.

Wilson, Graham K. *Business and Politics: A Comparative Introduction*. Chatham, N.J.: Chatham House, 1985.

———. "Why Is There No Corporatism in the United States?" In Gerhard

Lehmbruch and Philippe C. Schmitter, eds., *Patterns of Corporatist Policy-Making*, pp. 219–236. Beverly Hills, Calif.: Sage, 1982.

Wilson, James Q. *Political Organizations*. New York: Basic Books, 1973.

Wilson, Richard W. *Learning to Be Chinese: The Political Socialization of Children in Taiwan*. Cambridge, Mass.: MIT Press, 1970.

Winkler, Edwin A. "National, Regional, and Local Politics." In Emily Martin Ahern and Hill Gates, eds., *The Anthropology of Taiwanese Society*, pp. 13–37. Stanford, Calif.: Stanford University Press, 1981.

————. "Roles Linking State and Society." In Emily Martin Ahern and Hill Gates, eds., *The Anthropology of Taiwanese Society*, pp. 50–88. Stanford, Calif.: Stanford University Press, 1981.

————. "Statism and Familism on Taiwan." In George C. Loege and Ezra F. Vogel, eds., *Ideology and Competitiveness*, pp. 182–183. Boston: Harvard Business School, 1987.

Winkler, J. T. "Corporatism." *Archives of European Sociology* 17 (1976): 100–136.

World Bank. *World Development Report, 1985*. Washington, D.C.: World Bank, 1986.

Wright, Arthur. "Introduction." In Arthur Wright, ed., *Confucianism and Chinese Civilization*, pp. vii–xv. Stanford, Calif.: Stanford University Press, 1975.

Wright, John R. "PACs, Contributions, and Roll Calls: An Organizational Perspective." *American Political Science Review* 79 (June, 1985): 400–414.

Wright, Lindsay. "The Future of Democracy: Corporatist or Pluralist?" In Raymond D. Gastil, ed., *Freedom in the World: Political Rights and Civil Liberties*. pp. 73–95. New York: Freedom House, 1985.

Yang, Lien Sheng. "The Concept of *Pao* as a Basis for Social Relations in China." In John K. Fairbank, ed., *Chinese Thought and Institutions*, pp. 291–309. Chicago: University of Chicago Press, 1957.

Zeigler, Harmon. "Interest Groups and Public Policy: A Comparative, Revisionist Perspective." In Roger Scott, ed., *Interest Groups and Public Policy: Case Studies from the Australian States*. Melbourne: Macmillan of Australia, 1980.

————. "Interest Groups in the States." In Virginia Gray, Herbert Jacob, and Kenneth Vines, eds., *Politics in the American States*, pp. 97–132. 4th ed. Boston: Little, Brown, 1983.

————. *The Politics of Small Business*. Washington, D.C.: Public Affairs Press, 1961.

Zeigler, Harmon, and G. Wayne Peak. *Interest Groups in American Society*. 2nd ed. Englewood Cliffs, N.J.: Prentice-Hall, 1972.

Zeigler, Harmon, and Keith Poole. "Political Woman: Gender Indifference." *Public Opinion*, Aug./Sept., 1985, pp. 48–62.

INDEX

Almond, Gabriel, 79
Aristotle, 22–23
Asian countries, state corporatism in, 117–146; characteristics of governments, 126–128(tables); commitment to a single political party, 132–146; Confucian political culture, 121–132; labor unions in, 74. *See also names of individual countries, e.g.* Taiwan
Australia, corporatism in, 113–114, 210 n.61
Austria, corporatism in, 81, 85, 91, 93, 98, 103; and governmental policy initiative, 114
Authoritarianism. *See* State corporatism
Automobile industry, Taiwanese, 172

Barrett, Richard, 156
Barry, Brian, 73
Bauer, Raymond, 58
Bentley, Arthur, 5
Berger, Peter, 120
Berry, Jeffrey, 63
Brazil, 193
Bureaucracy, 163–184; in Confucian China, 24–26, 163, 201 n.53; institutional arrangements and priorities in, 164–172; loyalty vs. merit in, 178–184; recruitment and cohesion, 172–178;

Taiwan's Kuomintang Party, 136–139. *See also* Government(s)
Business interest groups, 57–58; cooperation with state bureaucracy, 164–172; recruiting for, 37–38
Business Roundtable, 58, 194

Calhoun, John C., 23
Cameron, David, 92
Canada, 84
Capture theory, 21, 191
Castle, Francis, 80
Cawson, Alan, 18
Chamber of Commerce, 57–58
Chen Cieng, 136
Chiang Ching-kuo, 122, 129, 136, 144, 155, 175, 217 n.96
Chiang Kai-shek, xii, 122, 136
Chile, 193
China, Confucianism in: bureaucracy and, 24–26, 163, 201 n.53; vs. Japan, 26; Ming dynasty, 198 n.6. *See also* People's Republic of China; Taiwan
Christianity, and corporatism, 19–20, 197 n.6
Civil liberties, in Asian corporatist countries, 122, 123–124, 128–129, 138–139, 215 n.57
Civil service, 24–26, 163. *See also* Bureaucracy

Collective good, 7, 8. *See also* Public good
Collier, David, 72–73, 115
Collier, Ruth Berins, 72–73, 115
Common Cause: membership renewal, 39; message of, and group participation, 52–54; origins/organization of, 34–36
Comparative Politics: A Developmental Approach, 79
Comparative Public Administration, 179
Confederation of British Industry, 10
Conflict: Confucian avoidance of, 25; pluralism and, 23
Conflict regulation/resolution, xiv; and economic growth, 187; fragmentation and, 104–105. *See also* Interest group intermediation
Confucianism, 107, 117–119, 121–132; economic growth and, 187–188; ethical tenants of, xiv–xv, 197–198 n.6; as organic statism of harmony, 23–32
Corporatism, 15–17; characteristics of, and culture, 80–82, 112–116 (*see also* Culture and corporatism); components of, 17–23; modern transformation to, 190–191; vs. pluralism, x, 15–23, 191–194; and policy (*see* Policy, governmental). *See also* Societal corporatism; State corporatism
Costa Rica, xii; government's role in the economy, 197 n.2; income distribution in, xiv
Crouch, Colin, on corporatism and stability, 111–112
Culture and corporatism, 19–20, 80–82, 105–116; change/stability in Spain and Japan, 105–107; governability and, 105, 107, 108–110; stability, 110–112; varieties/classification of corporatism, 112–116. *See also* Confucianism

Dahl, Robert, 42
Darnton, Robert, 29
Deaver, Michael, 190

Debt, and corporatism, 99–105
Democratic Justice Party (South Korea), 132
Democratic People's Party (Taiwan), 145, 147–148
Democratic Progressive Party (Taiwan), 145, 218 n.1
Deng Xiaoping, 144
Dexter, Lewis A., 58
Dogan, Mattei, 163
Dye, Thomas R., 79, 80

Economic growth, and corporatism, 82–87; Asian governments, 127(table); conflict resolution and, 187; Confucianism and 187–188; fiscal soundness and, 99–105; government policy initiative and Taiwanese, 181–183
Economic planning, governmental, 69–70
Edelman, Murray, on types of group activity, 43
Edsall, Thomas, 58
Encompassing organizations, ix, 124–125; Asian political parties as, 147–162; in Confucian political culture, 124, 125–132; corporatism's fiscal soundness and, 102–103; labor unions as, 76
Entrepreneurs, and group formation, 14; two examples of, 34–36; varieties of behavior in, 40–42
Equity. *See* Income distribution
Estes, Richard J., 95
Ethnic disputes, Taiwan, 155–162, 178

Family, and Confucianism, 24, 27–30, 212 n.28
Fascism, association with state corporatism, xi, 15, 22, 191
Federal Republic of Germany, 205 n.40, 218 n.1
Feminist groups, 47. *See also* National Organization for Women
Fields, Gary, xiii
Flanagan, Scott, 148; on bureaucratic personalism, 174
France, corporatism in, xvi, 69, 109,

113, 191, 205 n.40
Friedan, Betty, 34–36

Galbraith, John Kenneth, 70
Gardner, John, 34–36
Gini index, in Taiwan, xiii–xiv, 131, 157
Gold, Thomas, on Taiwan politics/ economics, 187, 188
Goods, supply/demand for, and group membership, 58–60; demand curves, 60–65. *See also* Collective good; Public good; Selective goods, and group membership
Government(s): budget priorities of, and corporatism, 93, 94, 95 (table); characteristics of Asian, 126–128(tables); Confucian view of, as family, 27–30; economic planning by, 69–70; policy (*see* Policy, governmental); spending by, and corporatism, 83, 84(table), 85, 86(table); stability of, and corporatism, 105–107, 109(table), 110(table), 111(table), 112. *See also* Bureaucracy
Governmental process, in pluralism vs. corporatism, 30–32; governability, 105, 107, 108–110. *See also* Bureaucracy; Interest group(s)
Governmental Process, The, 6
Great Britain, corporatism in, 113; and economic planning, 69
Gross national product (GNP): growth in, and corporatism, 82–87; per capita and income distribution, xiii; in pluralist vs. corporatist societies, 81–82; ratio of debt to, 100 (table)
Groups. *See* Interest group(s)

Hall, Peter, xvi, 90, 112
Hansen, John, 11, 12–13
Heady, Ferrel, 179
Heclo, Hugh, 104
Hibbs, Douglas, 111
Holt, Robert T., xv
Hong Kong, 155, 220 n.24
Hsiung, James, 119

Hsun-Tzu, 25
Hu, Leonard Shihlien, on Confucianism and political democracy, 118
Hu Fu, 123
Hung Chao-tai, 121
Huntington, Samuel P., on political values, 188, 189

Income distribution, 186; corporatism income policies and, 96–99; inequality in, and corporatism, 70–71; per capita GNP and, xiii; in Taiwan, xiii, xiv, 156–158, 160, 221 n.42
Index of Social progress, 95
Individualism and pluralism, 3–7; flaw of economic models of, 9–11; interest groups and, 5; rational individual choice, 8–9; rise/ decline of traditional group theory, 5–6
Inequality, in corporatist societies, 70–71
Inflation, and corporatism, 90–91 (table), 101
Institutional Revolutionary Party (Mexico), 131, 184
Interest group(s): competing theories of the origins of, 33–36; in Confucian societies, 30–32; message misrepresentation of, 51–57, 72; and pluralist theory, 5; private sector, 36–42; size of (*see* Size of interest groups); traditional group theory and, 5–6
Interest group intermediation: in Asian bureaucracies, 180–184; corporatist, 18–21; in corporatist vs. pluralist societies, 30–31; fragmentation and, 104–105; in societal corporatism, 71–72, 189–190
Interest group membership, 7–14, 185–186; competition and market for, 57–65; creating vs. joining a group, 13–14; entrepreneurs and, 14; flaw in economic models of, 9–11; income, and

reasons given for, 11–13; individual choice in, and group size, 45–51; overlapping (see Overlapping group membership); personal motives and organizational goals, 38–40; rational indivudal choice and, 8–9; reasons for joining Taiwan's Kuomintang Party, 140–146; renewal rates, 39 (table), 64 (table)
Ireland, corporatism in, 81, 84
Ishida, Takeshi, 106
Italy, 69

Japan, xii, xvi; bureaucracy of, 172–173, 174–175; business/bureaucracy coordination in, 164–165; change/stability and corporatism in, 105–107; Confucianism in, 26, 107, 122, 126; income distribution in, xiv; labor unions in, 74; per capita GNP in, xiii. See also Liberal Democratic Party (Japan)
Japan, corporatism in, 81, 92, 93; and governmental policy initiative, 114; "private" nature of, 96, 206 n.55
Japan Socialist Party, 133
Johnson, Chalmers, 122, 164, 176

Kahn, Herman, 119
Kao, Henry, 215
Katzenstein, Peter, on corporatism in Switzerland, 97
Keidanren, 164–165
Kim, Ilpyong, 122
Korpi, Walter, 73
Kuomintang Party (Taiwan), xii, 132, 133, 134–139, 187, 224 n.2; efforts to reduce corruption by, 175–176; ethnic disputes in, 155–162; factions and intraparty disputes, 148–155; recruitment and integration, 142–146; relationship to government, 139–142

Labor and labor unions: as a legitimate

participant in corporatism, 72, 73–77; as oppressive to the working class, 70–71; origins of, 13–14; in Taiwan, 130, 170, 213–214 n.43; wealth, economic growth, and, under corporatism, 86–87. See also Strikes, labor
Land reform in Taiwan, xiv, 135–136, 215 n.62
Latin American, corporatism in, 191. See also Mexico, corporatism in
Lau, Lawrence, on the difference between Taiwan and South Korean governments, 169–170
League of Women Voters, 12
Lee Kuan-yew, 120
Legislative Yuan (Taiwan), 147
Legislatures, relationship to bureaucracies and interest groups, 194
Liberal Democratic Party (Japan), 132, 133, 190
Liberty Federation, 60
Lien Sheng-yang, 152
Lindblom, Charles, 69
Lin Piao, 118
Liu, Henry, 129, 152, 216 n.77, 219 n.17
Logic of Collective Action, The, 75
Lowi, Theodore, 21

McFarland, Andrew, 52
MacFarquhar, Roderick, on Confucianism, 119
Madison, James, 23, 70, 198 n.6
Madsen, Henrik, 104
Maier, Charles, 190
Malaysia, per capita GNP in, xiii
Mandarins of Western Europe, The, 163
Mao Tse-tung, 30, 118, 144
Marsh, David, 10
Marxism, 20, 22, 30, 70, 73–74, 80
Mencius, 25, 29
Mesocorporatism, 115
Mexico, corporatism in, 17, 131, 183–184, 193
Michels, Roberto, 51
Ministry of Economic Affairs (Taiwan), 168, 169, 176–178; personnel characteristics, 179(table)
Ministry of International Trade and

Industry (Japan), 165–166
Moe, Terry, 11–12, 55, 63
Moral Majority, 60
Morgan, John, 95
Morishima, Michio, 107

National Association of Manufacturers
    (NAM), 57–58
National Organization for Women,
    12; origins/organization of,
    34–36
National Taiwan University, 179
New Right groups, 47, 60
New Zealand, corporatism in, 85
Nordlinger, Eric A., 113
Norway, corporatism in, 103

O'Donnell, Guillermo, 191
Offe, Claus, 57
Olson, Mancur, xvi; on corporatism
    and economic growth, 102,
    103; on group membership, 7,
    8–9, 10, 13–14; on group size,
    43; on interest groups and
    government, 21; on labor
    unions, 75–77; on Taiwanese
    economic growth, 182
Organic statism, 15–16; Confucianism
    as, 23–32; and corporatism, 16–
    17, 22
Overlapping group membership, 5, 43,
    202 n.20; crosscutting cleavages
    as, 45–51

Panitch, Leo, on class bias in corporat-
    ism, 70–71, 97
Peak associations, x, xi, 31; in Asian
    societies, 164–172. *See also*
    Business interest groups; Labor
    and labor unions
People's Action Party (Singapore),
    123, 132, 147
People's Republic of China, xii, 138;
    Confucianism in, 30, 117, 201
    n.63
Perlmutter, Amos, 18
Personalism and reciprocity, in Taiwan,
    152–153; bureaucratic corrup-
    tion and, 173–176

Philippines, 130; per capita GNP in,
    xiii
Pilot agencies, 176
Pluralism, 3–65; basis for group mem-
    bership and, 7–14; competition
    and the marketplace under, 57–
    65; conflict and, 23; vs. corpo-
    ratism, x, 15–23, 191–194;
    corporatism and Confucianism
    and, 23–32; defined, ix, 3;
    individualism and, 3–7; interest
    intermediation and, 31; message
    misrepresentation problems, 51–
    57; normative, 21; private
    sector organizations under, 36–
    42; size of groups under, 42–51;
    A. Stepan on, 16; theories of
    group origins under, 33–36
Policy, governmental, xi, 89–116;
    budget priorities, 93–95; culture,
    corporatism and, 105–116;
    fiscal soundness of corporatism
    and, 99–105; income distribu-
    tion, 96–99; inflation and, 90–
    91; initiation of, in Asia,
    181–183; predictors of societal
    corporatism output, 79–80;
    unemployment and, 91–93
Political action committees (PACs),
    U.S., 55–56, 190
*Political Basis of Economic Development,
    The*, xv–xvi
Political economy, Confucian views of,
    26
Political parties in Asia: Confucian
    commitment to a single, 132–
    146; ethnic disputes in Taiwan-
    ese, 155–162; factions and
    intra-party disputes in Taiwan,
    148–155
Politics, Economics, and the Public, 79
Poole, Ithiel de Sola, 58
Portugal, 183–184
Powell, Bingham, 79
Private sector organizations, under
    pluralism, 36–42
Privatization trend, 193–194
Public good: concept of, 21–22; corpo-
    ratist views of, 22–23. *See also*
    Collective good

Pye, Lucian, on Confucianism, 28,
119, 121, 122, 126, 130

Rawls, John, 70
Reagan, Ronald, administration of,
193, 227 n.24; income distribu-
tion inequality under, 99; soci-
etal corporatism and, 195;
spending reduction program,
200 n.42
Reich, Charles, 75, 94
Reich, Robert, on American politics
and economy, 192-193
Religion of China, The, 119
Richardson, Bradley, 148; on bureau-
cratic personalism, 174
Riker, William, 51
Rise and Decline of Nations, 21, 76
Rose, Richard, 90

Salisbury, Robert, 33; on reasons for
joining a group, 41-42, 59
Schiffman, James, on South Korea vs.
Taiwan, 171
Schmidt, Manfred, 74; classification
of corporatism, 77-78, 205
n.40; on unemployment, 92
Schmitter, Philippe: on corporatism,
17, 18, 67-68, 81, 104; on
governability and stability,
108-109
Schott, Kerry, on unemployment/
inflation, and corporatism, 101
Selective goods, and group member-
ship, 7, 8, 9, 10; demand curve
for, 60-65; supply/demand of,
58-60
Shao, Maria, on South Korea vs.
Taiwan, 171
Share, Donald, 68, 105
Shared attitudes in group membership,
5, 7, 10
Shockley, William, 212 n.28
Sierra Club, 54
Silin, Robert, 180
Singapore: Confucianism and govern-
ment in, 117, 118, 123-124,
126-130, 212 n.28; per capita
GNP in, xiii; political parties

(see People's Action Party
(Singapore))
Size of interest groups: logic of individual choice and, 45-51; participation and, 52-54; stability
and, 54-57; strategy and, 43-45
Societal corporatism, ix, 67-87, 186-
187; classification of, 77-79,
205 n.35; costs and benefits of,
68-72; defined, x, 17; interest
intermediation in, 18-21, 30-
31; legitimate participants in,
72-77; significance of, 77-87
Solomon, Richard, 24; on Confucian
values, 120
South Korea, xii, xvi; authoritarianism
of, vs. Taiwan, 169-171; bureaucracy and business in, 165,
166, 168; Confucianism and
government in, 122, 126-130;
income distribution in, xiv;
labor strikes in, 214 n.43; per
capita GNP, xiii; political violence and martial law in, 122,
212 n.23
Spain, xvi; corporatism and change/
stability in, 105-107, 208 n.38
Spontaneous theory of group origins,
33, 44-45
State corporatism, ix; association with
fascism, 15, 22, 191; defined,
x-xi, 17; interest intermediation
in, 18-21, 31; in Taiwan (see
Taiwan)
Stepan, Alfred, on corporatism and
pluralism, 16, 20, 22
Stockman, David, 200 n.42
Strikes, labor: as a measure of corporatism, 78-79, 205 n.38; in Tai-
wan, 130, 213-214 n.43
Students for Democratic Society, 45
Sun Yat-sen, 118, 134, 145-146; his
"Three Principles of the People,"
147, 179, 182
Sweden, corporatism in, 84, 103;
fragmentation and, 104-105
Swedish Employers' Association, 103
Swedish Trade Union Confederation,
103

Switzerland, corporatism in, 17, 81, 84, 91, 92, 93; and governmental policy initiative, 114; "private" nature of, 96–97, 206 n.55

Taiwan, xii–xiv; bureaucracy, loyalty vs. merit in the, 178–184; bureaucracy-business coordination and economic affairs in, 165–172, 176–178, 222 n.19, 223 n.25; bureaucracy recruitment/cohesion, 172–178; Confucianism in, 29–30, 119, 120, 122–123, 201 n.63, 211 n.12, 212 n.28; corruption in, 173–176, 216 n.70; credit scandal in, 152, 219 n.18; ethnic disputes, 155–162, 178, 180; government of, and Confucianism in, 126–132; government of, relationship to Kuomintang Party, 139–142; income distribution in, xiii, xiv, 156–158, 160, 221 n.42; interest in politics vs. business in, 161, 162 (table); land reform in, xiv, 135–136, 215 n.62; literacy/education, 223 n.33; martial law in, 138–139, 149, 171, 219 n.14; media censorship in, 138, 216 n.77; military in, 151–152, 219 n.14, 219 n.15; per capita GNP in, xiii; personalism and reciprocity in, 152–153; political parties (*see* Democratic People's Party (Taiwan); Kuomintang Party (Taiwan)); "soft" authoritarianism in, 153–155
Taiwan Textile Federation, 169
Tanaka, Kakuei, 174–175
Tangwai Research Association, 152
Taxing policies, 93–94; in Taiwan, 158
Thailand, per capita GNP in, xiii
Thurow, Lester, 99
Tokyo University, 179

Trade associations, 57–58
Truman, David, his interest group theory, 5–6, 13, 14, 43, 202 n.20
Tufte, Edward, 42
Turner, John E., xv
Tu Wei-ming, 28–29

Unemployment, and corporatism, 91, 92(table), 93, 101; and civil disorder, 111 (table)
United Auto Workers, 45
United States: corporatism in, 68; government-initiated interest groups in, 192; per capita GNP, xiv, 81; pluralism in, 3, 33–65

Vietnam Moratorium, 44–45
Vogel, Ezra, 75, 130

Walker, Jack, 45
Ward, Michael Don, 96, 97, 98, 110
Ward, Robert E., on postwar Japan, 132–133
Watson, Michael, on failure of economic planning, 69–70
Weakland, John, 153
Wealth: distribution of (*see* Income distribution); spending of, by government, 83, 84 (table), 84–85, 86 (table)
Weathermen, 45
Weber, Max, 119
Wei Yung, 150–151
Whyte, Martin, 156
Wilensky, Harold, 195–196
Williamson, Peter, 19, 74, 115
Wilson, Graham, 58, 89
Winkler, Edwin, 137
Winkler, J. T., 18
Women, status of, and Asian governments, 128 (table), 214–215 n.51
Wu Teh-yao, 118

Yue Loong, 172